ART CARNEY

A BIOGRAPHY

ART CARNEY

A BIOGRAPHY

MICHAEL SETH STARR

FROMM INTERNATIONAL PUBLISHING CORPORATION
NEW YORK

First Fromm International hardcover, April 1997

Copyright © 1997 by Michael Seth Starr

Library of Congress Cataloging-in-Publication Data

Starr, Michael, 1961–

    Art Carney : a biography / by Michael Seth Starr.

       p.   cm.

    ISBN 0-88064-173-8

       1. Carney, Art, 1918–   . 2. Comedians—United States—Biography. 3. Actors—United States—Biography.   I. Title.

PN2287.C273S72   1997

791.45'028'092—dc20

[B]   96-43716

10 9 8 7 6 5 4 3 2 1

To Gail Ellen and Rachel Lara,
the two most important women in my life.

And to the two souls we lost during the writing of this book.
May they rest in peace.

CONTENTS

ACKNOWLEDGMENTS

I would like to thank the following people who agreed to be interviewed for this book: Joanna Cassidy, Willie Deverman, Cynthia Harris, Raymond Edward Johnson, Morey Amsterdam, Elizabeth Ashley, Robert Benton, Jane Kean, James Karen, Gus Trikonis, Sheila MacRae, Jack Philbin, Walter Stone, Joyce Randolph, Lily Tomlin, Jack Haley Jr., David Niven Jr., Horace Heidt Jr., Phil Bruns, Phil Leeds, Paul Dooley, Sidney Armus, Neil Simon, Paul Mazursky, Al Lewis, Melanie Mayron, Martin Brest, Jackie Cooper, Steve Allen, Howard Zieff, Paul Bogart, Sir Peter Hall, Beulah Garrick, Barbara Barrie, Joseph Sargent, Joan Reichman Canale, Leonard Stern, Sydell Spear, Frank Marth, George Petrie, Joe Cates, Pete McGovern, Larry Haines, Carol Shelley, Alvino Rey, Rod Parker, Ronald Wayne, Charles Hallahan, June Taylor, Larry Gelbart, Sheldon Keller, Robert Hilliard, Frank DeVol, George Maran, Donna Conkling, Mitzi Gaynor, Coleman Jacoby, Harry Crane, Phyllis Thaxter, Larry Storch, Thomas Ryan, Mimi Hatton, Bob Weiss, Millie O'Toole, Frankie Carle, Bruce Solomon, Janis Paige, Theodore Bikel, Julius LaRosa, Morton Gottlieb, Harvey Medlinsky, Barbara Myers, John Considine, Jackson Beck, Barnard Hughes, Richard Sarafian,

Lon Clark, Robert Dreyden, Arnold Stang, Henry Morgan, Elaine Stritch, Ronnie Kemper, Peggy Lee, Stanley Ralph Ross, Nandrea Lin Courts, Jack Klugman, Brett Somers, Abby Lewis, Louise Sorel, Jack Smight, Salem Ludwig, Rosemary Forsyth, Tom Ligon, Porter Van Zandt, Will Mackenzie, Emory Bass, A. J. Russell, Robert Abbatecola, Walter Sherman, Michael Altieri, Al Tepe, Geraldine Fryer, Vince Pizzi, Barney Sokoloff, Madeleine Lee, Jack Grimes, Phil Marano, Heywood Hale Broun, Norma Roberts, Aaron Ruben, Ronald Biscow, Roy Alfred, Anna Manahan, Rhoda Goldberger, and Bryan Forbes.

I would also like to thank Thomas Thornton, my first editor on this project, for his enthusiasm, support, and encouragement; Fred Jordan of Fromm International for his valuable criticisms and line editing; Chris Slavik, for her help in locating CBS archival photographs; Virginia Frye, of the CBS research department; and Kristine Krueger, of the American Academy of Motion Picture Arts and Sciences, who provided me with the text of Art Carney's Academy Award acceptance speech.

Special thanks to Morey Amsterdam, Millie O'Toole, and Horace Heidt Jr. for providing me with valuable photographs. I would also like to thank my editor at the *New York Post,* Adam Buckman, for giving me the break of a lifetime.

Last—but certainly not least—a special thank-you to my wife, Dr. Gail Starr, who has always encouraged me to reach for the sky. I love you.

ART CARNEY

A BIOGRAPHY

INTRODUCTION

It's David Letterman's domain these days, the squat brick theater on Broadway that once echoed with the sounds of Ed
Sullivan's "really big shew," of frenzied teenagers screaming
for a young Memphis kid named Elvis Presley, for the Beatles
and the Rolling Stones.

If you walk past the theater now—and if the wind is blow-
ing in off the Hudson and conditions are just right—you might
hear a faint roar emanating from within. It's the roar of television
history, of a bellowing Brooklyn bus driver named Kramden
threatening to send his wife Alice "to the moon!" It's the roar of
Kramden percolating into a slow-burn boil and exploding at his
best friend, Norton, who's methodically chalking a pool cue or
"addressing" a golf ball: "Helloooooo, ball!"

The show, of course, was *The Jackie Gleason Show,* the star
the Great One himself, a B-movie Hollywood actor, mediocre
nightclub comic, and television retread who moved into New
York's Adelphi Theatre in 1950 and—for the next six years—produced some of the most brilliant sketch comedy ever presented
on the small screen.

Jackie Gleason had his beloved stock characters—Fenwick
Babbitt, The Poor Soul, Reginald Van Gleason, Joe the Bartender,
Rudy the Repairman—and he had the bombastic charisma that
America pined for during the feel-good Eisenhower years. What

he didn't have—Sid Caesar's literate writers fleecing Hollywood's sacred cows, or the innovative sitcom genius of Lucille Ball and Desi Arnaz—Gleason more than compensated for with sheer energy. When the Great One roared, his audience roared with him.

But Gleason's biggest asset, bigger than anything the ostentatious Great One could ever hope to buy, was his costar. It takes two to tango in sketch comedy, and Gleason had the greatest dancer of them all, an agile, rubber-limbed comedian whose talent often overshadowed Gleason's, a show business recluse whose sweetness and introverted nature masked the ferocity of a brilliant actor.

This isn't a book about Jackie Gleason. And if the Great One were alive today he'd no doubt loathe his status here as the second banana, a tag so often applied—and misapplied—to our real star.

He's been known in various guises since 1941. He was FDR, Al Smith, and many others on radio's *Report to the Nation*. When the new medium of television was born, he became Newton the Waiter on *The Morey Amsterdam Show* and, later, Ed Norton on *The Honeymooners*.

Perhaps you remember him as Broadway's original Felix Unger in *The Odd Couple*, or in his Oscar-winning role with a marmalade cat in *Harry and Tonto*.

He is, of course, Art Carney.

The television partnership formed by Jackie Gleason and Art Carney—most memorably Brooklyn bus driver Ralph Kramden and his dim-witted pal, sewer worker Ed Norton—remains, to this day, the most powerful comedic union ever conceived for the small screen.

Gleason and *The Honeymooners* played a major role in the shaping of Art Carney's life and career. It was Gleason who precipitated Carney's meteoric rise to television prominence in the early 1950s, allowing his comic aide-de-camp to blossom on *The Jackie Gleason Show* and tackle varied dramatic and comedic parts in anthology shows like *Playhouse 90, Studio One,* and *Kraft Television Theatre*.

And it was Gleason who—like some suntanned, rotund

white knight—rode to Carney's rescue a decade later, persuading the clinically depressed, alcoholic actor to visit Miami for a *Honeymooners* reunion that resurrected Carney's sputtering career.

But *The Honeymooners* and Ed Norton are only a part of Art Carney's story. Like the "overnight success" who in fact paid his dues in spades, Art Carney didn't just materialize out of thin air ready to stake his claim as a television legend.

1

"ART BY ART"

Art Carney's road to success began in Mount Vernon, New York, a middle-class community located about ten miles north of Manhattan in Westchester County. A bustling, tree-lined city populated by a mixture of Irish, Jewish, and German immigrants, Mount Vernon flourished as a favorite "country" retreat peopled by some of New York's wealthiest residents, who favored its easy proximity to Manhattan.

It was around 1915 that Massachusetts native Edward Carney moved his wife Helen and their five young sons into Mount Vernon, buying a home at 345 Bedford Avenue, directly across the street from DeWitt Clinton Grammar School.

With the boys running roughshod over the old Victorian house, Helen and Edward had their hearts set on giving Jack, Ned, Phil, Fred, and Bob a baby sister. So if the very late arrival of Arthur William Matthew Carney on November 4, 1918, was a joyous occasion, it was one tinged with just a little disappointment.

"With five boys in the family, we hoped and prayed that this time it would be a girl," Helen Carney would later recall. "Somehow, word got around by mistake when Artie arrived that he *was* a girl. I was kind of heartbroken at first, when I found out.

"When we got over the disappointment of his being a boy, he was babied a bit. But he was saved from spoiling because we didn't have time for it, with so many. I think a certain amount of wholesome neglect is good for kids."

But with this newest addition to their already large family, the Carneys didn't have much time to reflect on what could have been. The Carney house—the last Mount Vernon residence to be lit by gas—was forever bustling with activity. As a boy, Art could remember his father shaving by gaslight, and with nine rooms plus three extra rooms in its attic and a huge front porch decorated with Victorian curlicues, the old Carney house was, Edward Carney remembered, "an architect's nightmare" basking in its own ornate splendor.

The Carney clan followed a circuitous route to Mount Vernon. Edward Michael Carney was born in 1879 in Lawrence, Massachusetts, spending about ten years in Manchester, New Hampshire, attending Christian Brothers' School before returning to Lawrence and graduating from Lawrence High School in 1899. A journalist by trade, Edward spent three years as a local newspaper reporter before trading his typewriter for actuarial tables, becoming resident manager of the Equitable Life Assurance Society's Lawrence office.

Three years later, Edward switched jobs again—this time to public relations—and moved his family to New York, where he worked for a number of firms, including the American Telephone and Telegraph Company, *Collier's Weekly,* and the U.S. Worsted Company.

After managing the Empire State Building observatory, Edward cofounded an advertising agency, Carney & Kerr, that lasted four years, until the outbreak of World War I. After the war, Edward returned to journalism in a supervisory capacity, overseeing twenty-eight newspapers in the Hearst chain and editing the company's in-house executive publication. His job brought him into daily contact with boss Randolph Hearst and Colonel Frank Knox, Hearst's general manager, who later became Secretary of the Navy.

Like many other businesses, the Hearst newspaper chain was hit hard by the Depression. In 1932, forced on a bank "holiday" by Hearst's Depression-era retrenchment program, Edward left the company to become public relations director for the Mount Vernon Trust Company, a post he held for twenty years before retiring. He also served as public relations counsel for Mount Vernon Hospital.

By 1951, when he was honored as Mount Vernon's Most Distinguished Citizen, Edward Carney had been involved in almost every facet of the city's civic, fraternal, and religious life. His sons jokingly called him "Civic Virtue" Carney.

The public spotlight shone far less brightly on Helen Farrell Carney, who preferred to remain in the background raising her family. But while she was the antithesis of her garrulous husband, Helen was no less influential in her sons' lives. "Mrs. Carney is an avid reader of books, reading anything she can lay hands on," the local newspaper reported in a 1935 feature article devoted to Helen. "She is not especially fond of social life, nor does she play bridge for which she has no interest."

The daughter of John and Bridget Farrell, Helen, like Edward, was born in Lawrence, Massachusetts. Her musical talent was apparent at an early age, and encouraged by her father, Helen was soon playing the violin. By the age of seven she was renowned throughout New England for her violin prowess; in her early teens Helen was accepted into training by violin master Franz Kneisel, who for many years conducted the Boston Symphony Orchestra and led his Kneisel String Quartet.

Kneisel was a stern taskmaster, demanding four hours of violin practice each day. But he was so impressed with Helen's ability that he persuaded her to buy his beloved Crancino violin, crafted in the early eighteenth century by Italian master violin maker Giovanni Crancino. It was an honor not bestowed lightly. "She plays like a man, with great power," noted one critic of Helen's violin talent.

Upon meeting Edward Carney, Helen put down her violin to concentrate on raising her six sons, only occasionally removing the Crancino from its case when coaxed by her family. When the Carneys took a Cape Cod vacation in August 1935, Helen placed the Crancino in a bank vault for safekeeping.

"I suppose if I wanted to I would play, but I never have

really wanted to," Helen said at the time. "I wanted to learn to drive a car, and in spite of all my family's protests that I was too nervous and couldn't possibly learn, I secretly took lessons, and perhaps the greatest thrill of my life came when I showed my husband and the boys my driver's license."

So it was a loving, generous, and talented family into which young Art Carney made his belated debut. Oldest brother Jack, twelve years Art's senior, was a star athlete at Rutgers University and later became an agent with show business conglomerate MCA, playing a pivotal role in Art's career and producing *Arthur Godfrey's Talent Scouts* for television. Jack was followed, in descending chronological order, by Ned (Edward Michael Jr.)—a dentist who practiced in New York—Philip, Frederick, Robert, and Art.

"We weren't too well-off," Art said later. "There wasn't much money. I got a lot of hand-me-downs like all the youngest kids get. But when I look back, I had a very happy childhood."

Important to young Art's emotional development, perhaps because of the age difference between him and his brothers, was a family member unrelated by blood but considered an honorary Carney nonetheless. His name was Philip Richardson—Uncle Rich or Uncle Phil to the Carney boys—and he lived with the Carneys through Art's adolescence. He was an avuncular, non-judgmental, gentle man whom Art would remember years later as the biggest influence in his life.

A former mayor of Woburn, Massachusetts, Uncle Rich had given Edward Carney his first newspaper job and remained friendly with his former employee. When Edward and Helen moved the family to Mount Vernon, Rich was invited to live with them.

"Rich had an unhappy and childless marriage, and when he was about fifty he was alone. Naturally, he came to live with us. My parents wouldn't have it any other way," Art recalled. "He quit newspapering and, until he retired at sixty-five, worked for the American Telephone and Telegraph Company."

Edward Carney was a devoted family man, but with a full-time job and his many civic commitments he found it difficult to be everywhere at once. Uncle Rich, unhappy in marriage, refocused his energies on the Carney boys, helping Edward and Helen manage the family.

"My parents were unstinting in their love for us," Art said later. Art once sold a valued set of drums to buy his mother an Easter plant; and one of his brothers, talking to a magazine reporter in the mid-fifties, told how "Artie was always an affectionate little kid. He still signs notes to Mom with X's and O's for kisses and hugs."

But Rich added a new dimension to that love.

Art said, "I was the youngest, so the relationship between Rich and me was the longest and, I like to think, the deepest."

Art described Uncle Rich as "a medium-sized, gray-haired General MacArthur without the severe face but with the same meticulous air of distinction." Uncle Rich was young Art's hero, playing marbles with Art before dinnertime and taking him for Friday walks to Aunt Mabel's, where Art would stuff himself with chocolate mints and cheese crackers, washing it all down with ice water.

"Once, on the way there, I thought I smelled gas coming from the ground. I yelled, 'Gas! Gas!' Rich didn't think I was crazy," Art said. "Anybody else would have, but not him. He went over, bent down, sniffed very seriously. Sure enough, there was part of an old gas pipe there with a strong gas smell. From then on, every Friday night when we got to that spot we'd both stop, bend down, sniff, look up knowingly, and walk on happily, sharing our great, dark secret."

Rich played baseball with Art, bought him his first two-wheel bicycle, and sat glued to the radio listening with Art to his favorite show, *Amos 'n' Andy*. While Rich did his Sunday *Times* crossword puzzle—"Starting with one across and just working his way clear on through," Art recalled—Art would use Rich's old-fashioned brushes to comb the older man's hair.

"I worked on his hair, winding it up and looping it around and making all sorts of fancy twirls," Art remembered. "And he'd just sit there working his puzzle and not saying a word. When I got finished with his hair, I'd call my mother to come take a look, and I'd bring a mirror for Uncle Rich."

Next to his passion for crossword puzzles, Rich took great

pride in his artwork, mostly charcoals and watercolors. He encouraged Art's creativity, gently nudging the shy boy into his first public performance.

By the age of nine, Art was already showing a remarkable talent for mimicry, impersonating teachers and friends with uncanny accuracy. Although his musical talent didn't match his mother's—his piano playing never progressed beyond the key of C, despite years of lessons—Art could impersonate almost anyone and decided to stage a one-man show in the family's Bedford Avenue parlor room.

Rich, blessed with graceful, stylish handwriting, handled the invitations, sending out twelve notes, mostly to Mount Vernon relatives: "You are invited to a special evening of entertainment by Mr. Arthur Carney called 'Art by Art.' " Art jumped on his bicycle and hand-delivered the invitations, then prepared for his dramatic debut.

"Uncle Phil was the emcee. I played the piano, the slide whistle, the flexatone, sang, danced, and even drew a picture," he recalled. "As I look back, I wasn't much good at anything, so I must have been a pretty conceited kid."

Art once said of Rich: "It seemed he never had any problems of his own. He did. Plenty. But he never burdened anyone with them. I suspect he eased his problems by being with kids, especially me."

One thing Rich couldn't help Art with was school, where Art's academic record was less than stellar. Although the family's home was directly across from DeWitt Clinton Grammar School Number 9—he had to walk only a few hundred yards to reach the schoolyard—Art still found it difficult making it to class on time. He was often late to school with one excuse or another, much to the chagrin of his frazzled teachers.

"When I used to have friends over, I would try to get rid of Arthur, who would usually just sit and play the piano," brother Phil recalled. "I'd say, 'There's my dumb brother.' I never thought he'd get out of grammar school."

But Art's classmate Norma Roberts remembers Art as a sharp student—at least in grammar school. Each DeWitt Clinton class was divided into A and B sections, she recalled, with students placed into either group according to their interests, grades, and learning skills.

"Art was an excellent student in the B section of the class. I was in the A section, but we used to come in after they had taken the same test in arithmetic and Art very often had perfect scores on his arithmetic tests," Roberts recalled. "He was not a stupid boy, and I always had a soft spot in my heart for him because he was a sweet kid. He was really very quiet in school."

Although shy at home, Art blossomed at DeWitt Clinton, impressing classmates with his vocal mimicry and transforming himself into a brash class clown who continuously generated laughs and a steady string of bad grades.

"I was the one who almost ruined the family name," he would joke. But Art's mediocre report cards were a blessing in disguise. DeWitt Clinton required parents to sign their child's report card, and Edward Carney's exaggerated hand movements—the way in which he put pen to paper, stopping . . . starting . . . stopping . . . starting—inspired Art. He would later incorporate his father's movements into Ed Norton's maddening ballet that so infuriated Ralph Kramden.

"He loved to move things around, my father," Art said. "Like I'd bring him my report card and he couldn't just look at it and sign it. He had to lay it on a table and then he'd take out his eyeglasses and clean the lenses and put the glasses on and move the report card an inch further up and then he'd adjust the salt and pepper shakers over there and he'd straighten his cuffs and take out his fat, long Waterman fountain pen and unscrew it and move around the sugar bowl and restore the salt shaker to its original position."

Art's father also joined his youngest son on stage during PTA nights and student assemblies—the effusive bank VP and his shy kid performing musical numbers and skits.

"Mr. Carney was a very outgoing, cheery fellow, and he'd cavort just as much as Art, who was very respectful in class and, on the whole, very sober," classmate Norma Roberts recalled. "But when it came to putting on those shows, Art and his father—and sometimes one of Art's older brothers—were always great. Art was a whiz on the ocarina and the penny whistle, and his father was good at all those things, too. Mr. Carney was the kind of person everybody liked, so he made an ideal public relations man for a bank in a small town."

When he was about twelve, Art and some classmates were standing in line waiting to sharpen their pencils. Spying a bust of Beethoven in the corner, Art ran over, withdrew a white handkerchief from his pocket with an Ed Norton–ish flourish, and blew Beethoven's nose. He was adept at getting his pal Harold "Whitey" Fryer into trouble at school, bringing in a set of false teeth (no doubt supplied by brother Ned, the dentist) and turning in his seat to flash his phony choppers at his giggling classmate.

But it was with his uncanny talent for mimicry that Art soon made a name for himself in the schoolyard.

"Starting with his teachers in school, Art could mimic anyone he ever met," a friend said. "He picked up the talk of the kids on the street corners of Mount Vernon." Later, when he moved out of the house, Art would call his mother pretending to be any one of his five brothers. Woe be Ned, Bob, Fred, Jack, or Phil if they phoned home; they'd have to prove they weren't Art before Helen Carney would believe them.

"I had absolutely no ambitions to become an actor," Art recalled. "When I was growing up in Mount Vernon I was too scared of learning lines to try out for the high school plays. I was afraid that if I ever got up on that stage I'd forget every line I had and just stand there frozen with fright.

"Yet I was always fascinated with actors and personalities who were in the public eye. I had this intuitive ability to mimic famous people. I would go to the newsreels to study the people who were making the headlines. I'd listen to the radio and study their voices. I didn't *really* do caricatures of famous people. I really zoomed in on them, getting voice mannerisms and inflections."

Art's vocal talents didn't go unnoticed at DeWitt Clinton. While his grades plummeted, he showed remarkable poise and confidence in his ability to make people laugh, winning a school talent contest by imitating cigar-chewing comic Ned Sparks. And Art's Franklin Delano Roosevelt impersonation—which would later earn him his first newspaper notices and first dramatic radio gig—was always a crowd pleaser.

School, somehow, always seemed to get in the way.

"I recall he was frequently up to no good with various pranks," recalled boyhood friend Robert Abbatecola, whose father owned a tailor shop frequented by Edward Carney. "He once put horse manure, in plentiful supply back then, in a gift box tied with fancy paper and ribbons and gave it to one of the teachers he didn't like. Artie was also not your average model student. He was usually late, although he lived almost directly across from the school. He was also circumcised rather late in life—when he was about twelve or so—and he had a great time standing in a window of his house and showing off his 'wound' with lots of smart repartee."

Boyhood pal Michael Altieri recalled eating dinner one night at the Carney house. "His father, who was very, very formal, had turned his soup bowl over waiting to be served. And Art had put a fake turd underneath there."

Art's main nemesis at DeWitt Clinton was the school's principal, Minnie S. Graham, a Scottish spinster whose stern demeanor masked a heart of gold that endeared her to students and to the community. DeWitt Clinton was later renamed the Minnie S. Graham School in her honor.

"Oot, Carney, oot!" Miss Graham would yell at Art after one of his many visits to her office. "Ye'll niver amount to anythin'!" More than two decades later, when he was a famous television star, Art returned to Mount Vernon to host Miss Graham's retirement party. "Oh no, it's not you again!" she shrieked in mock horror when Art emerged on the stage. "Ye drove me crazy, but I loved ye just the same." It brought down the house.

But Art's schoolyard pranks didn't just annoy Miss Graham and his teachers; his brothers, too, grew progressively irritated with Art's ceaseless impersonations. When Art was fifteen, his brothers thought they had finally found a way to shut him up.

"I fancied myself hot stuff as an impersonator," Art said. "When my brothers became fed to the ears with my impressions, they figured that a night before the critical eyes of Mount Vernon's Brother Elks would do me a world of good."

Art's Elks Club debut was less than memorable. He was extremely nervous, and his impersonation of macho football star

Bronko Nagurski sounded oddly falsetto. It didn't matter—the Elks apparently were hungry for *any* entertainment and invited Art back again and again. Soon thereafter, other civic organizations (no doubt influenced by Edward Carney) followed suit.

But while he was slaying 'em at Rotary clubs and women's clubs around Mount Vernon, Art was becoming involved in his own fraternal organization. The Bedford Boys, a society he helped to found, is where Art would meet some of his closest lifelong friends.

Next to mimicry, baseball was Art's true love. A pitcher with a wicked curveball, Art played on several neighborhood baseball teams before meeting Al "Wigwam" Tepe, a new kid from Fanwood, New Jersey, who also attended DeWitt Clinton.

"I first got to know Artie when I played on a rival baseball team, the Rebels, and he struck me out four times—and I was supposed to be the prime slugger," Tepe recalled. "We were fast friends after that. We used to get together after school. His brother Ned, the dentist, had a bunch of false teeth, and we always used to go to Artie's house and see how we could make foolish disguises with false teeth, masks, and wigs."

Art's friendship with Al Tepe blossomed, and the duo soon perfected an *Amos 'n' Andy* routine based on their favorite radio show. Art loved to visit Al's house and listen to his German-born mother and aunt converse in their native tongue.

"Artie would say, 'How do I say "What are we eating tonight?" ' And they'd say, 'Was essen wir heute Abend,' " Tepe said, laughing at the memory. "And he still says that to me on the phone to this day!"

Before long, Art asked Al to join his baseball team. Art, Al, and Whitey Fryer then decided to form their own team, which they envisioned as a secret society complete with passwords.

"We went up in the top of Artie's old wooden garage one night and had a secret meeting," Tepe recalled. "We had a quarter in the treasury, and we had a candle in there, and we said we wanted to form an organization. But what should we call it? We finally decided on the Bedford Boys. And after we celebrated we took the quarter, went over to Kossoffs candy store, and bought five Eskimo Pies."

The Bedford Boys, named after the street where Art and many of his pals lived, soon began to attract members raided from other local baseball teams. The Bedfords, as they came to be known, built a treehouse in a vacant lot. It was a hideaway where they could play cards, roughhouse, and engage in 1930s-era male bonding. Over the next six years, the Bedfords amassed a complete roster of baseball players. Art grew especially close to teammate Victor Biscow, whose horribly off-key rendition of Joyce Kilmer's poem "Trees" kept Art in stitches. Robert Abbatecola and Barney Sokoloff, who lived on Garden Avenue directly behind the Carney house, served as team mascots and valued nonplayers.

"The club was ultraprivate and very exclusive," Abbatecola recalled. "Even my own brother couldn't get in. Basically we were a baseball club, but there was a lot more: secret passwords, meetings, etc. We stuck around together and horsed around together."

Although anti-Semitism was rampant in Mount Vernon, notwithstanding the town's heavy Jewish population, the Bedfords were remarkably integrated, counting among their members Jews, Italians, blacks, Swedes, and just about any other ethnic group contributing to the city's multicultural mix.

The Bedfords played a tough, seventy-game schedule every spring and summer, competing against teams in Mount Vernon, throughout Westchester County, and even in Brooklyn and the Bronx.

But Art, Al, and Whitey were only about twelve years old when they founded the Bedfords; they needed guidance, organization, and above all money for uniforms, bats, and balls.

They found all this—and much more—in Charles Farrell, an unmarried, wealthy executive with New York's Hanover Bank who lived in town and had spent years managing the New York Athletic Club baseball team. Farrell's house abutted part of DeWitt Clinton's schoolyard, where the Bedfords practiced. He would watch the novice team with great interest, convinced he could mold the boys into a first-rate, amateur-rank baseball team.

"Mr. Farrell saw us practicing in back and he came out one

night and said, 'You guys don't know what you're doing,' and that's how things evolved," Al Tepe remembers. "He started hitting grounders to us with a fungo bat, and we used to go over to his house practically every night and sit in his big screened, wraparound porch. He became our manager, and he'd come out on the hottest day of the summer with his silk suit and high, starched collar just like Connie Mack."

But Charles Farrell was more than a manager; to Art and most of the other team members he was a surrogate father for boys whose real fathers sometimes worked two or three jobs to make ends meet. In some cases their fathers were absent altogether.

"All of the kids I knew on the team either didn't have a father or didn't have a close relationship with their father," Tepe said. "I don't think Artie's father was too close to his kids because he was always doing this or that and was involved in things in town."

If Charles Farrell was a father figure, he treated his young charges likewise. He refused to give the boys money for uniforms and equipment, instead instituting an annual raffle (for a football and porcelain baby doll) to raise the necessary funds and instill in team members a sense of family and closeness that remains to this day.

The Bedford Boys also benefited from Farrell's bank and Athletic Club connections. Baseball star Frankie Frisch, nicknamed the Fordham Flash, was a member of the St. Louis Cardinals' "gashouse gang." He was a friend of Farrell's and often came to watch the Bedfords play when his Cardinals visited New York. Consequently, several Bedfords were offered minor league contracts. Star pitcher Frank Carretta—who routinely fanned between fifteen and eighteen batters a game—played briefly with the New York Giants before retiring to his family's laundry business. Michael Altieri signed with the Cardinals in 1938. Al Tepe also signed a Cardinals contract but had his major league dreams derailed by a career-ending ankle injury.

Art's baseball career began and ended with the Bedfords; he was too busy embarrassing proper ladies at Kossoffs candy store with his whoopee cushion or drilling holes in the store's pinball machine to give a professional baseball career much thought.

Art entered A. B. Davis High School in the fall of 1933, continuing to ignore his homework while sharpening his impersonations. To earn some extra money he worked a paper route and clerked in a local jewelry store.

"I remember he used to entertain at the school assemblies and do impersonations of FDR," said classmate and baseball rival (of the Seneca Indians) Larry Haines, who later worked with Art in radio and became a television soap opera star. "Even then he was marvelous."

Art and Haines (then known as Larry Hecht) weren't the only classmates headed for show business careers. A. B. Davis High also boasted a frenetic kid named Dayton Bolke, who was later known as Dayton Allen when he starred as part of Steve Allen's comedic ensemble. And classmate Elliott Reid would become a well-known radio and TV actor.

It was around this time, 1935, that Art bought the beaten-up hat he'd wear as Ed Norton on *The Honeymooners.*

"It was the first felt hat I ever bought; it cost me five dollars and I haven't cleaned it since, not in thirty years," Art later told columnist Earl Wilson. "That hat is the only prop I still use. It still retains its shape."

As he reached his high school years, Art's relationships—with his brothers and Uncle Rich and Charles Farrell and the Bedfords—had been predominantly male. Helen Carney, Minnie S. Graham, and unsuspecting female prank victims notwithstanding, women had played a minor role in the shaping of Art Carney's life and personality to that point.

But all that changed during Art's senior year at A. B. Davis when he met Jean Myers, a pretty, talented blond singer who later studied at New York's Juilliard School. In his typically unassuming style, Art's pursuit of Jean was circuitous. He let time, circumstance, and Jean's campaign for class vice president solve the dilemma of asking her out for a date.

Jean's campaign manager asked Art—who had taken public speaking classes to overcome his stage fright—to deliver Jean's nomination speech. But Art faced a problem: another girl had asked him to speak on her behalf. He resolved the situation by putting their names in a hat and drawing Jean's name. Summoning the courage and oratory brilliance of his heroes FDR and Al Smith, Art gave the speech of his life, and Jean Myers was elected.

But Art's romantic pursuit of Jean wasn't that easy. His public speaking bravura seemed to disappear whenever he was in Jean's company.

"She made pretty good fried-egg sandwiches, and pretty soon I was dropping around to play duets with her father, who was a concert pianist," Art recalled. "Things rocked along like that for a while, and then one day I said to her: 'You know, I don't come around here just to play double piano with your father.' "

While his romance with Jean blossomed, Art continued to perform for civic organizations and participate in school functions, winning a second amateur contest with impersonations of radio comedian Colonel Stoopnagle, actor Edward G. Robinson, FDR, Al Smith, Major Bowes, and Lionel Barrymore.

"Arthur W. Carney, one of the entertainers, will give impersonations and eccentric dancing," was how a newspaper in 1936 described one of Art's fund-raising performances. The article was topped by a photograph of a studious Art in suit and tie.

"Art was quite a mimic, even as a kid," his boyhood friend Larry Haines recalled. "His brother Ned, the dentist, made some sort of slip-on jacket for his teeth, which he put in when he did FDR, and he had the glasses and the long cigarette holder. I remember it vividly. He was marvelous."

Art, however, downplayed his early performing accomplishments.

"It was about all I accomplished in school," he said. "I never joined the dramatic club like [brothers] Phil and Fred. I didn't think I was an actor—all I could do was imitations."

Art's grades continued to falter, and his poor academic record kept him from graduating with Al Tepe, Whitey Fryer, and the rest of his pals in June 1936. In those days students were held back for only half a year, so Art finally graduated from A. B. Davis High School in January 1937.

"The only subjects I was any good at were typing and music appreciation," he said. "I had to stay in high school an extra semester to graduate, and I'd probably be there still if a kindhearted history teacher hadn't made me a present of a passing grade."

But graduate he did, and in a harbinger of things to come, Art Carney left A. B. Davis with a flourish: He was voted Wittiest Boy in the annual *Maroon & White* yearbook poll.

It was a nice honor, but it didn't pay the bills. Being funny was one thing; making a living at it was another.

2

REACHING NEW
HEIDTS

Notwithstanding Rotarian lunches and the like, Art's show business career had been limited to amusing friends, schoolmates, and family members with his uncanny impersonations. His graduation from A. B. Davis in January 1937 left Art, now eighteen, with few options. What would he do now? Many of the Bedford Boys had left for college or moved away, and while Art continued to romance Jean, she was still in high school and not yet ready for a permanent commitment.

"I didn't know what to make of myself," Art said. "I'd had a paper route, clerked in a jewelry store, and tried a few other odd jobs, but nothing that looked like a way to make a living."

Art hadn't considered a show business career; he had downplayed his talents and refused to take himself too seriously. His brothers Phil and Fred had already embarked on acting careers, Phil entertaining cruise-line passengers and Fred training with Maurice Evans's Shakespeare company.

But all those years of impersonations finally paid off for Art. And his introduction to the world of big-time show business came from a most unlikely source: his oldest brother, Jack.

Jack, now thirty, was working for the show business talent

agency Music Corporation of America (MCA) when Art graduated high school. A company bigwig familiar with MCA's stable of talent, Jack knew that bandleader Horace Heidt was looking for a mimic/announcer to complement his Musical Knights, a Big Band touring troupe that played some of the country's largest clubs. Heidt and his Musical Knights also appeared on various radio programs, including *Answers by the Dancers, Treasure Chest, Celebrate Anniversary Night with Horace Heidt,* and, in 1938, *Pot o' Gold.*

Jack, of course, was all too familiar with Art's range of impersonations, and he convinced Heidt to audition his kid brother, hoping to snare Art a spot in the renowned, quirky band. Although Heidt prided himself on off-center acts like "blind" whistler Fred Lowery (one eye fake, the other legally blind) and stone-blind xylophonist Pierce Knox, his band also featured some of the country's finest musicians: Frank DeVol, pianist Frankie Carle, guitarist Alvino Rey, and singers the King Sisters. "The kid does imitations," Jack told Heidt. "Maybe you could use him."

In the summer of 1937, more to appease Jack than to discover another great talent, Heidt agreed to audition Art, now eight months removed from high school. The audition took place in Manhattan's Adelphi Theatre. It was the same theater where, fourteen years later, Art would meet Jackie Gleason.

"Jack brought me down to what is now the Ed Sullivan Theatre, and knowing that Heidt was looking for novelty acts, and knowing I was a novelty, I did my stale act of impersonations for Heidt," Art recalled.

Nearly sixty years later, guitarist Rey vividly remembered that day. "Heidt was always looking for new people, new talent, and we went into the theater on Seventh Avenue to listen to people trying out and one kid came up, and he happened to be Art Carney. I can remember that. I told Art years later what his first imitation was, which is ridiculous—he had an imitation of an electric car, which in those days had brakes that ran on air, so when they'd run out of air a compression motor would go on. Of all his imitations, Art had one of that motor. He's the only one I ever heard do a dumb thing like that!"

Whatever his doubts, Heidt hired Art on the spot and ordered him to join the band three weeks later in Washington, D.C. Frank

DeVol, a comedian/musician who'd joined Heidt in the early thirties, remembered when Heidt introduced Art to the troupe.

"We were at a vaudeville theater, and we were all tired and rehearsing in our uniforms," DeVol recalled. "Heidt said, 'I want you to hear a man who was sent over from MCA.' So this young guy just out of high school comes in with a felt hat that creased down the middle and a rubber cigar, and he did all the people who were stars at that time—FDR, Edward G. Robinson, Ned Sparks with the cigar. He did a number of voices and he was terrific."

Heidt offered Art fifty dollars a week, which was a princely sum to the unemployed odd-jobber. Now Art had a chance to make a living doing the impersonations and comic riffs he'd perfected back in Mount Vernon. "I felt like I'd struck gold," Art said later.

When Art joined Heidt in 1937, the Big Band sound had swept the country, and Heidt's popularity nearly equaled that of other bands led by Fred Waring, Guy Lombardo, and Tommy Dorsey. But Heidt had another well-publicized weapon: his *Pot o' Gold* radio show, which awarded cash to contestants who answered their telephone. *Pot o' Gold* was giving top-rated radio comedian Fred Allen a run for his money, and Heidt was able to attract powerful sponsors like Alemite, Shell, and Tums. Meanwhile, the Musical Knights were drawing big crowds in posh hotels like New York's Biltmore—where their show was broadcast from the Bowman Room and the Roof Garden— Chicago's Drake, and Los Angeles's Cocoanut Grove (later renamed the Ambassador).

Heidt was a consummate self-promoter. He mailed business cards to everyone who attended a show, kept minutely documented scrapbooks, and employed a publicity man to scout future performing sites and arrange local radio and newspaper interviews with band members. Although Heidt admired Art's talent and wit, he was, for most of Art's three-year stint with the band, forever clashing with his brash impersonator. Art loved practical jokes and radiated the sense of humor Heidt seemed to lack.

According to those who worked for him, Heidt was a bullying boss and mediocre musician with a nose for talent and an inclination toward kitsch. But he knew what his audience

wanted, and had assembled an impressive band while developing an intricate floor show mixing novelty acts, dance numbers,
and straight-ahead music.

"It was like a Fred Waring show band," recalled Donna
Conkling, who toured with Heidt as one of the King Sisters.
"When he played a hotel, Horace had a glee club, and he always
had this big bandstand that went up a bunch of tiers, and the
glee club would sit on the stand and sway back and forth. He did
a floor show, and Alvino [Rey] was always featured because he
did a lot of tricky stuff with his guitar. He had a harpist named
Elizabeth Hughes, who did duets with a tall, handsome basso
profundo, and a young couple that did the jitterbug."

Art and fellow mimic Ollie O'Toole provided comic relief,
performing impersonations for about fifteen minutes each night.
Heidt placed the men on opposite ends of the stage and flashed
the spotlight back and forth, with Art and Ollie providing duel-
ing impersonations. Art never failed to bring down the house.

"I traveled up and down the country with Horace, and
every time the band would stop playing I'd jump up, thumb my
vest, and bust into an imitation of Lionel Barrymore," Art said.
"In three years with Heidt I wore out sixty vests."

Heidt pianist Ronnie Kemper, who later wrote "I'm a Little
Teapot" and hit it big with "Cecilia," remembered that Heidt
would get the audience involved in the Carney-O'Toole shenanigans.

"Heidt would say, 'Now here's the battle of the impersonators.' Art would do somebody and then Ollie would do somebody like Billy Barty or Chaplin. Heidt would always make it so it
was a tie. 'Well, it's kind of hard to say, but judging by your
applause it looks like both of them are winners.' And the crowd
would go mad."

But the fun that Art and Ollie had on stage wasn't because
they were close personal friends—at least not at first.
Notwithstanding Art's hasty audition, Heidt always frowned upon
on-site auditions. But he immediately hired Ollie when the young,
reed-thin impersonator/disc jockey auditioned in Pittsburgh with a
medley of Irish ballads and as a ranting, incoherent Adolf Hitler.
Art immediately questioned the logic of having *two* impersonators

in the band, and he sniped behind Ollie's back, convinced that Heidt was tormenting him. He finally relaxed when Ollie assured him he wasn't gunning for Art's job. Shortly thereafter, Heidt paired the duo in the well-received "Battle of the Impersonators" and a lifelong friendship was formed.

Art's FDR and Al Smith impersonations, meanwhile, began to attract notice, even from Smith himself. After performing for Smith at a Biltmore Hotel fundraiser, Art sat down. The legendary politician, seated at the dais, stood up and looked directly at Art. "I wanna congratulate the young impersonator," he said. "My boy, you sound more like me than I do myself. Every year somebody takes me off. This is the best one I've heard yet."

And Smith wasn't alone in his praise. With the Heidt troupe's exhaustive touring schedule exposing Art to major and minor markets in the United States, his vocal mimicry soon merited mention in nearly every newspaper review of Heidt's stage show.

"Alvino Rey still cracking 'em with his steel guitar wizardry, and despite gradual passing of mimics, Art Carney can still tie up the proceedings with his accuracy on the biggies," *Variety* noted on November 18, 1938. "Starts with Lionel Barrymore and Ned Sparks, finishing strong on President Roosevelt and Al Smith. Latter right on the nose, and benefiting additionally by excellent material."

The *Indianapolis Times,* in a 1938 review, incorrectly noted Art's age as seventeen—he was twenty—but nonetheless paid particular attention to his talents.

"Art Carney . . . does impersonations. Not too many, and very good. Lionel Barrymore is one of his best, but the audience went for Art's impression of the president, especially when he suggested relief of unemployment by a project which would move the Atlantic Ocean into the Pacific by means of a nationwide 'bucket brigade.' "

And one of New York's daily newspapers cited a homegrown talent: "Amateurs who have talent in singing, playing and other forms of entertainment will be given a chance to attain stardom on Horace Heidt's Alemite program. Art Carney, impersonator, was given such an opportunity several weeks ago by

Horace Heidt, and 'clicked' so heavily that he has been made a regular member of The Brigadiers."

"Art had a very cute act and was very popular with the band," recalled band member Donna Conkling. "Frank DeVol and Art were always kidding each other, doing gags and the like. They'd come walking in on their knees like Toulouse-Lautrec, dumb things like that. They were always pulling jokes."

Art, Frank DeVol, Ollie O'Toole, Fred Lowery, and Charlie Goodman used their sophomoric humor to alleviate the strain of the band's constant bus and train travel, and the stress of working up to five daily stage shows and the *Pot o' Gold* and *Treasure Chest* radio shows. Band members remember Heidt as a humorless disciplinarian who ran a tight ship and insisted on perfection from his employees. Drinking and smoking were strictly prohibited—at least when Heidt was around.

"We used to meet down at the ice cream shop in the bowels of the New York Central, and at 9:30 P.M. we had a half hour intermission and all the bands would meet there," Donna Conkling recalled. "Art was a really good boy, a good Catholic; us King Sisters were good Mormons, and Frank DeVol was a Christian Scientist who would order a Christian Science Collins. We'd meet Paul Weston, who was arranging for Tommy Dorsey, and Penny Gardener from Guy Lombardo's band. We had a gang of really nice people. Art was one of that group."

It was during this period that Art began drinking. It was a problem he would eventually discover he shared with three of his brothers, including Jack, and a problem that would escalate over the years, leading to depression and pill addiction.

For now, though, Art's drinking seemed to be recreational, a way to pass the time and monotony of long road trips and endless rehearsals. Art's roommate on the road was blind whistler Fred Lowery, whose "breakfast" was a real eye-opener.

"He would order gin and grapefruit juice for us in the morning and, gee, it was great," Art recalled. "We would go on and do five or six shows. No responsibilities, no remorse. I was an alcoholic even then."

The drinking didn't interfere with Art's work, and Heidt never knew just how spirited his blind whistler and ace mimic were from time to time. Art's popularity with the Heidt troupe was universal; he was the kid, and to an older, married man like Frank DeVol, Art represented an eternally impish sense of humor.

"Art was a funny, funny man who saw fun in so many things," DeVol recalled. "One time we were driving at night, looking for a particular house number, and we had Fred Lowery, the blind whistler, with us. I was driving and Art was in the middle, so Art says, 'Stop the car and let Fred look for it.' "

Art and Lowery struck up a strong friendship. Art became Lowery's self-proclaimed "seeing-eye guide," though he was always amazed at Lowery's ability to enter a room and immediately find the light switch. "So help me, Fred walks in and finds the switch with no trouble at all," an amazed Art would tell his Heidt bandmates. "No groping, no stumbling, no falling over chairs. I kid you not; ol' Fred's like a cat the way he can see in the dark."

Lowery was Art's coconspirator in various practical jokes they instigated to curtail the tedium of touring. Once, after downing a few beers at a corner saloon, Art concocted a memorable scenario: He would "mug" Lowery in midtown Manhattan, in broad daylight, to see if New Yorkers would come to the aid of a blind man having his pocket picked. Slightly drunk, Art and Lowery walked to the corner of Forty-second Street and Fifth Avenue at five o'clock, the height of rush hour, and stopped just outside the main gates of the New York Public Library. As Lowery, wearing his dark glasses, stood on the corner, Art approached and jabbed a finger in his back, shouting, "This is a stickup!"

"Abruptly help arrived, in the form of two husky New York cops," Lowery recalled in his memoirs. "One of them wrestled Carney to the sidewalk. The other grabbed my arm and demanded to know what the trouble was. During the next few minutes Art and I tried to explain our foolish stunt, but the more we talked the more ridiculous we sounded. The policemen weren't impressed, not even when we identified ourselves as members of Horace Heidt's band."

The police called Heidt, who came to post bail and fired Art and Lowery on the spot. He later changed his mind and rehired the duo, admitting to Lowery why he was *really* angry. It seems that when the cops called Heidt, he had been in the midst of romancing a woman at the Biltmore Hotel.

Art and Lowery had many memorable experiences while rooming together. It was with Lowery that Art had the breathtaking experience of sharing a Cocoanut Grove table with Clark Gable, Vivien Leigh, Leslie Howard, and Olivia de Havilland, who were starring in the recently released movie *Gone With the Wind*. Gable, Leigh, et al. had been at the Cocoanut Grove watching Heidt and his Musical Knights. Afterward, they invited Heidt, singer Larry Cotton, Lowery, and Art to join them for a round of drinks. Lowery remembered that Gable complained loudly and often about having to promote *Gone With the Wind*.

Although Art's relationship with Heidt resulted in his first show business success, it also enveloped him in yet another male-bonding fraternity (shades of the Bedfords). Hanging around with Frank DeVol, Ollie O'Toole, Fred Lowery, and Frankie Carle was nice, but it meant long weeks on the road away from Jean, who was accepted into New York's Juilliard's Academy after graduating from A. B. Davis High School in 1937.

Art and Jean had continued to date, and by 1940 they were deeply in love and contemplating marriage. The long stretches away from each other had only strengthened their feelings, and Art was beginning to think about the couple's future. Lowery and the guys' practical jokes aside (they once hired a hooker for Art as a "gift" while the band was in Milwaukee), Art was tiring of life with Heidt. Although Heidt had tripled Art's weekly salary to $150, he still insisted that Art perform the FDR/Al Smith routines he knew by rote. Art, meanwhile, wanted to expand his repertoire. His relationship with Heidt, rocky as ever, left him feeling uncomfortable and underappreciated. When Heidt hired Ollie O'Toole as his second impersonator, he began to feel crowded. Now Art decided to quit the band.

Before he quit, however, Art took care of his top priority: getting married.

Art had helped Lowery write love letters to his girlfriend (Lowery dictated, Art wrote). When the band reached Chicago's New Lawrence Hotel in August 1940 for a five-week gig at the

Edgewater Beach Hotel, Art confided to Lowery that he loved Jean and was considering marriage.

"I don't know what to do," Lowery remembered Art telling him while the two men talked in a bar. "I'm tired of playing around. I want a home and family, but I keep hesitating. I can't give up show business, and I'm not sure that Jean will ever be able to adapt to it. I don't want to make a mess of our lives." Without further ado, Art phoned Jean, who was vacationing with her family in Maine, and proposed over the telephone.

"It was a big deal to get a long-distance call. I could hear click-clicks going all over the place, people listening in," Art said about that fateful call. "I didn't care. I told her to come out to Chicago so we could get married, and she did."

It wasn't very romantic, but at the very least Jean could now replace Lowery as Art's traveling companion and join the wives of Frank DeVol and pianist Frankie Carle on tour with Heidt.

Jean and her parents left Mount Vernon on a Saturday morning and drove to Chicago, arriving Monday afternoon. On August 15, 1940, one week after Jean's arrival in the Windy City, Art and Jean were married in St. Thomas of Canterbury Church, with their parents and a few close friends in attendance. The very next day, the new Mr. and Mrs. Arthur Carney were off with Heidt to Los Angeles.

But Art was growing restless and tired of the constant disagreements with Heidt. Although Art and Heidt weren't overtly antagonistic—they would remain lifelong friends—Art decided to leave the band and strike out for greener professional pastures as a solo act.

Art had one more commitment to fulfill before ending his association with Heidt. Ironically, Art's bread-and-butter FDR impersonation was remotely connected to his first big-screen appearance.

President Roosevelt's son, James Roosevelt, was attracted to Hollywood's glitz and glitter and was trying to make a name for himself as a big-time producer. Unfortunately, James Roosevelt's efforts had amounted to a string of B-movie flops, and he now had the brilliant idea of transplanting Heidt's *Pot o' Gold* radio show, or a version thereof, to the big screen. Heidt and the

Musical Knights would provide the background for stars Jimmy Stewart and Paulette Goddard.

Heidt had begun the half-hour *Pot o' Gold* program in 1938. According to Heidt lore, Horace and crew were leaving Cincinnati's Gibson Hotel after being fired when a newsboy approached. "Mr. Heidt, I have an idea for you," he said. "Why don't you give money away on the radio? Everybody would tune in."

Thus was born *Pot o' Gold,* radio's first-ever giveaway program. Tums sponsored the show, in which Heidt thumbed through phone books from different cities, dialing random numbers. If Heidt's call was answered, the person would receive a thousand dollars. Art worked as a *Pot o' Gold* announcer when the show aired outside New York and in Hollywood.

For his *Pot o' Gold* movie, Roosevelt hired director George Marshall and managed to corral Stewart and Goddard, who were well known in 1940 but hadn't yet achieved superstardom. Veteran character actor Charlie Winninger and Irish actress Mary Gordon also were recruited.

"James Roosevelt produced *Pot o' Gold* about as well as I did; he just put his name on it," Frank DeVol recalled. "We had a very good cast, but it was a terrible picture. Art, Ollie O'Toole, and I were all in the picture, but we didn't have speaking lines or anything. We were in the band and sang 'A Knife, a Fork and a Spoon,' some piece of crap, but we had so much fun because we weren't in all the scenes. They had a big street scene for us, kind of an Argentinean thing they did. They had a stock of bananas, and we started eating those bananas, and we were down to about four bananas by the time we were through."

Filming on *Pot o' Gold* began in Hollywood in the fall of 1940. A silly, corny movie, *Pot o' Gold* told the story of Jimmy Haskel (Stewart), a financially strapped music-store owner whose Uncle Charles (Winninger) owns a successful health-food business and hosts a boring radio show, *The Haskel Happiness Hour.* Uncle Charlie wants Jimmy to join the family business, Haskel Health Foods, but Jimmy refuses. He changes his mind, however, when the bank threatens to foreclose on his music store.

Unbeknownst to Jimmy, Uncle Charlie is engaged in a raucous feud with his neighbors, the McCorkles, led by feisty Ma

McCorkle (Gordon). Ma McCorkle's daughter, Molly (Goddard), sings in Horace Heidt's band. The band lives in the McCorkle house, opposite Haskel Health Foods, and practices on the roof, annoying Uncle Charlie, a music hater who wants to buy the McCorkle place and expand his factory.

In a series of farcical events, Jimmy falls in love with Molly, ships Uncle Charlie off to Canada, and takes over *The Haskel Happiness Hour.* Jimmy gives Horace Heidt and His Musical Knights the chance to play to a nationwide radio audience and introduces the *Pot o' Gold* contest on his now popular radio show.

Blink once and you'll miss Art's *Pot o' Gold* appearances; blink twice and you'll swear he's not even in the movie. But Art is there, and if you look hard enough you'll see him jitterbugging in an early street scene and saying his first-ever line of movie dialogue—"Take it easy, will ya¢!"—while being shoved aside in a courtroom by Charlie Winninger. Art is also at the dinner table singing "A Knife, a Fork and a Spoon" in a rousing tribute to Ma McCorkle's Irish stew:

A knife, a fork and a spoon
Will beat out a happy tune
You'll all feel chummy as you fill your tummy
With a knife, a fork and a spoon!

Art's biggest scene lasts about fifteen seconds and comes near the end of the movie. Jimmy has brought *The Haskel Happiness Hour* to the Eastchester Country Club to give away his first thousand dollars and make peace between the Haskels and the McCorkles. Art is the show's announcer, and with his hair slicked back above his visible widow's peak, wearing a fancy dark suit, he steps up to the microphone after Ollie O'Toole. In his best stentorian tones, Art announces: "And don't forget, ladies and gentlemen, before this program is over we will give away one thousand in cash. The method of giving it will be announced later."

Pot o' Gold closed soon after opening. It would be Art's last big-screen appearance for nearly twenty-five years. For now, Art had in mind only settling down with Jean, leaving Heidt, and establishing himself as a nightclub comic.

3

RADIO DAYS

A rt was convinced that his talents were better suited as a solo act in vaudeville and nightclubs, and he looked for a way to leave Heidt on his own terms. It didn't take long before an opportunity presented itself, and once again both Lowery and alcohol—always a lethal combination—were involved.

In early 1941 Art and Lowery were in Chicago, working with Heidt on the *Pot o' Gold* show from a studio in the Merchandise Mart. After rehearsing, Art and Lowery decided to have a few drinks and order dinner at a nearby restaurant.

"The 'couple of cocktails' evolved into several double Manhattans," Lowery recalled. "When the third round was served I ordered steaks and coffee for both of us. However, while I ate, Carney scarcely nibbled at his food. Instead, he indulged in two more doubles."

Despite his substantial boozing, Art seemed to be in surprisingly good shape when he and Lowery showed up later for the *Pot o' Gold* show. But the studio was warm, and the heat soon took its toll on Art's pickled brain. Before long he was slurring his speech.

"After the band's opening fanfare he stumbled up to the microphone and started his regular commercial pitch—a spiel that called for him to spell out T-U-M-S over the air," Lowery recalled. "He didn't get very far. 'Ladeeees an' gennulllmum,' he began, 'Tums for the tummy! That's spelled . . .' He paused as he struggled to remember how to spell the product name, then plunged ahead once more. 'That's T-M-L . . . No, dammit, that's not right. T-U-M-L. Oh, the hell with it!' Admitting defeat, Art turned away from the mike and made his uncertain way back to his chair on the bandstand."

Heidt was furious. Not only had Art embarrassed the Musical Knights and the entire *Pot o' Gold* show, but Heidt was certain Tums would cancel their lucrative advertising contract after Art's debacle. Sure enough, Tums officials called Heidt the next morning and ordered him to fire his drunk announcer. Heidt stalled Tums for a few days before finally relenting. But Art wouldn't give him the satisfaction. He beat Heidt to the punch, announcing he was leaving the troupe to go solo. Art's career as a Musical Knight was over.

In all the newspaper and magazine articles written about Art Carney over the years—in all the interviews he gave and in all his public relations biographies—the years 1941 and 1942 are strangely glossed over or summed up in a single sentence. There's a reason for this: These weren't very happy times for Art, who had left Heidt to seek fame and fortune in the unforgiving vaudeville/nightclub circuit.

Art was a mimic who was accustomed to performing fifteen minutes a night. He was also an extremely introverted man who had functioned as a small part of a larger entertainment unit. That all changed now. Art, intent on making a name for himself, was forced into the spotlight to perform sixty to ninety minutes of material each night. There was no life preserver, no Horace Heidt to choreograph his act or provide a steady paycheck.

"When I started in nightclubs I felt I was too exposed," Art said later. "I couldn't cope with the audience as individuals so close to me—eating, drinking, sometimes heckling. If I'm in a play or on television, I can treat the audience as a hunk, as a mass; I still never look at them as individuals."

Art wasn't alone in his growing frustration with nightclubs and their often hostile atmosphere. His angst was being shared by a rotund comic named Jackie Gleason. Gleason had failed both as a Hollywood actor and as a nightclub comedian. Only after changing his act did Gleason begin to make a name for himself through insult humor and pure swagger.

Although their paths didn't cross at this time, both Art and Gleason found their inability to tell jokes and/or comic monologues to be their undoing on the nightclub circuit. Gleason was able to adapt and find his niche; Art, however, loathed this existence and never once felt comfortable.

By 1941 vaudeville was dying. Art's act, a pastiche of the impersonations he'd performed with Heidt, was admittedly short on material and long on tedium. "They didn't try to hold me over," Art later said about a gig in New York's Hotel Pierre.

But Art's act wasn't really that bad, at least not according to a *Variety* critic who reviewed his ten-minute performance at Brooklyn's Flatbush Theater in March 1941.

> Formerly with Horace Heidt, Art Carney looks like a first-rate possibility for the combo houses and some niteries. Though there is nothing particularly new or startling about personality imitations, Carney succeeds in making his take-offs both sufficiently humorous and realistic to hold attention.
>
> In addition to familiar Lionel Barrymore and Franklin D. Roosevelt mimicries Carney also essays more difficult impressions of Jimmy Stewart and Major Bowes. The Major Bowes carbon is one of his best. Carney's work is mostly vocal, his patter is lively, well-written and ably presented. Takeoff on Al Smith for the finish is surefire.

Art's brother Jack, still with MCA, encouraged Art to stick with nightclubs, no matter how dreadful he felt about the crowds at his sporadic performances. "A nightclub act is a commodity you can sell," Jack told Art. "An actor is just another name in a file. We have ten thousand actors on file and only a handful ever work."

Art would later say he couldn't remember any of the jokes he told in his aborted, yearlong nightclub career, and he was probably telling the truth. Art Carney, nightclub comic, was not in much demand during 1941.

"I worked, but not too often," he said. "The act wasn't too good, anyway. I just didn't have any self-confidence." Art hated the traveling (which included Miami and New Orleans) and the time away from Jean. Above all, he hated the overbearing burden of being the top banana.

Art's unhappiness and his lack of progress as a nightclub performer soon turned to desperation. By the end of 1941 Art, now twenty-three, had reached a crossroads in his skidding professional career. His income wasn't nearly enough to support Jean and himself, and the couple was forced, much to Art's chagrin, to move in with Jean's parents back in Mount Vernon. Art borrowed money from his in-laws, which is never a comfortable situation. (He eventually payed it all back.) But far from criticizing Art, Jean's parents were extremely supportive, encouraging Art to pursue his entertainment career.

Art was intent on forgetting about show business, and he applied for jobs as a shipping clerk at Macy's and Gimbel's department stores. Both stores turned him down.

"At one point I was so desperate I had job applications in with every department store in town," Art said. "But [my in-laws] wouldn't let me work at anything but acting. They believed in me."

Just when Art thought he had reached rock-bottom, he was rescued, once again, by his brother Jack.

Jack had left MCA to join CBS in 1942. Using his extensive show business contacts and his savvy, Jack steered Art toward the CBS Radio studios in New York. Jack had heard that CBS's *Report to the Nation* was looking for actors. He thought Art and his litany of impersonations would be a perfect match.

With television still six years in the future and vaudeville just about dead, radio, especially in New York, was the medium of choice for working actors. The pay was good, and actors could work several shows a day in different genres (soaps, comedies, melodramas, serials); often they payed stand-ins to read their lines while they raced from studio to studio.

"You could start at ten in the morning doing a soap opera, then at night go on to play a maniacal killer," said Larry Haines, Art's boyhood friend, who had established himself as a busy New York radio performer.

New York was radio's mecca in the early forties. *Gangbusters, This Is Your FBI, The Man Behind the Gun, Amos 'n' Andy*—the world of big-time radio could be found within a few square blocks in midtown Manhattan.

The problem for an unknown radio performer like Art was getting noticed. The radio community was essentially closed, with a core group of actors being hired for most of the juicy, well-paying roles.

Art's radio experience was limited to intermittent announcing chores on Heidt's *Treasure Chest* and *Pot o' Gold* programs. While he certainly had an authoritative announcing voice, he had yet to demonstrate any dramatic acting skills.

That all changed in 1942, when Jack told Art about the opportunity on *Report to the Nation*, the Saturday-morning news show that reenacted current events using actors to imitate the era's famous voices.

According to show business legend, Art walked into the CBS executive's office and immediately burst into his FDR imitation. "Good Lord!" the executive blurted out. "He *is* Roosevelt!"

Whether or not the story is true isn't important. Art obviously had impressed the executive, who immediately signed him to a contract and cast him on *Report to the Nation*. Art had at last found his niche. With memories of his desperate Macy's and Gimbel's job applications quickly fading, Art began making a name for himself as the man of a thousand voices.

Report to the Nation had Art working in his element, and the imitations that had wowed them back in Mount Vernon and during his three-year stint with Heidt were now paying handsome dividends. Art became a *Report to the Nation* regular and wore dozens of vocal hats: FDR, Wendell Wilkie, Harry Truman, George Marshall, and General Dwight D. Eisenhower among them. Before long he caught the attention of other radio producers, and his steady work gained him admission into radio's fraternity. That meant playing gin rummy with other radio actors at Colby's Restaurant over at CBS, or in Kauffman and Bedrick at NBC; shooting the breeze; taking a quick nap between jobs; or grabbing dinner at Louie and Armand's or the Swiss Inn.

"Art had the gift of imagination, to create characters that

were far away from himself," said Lon Clark, who voiced *Nick Carter, Master Detective* and worked regularly with Art on *Report to the Nation, March of Time,* and *Columbia School of the Air.* "There was a man named William Adams who had been quite well known for doing FDR, but Art's FDR was superb; Art had a remarkable timbre in his voice that fitted FDR's tonalities."

Art's impersonation of FDR was so realistic that FDR's press secretary, Steven Early, was forced to write *Report to the Nation*'s producer. "Don't have any more imitations of the President on your show," Early wrote. "That man who imitates the President is too good. We don't want people to think the President is going on your show."

Report to the Nation became Art's first real acting experience, and it led to a flood of offers that kept Art working steadily for the next two years, on soaps, children's shows, educational shows, comedies, and dozens of other programs airing on CBS, NBC, WOR, ABC, and the Mutual Network.

Radio shows were logged haphazardly in those days, and it's impossible to list all of Art's radio appearances from 1942 to 1944. He was often featured as an unbilled supporting player, and like his colleagues he jumped from show to show and from network to network, sometimes acting in up to six programs a day. Some shows were even reenacted later that same night so they could air live on the West Coast.

The radio logs that do survive from that period show Art's versatility. He played the supporting role of Angus opposite Jean McCoy in NBC's *Lorenzo Jones* ("Now smile awhile with Lorenzo Jones and his wife Belle . . .") and appeared in ABC's *Land of the Lost* as Red Lantern, a glowing, talking fish who befriends two children and helps them retrieve their lost toys from the bottom of the ocean (magic seaweed enabled the kids to breathe underwater).

Art's role as Billy Oldham in 1943's *Joe and Ethel Turp,* a fifteen-minute CBS comedy based upon Damon Runyon–created characters, unleashed upon the world a prehistoric version of Ed Norton, who wouldn't appear in all his glory for another decade. Art also appeared in CBS's *The Jack Pepper Show; The Case Book of Gregory Hood; Casey, Crime Photographer* (costarring Betty Furness); and a few episodes of CBS's *Escape.* He substituted for William

Adams as FDR on the children's program *Let's Pretend* and did a few episodes of *Adventures of the Thin Man.*

Art also worked on *The Man Behind the Gun,* which reunited him with Mount Vernon boyhood pal Larry Haines. "We were at CBS at the time, and I was doing a soap opera called *The Second Mrs. Burton* and Art was in the studio next door doing another soap opera," Haines said. "They preceded us on the air—they were on from 10:00 to 10:30 A.M. and we were on from 10:30 to 11:00. But we were on the air, live, and Art and this other chap walked into the studio as I was playing a love scene and they got behind me and undid my trousers. I was helpless because we were broadcasting, but I'll tell you, I had to pinch myself to keep from breaking up. That was the kind of crazy stuff we used to pull on one another. Art loved zany, far-out humor."

The Man Behind the Gun, however, was anything but zany and far-out; it was a somber, serious half-hour program revolving around the wartime experiences of armed forces members. Written by Randy McDougall and directed/produced by William N. Robson, *The Man Behind the Gun* aired every week, "for the purpose of telling you that your boys and their comrades-in-arms are waging our war against Axis aggression." Art, as usual, played a variety of roles and helped the series win a 1942 Peabody Award.

Art's friendship with Larry Haines also led to his first and only stab at professional writing. The duo wrote a script for a comedy they called *Bobo and Gigi,* and they planned to audition before network executives, hoping to sell the program.

"It was just two guys, more or less the kind of character Art played on *The Honeymooners,* but there were two of us," Haines recalled. "We were the same kind of nutsy guys based primarily on guys we knew as kids in Mount Vernon. We did this audition show and we kept breaking each other up; it never got off and we never finished it. But we both ad-libbed most of it. I think the whole recording was more us laughing at each other than the audience laughing at us."

Art's voice could be heard most often on CBS's *The March of Time,* a documentary series narrated by Westbrook Van Voorhis, who opened the show each week with the memorable, "As it must to all men, death came this week to . . ."

The March of Time dramatized topical news events long before *Report to the Nation,* and was better known for the talent it attracted. Agnes Moorehead, Dwight Weist, and Everett Sloane all acted on the program. Art, of course, played FDR.

Equally popular was the loud, raucous CBS drama *Gangbusters,* on which Art had recurring roles playing hoods, cops, and anyone else needed that particular night. *Gangbusters* was famous for its clarion pronouncement: "Calling the police! Calling the G-men! Calling all Americans to war on the underworld!"

Gangbusters was so popular that the phrase "coming on like gangbusters" sprang from the show's loud opening, which featured machine-gun fire and wailing sirens. Each episode was based on a true crime story and ended with descriptions of criminals. Art worked on the show with Haines; a young actor named Richard Widmark also got his start on *Gangbusters.*

Said Haines, "That particular show had a split-week rehearsal; we would rehearse Saturday morning for several hours, then acetate discs would be brought back to the producer's office and he would listen and determine what should be cut, changed, or added. Then on the day of the show, Saturday, we'd come in in the afternoon and do two shows, one for the East Coast and a repeat show for the West Coast. It was live, but very rarely would there be a hitch."

Not so in Art's personal life, where a hitch of a different sort was about to present itself. Making a comfortable living— about two hundred dollars a week—as a steadily employed radio actor had bolstered Art's confidence, and he now dreamed of working with Fred Allen and other big-name comics.

Steady work also meant a steady paycheck. Feeling financially secure (though still living with Jean's parents), Art and Jean decided the time was right to start a family. In September 1942 their daughter, Eileen Wilson Carney, was born.

But Art didn't have much time to enjoy his new baby. With the Allies preparing for D day, Art was drafted in spring 1944.

4

"NEVER EVEN FIRED
A SHOT"

They say that timing is everything in show business, and
Art Carney certainly had great timing. With brothers
Ned (USNR Dental Corps) and Fred (Forty-sixth Special
Service Company, Italy) already in the service, Art was drafted
into the army and sent overseas. As a replacement with
Pennsylvania's Keystone Division, Art left on July 15, 1944, for
Normandy, France. Armed Forces Radio tried, to no avail, to get
Art transferred from behind enemy lines.

Although Art didn't reach the Normandy beaches until
August 1944, two months after D day, the Nazi war machine
had yet to be completely silenced. Nazi snipers were everywhere, and Private Art Carney—radio's Man Behind the Gun—
now played the part for real, joining the Twenty-eighth Infantry
Division at the Viere sector and praying he wouldn't have to use
his rifle.

Art's prayers were answered, but he paid a painful price for
his ticket home. On August 15, 1944—his fourth wedding
anniversary—Art had set up his machine gun on Saint-Lô and
was filling a canteen with water when, without warning, he was
blown off his feet by a Nazi mortar shell.

"Something whammed me, and I was on the ground with my right leg bent in a funny way," he recalled. "I moved the foot a little. It was still attached. Nothing hurt much. A piece of shrapnel had ripped into my right thigh, but it just felt numb, and I started hollering, 'Medic, medic!' Never even fired a shot and maybe never wanted to. I really cost the government money."

Art was carried off the Normandy beachhead in a stretcher, wrapped in a body cast, and transported to an army hospital in the English Midlands. Doctors there hoped the bones in his right leg would knit together properly, but they never did. His injured right leg was now three-quarters of an inch shorter, and Art was left with a permanent limp that became more pronounced when he was tired.

When he was first brought into the hospital, Art couldn't even see his right leg, which was wrapped in plaster and suspended in a traction device while Art laid flat on his back, completely immobile. Depressed, in pain, and longing to return home, Art's spirits were lifted considerably when boyhood pal Al Tepe, stationed in Africa as an air force captain, paid a visit to England.

"I got a letter telling me Artie was in the hospital—that he was shot and so forth—and asking if I was anywhere near him," Tepe remembered. "They mentioned the place, and I got on a plane and went over there. He was in traction at the time, and I came in and it was just a great reunion."

Back in Mount Vernon, Jean had good reason to be alarmed. Art had been reported as missing in action since August 11, and she didn't receive any concrete news of Art's condition until she received two of his letters on September 5.

"Although no details were given by the War Department in the recent telegram listing him as 'missing,' letters from Carney . . . said he was wounded in France on Aug. 15 and was transported to a U.S. Hospital in England," the local newspaper reported. "Although the extent of his wounds was not mentioned in his letters, he said he was 'out of danger—making good progress—receiving excellent care—will be normal and may be sent home.' "

In late fall of 1944, still in traction and still completely immobile, Art was shipped back to America. He was transported to McGuire General Hospital, a military installation (now a VA hospital) located near Richmond, Virginia, that specialized in treating amputees and paraplegics. Jean and two-year-old Eileen visited when they could, sometimes driving the three hundred miles with Jean's parents or Geraldine Fryer. "Thank heavens I was hit," Art once confided to Geraldine. "I didn't have to kill anyone."

Lying on his back twenty-four hours a day, Art had plenty of time to think, and friends who visited him at McGuire noted a new seriousness, a maturity and sense of purpose that Art had taken with him from Normandy after his brush with death.

"I don't know what difference it made in me," he said later, "but I learned one thing: No matter how badly off you think you are, there's always some other guy who's worse off. Also, at a time like that you think about all the mean tricks you've pulled, and you promise yourself that if you ever get out you'll never again be nasty to people who are close to you."

But being nasty wasn't in Art's gentle nature, and he refused to feel sorry for himself during his nine-month hospital stay, even when doctors were forced to rebreak his right leg after his bones had calcified. As he had done with the Bedford Boys, Horace Heidt's troupe, and his radio colleagues, Art soon endeared himself to his McGuire roommates, some horribly injured—burn victims, amputees—and others in dire need of emotional support.

Rhoda (Saletan) Goldberger worked as an occupational therapist at McGuire during Art's stay. A native New Yorker and theater junkie homesick for Manhattan, she struck up a friendship with Art after learning of his New York roots. They also had a mutual acquaintance, radio actress Minerva Pious, who was a member of Fred Allen's ensemble troupe and later worked with Art on *The Henry Morgan Show*.

"Art was hoping at the time to audition for the Fred Allen group," Goldberger said. "He said he was hoping to get better fast because he would like to be able to get to New York to audition."

As an occupational therapist it was Goldberger's job to keep the men busy with books, puzzles, and other activities. Shortly after Art's arrival, however, she began to feel left out. The men had all the entertainment they needed.

"Nobody was interested in what I was pushing because Art had them in stitches; he had taken over as a sort of master of ceremonies and he had everybody singing and telling jokes," she said. "And he had everybody so happy and busy that they didn't want any part of me. I always wanted to go up there and was delighted to be there because the atmosphere was so great. It was a very happy place to be."

But Art's role as resident clown was balanced by the maturity he had gained through his near-death experience. Art was seven or eight years older than his McGuire roommates, and a married father. As his oldest brother Jack had been to him, Art now became a paternal figure, particularly to one young man in the adjoining bed.

"The boy in the bed next to him was going through some sort of romantic crisis. He was weeping in his bed, and Carney took over the role of big brother, father, and mentor and saw him through whatever this was," Goldberger recalled. "Among his other wonderful, warm qualities was his ability to listen and help this boy deal with whatever terrible tragedy was going on in his twenty-year-old life. Carney was there in the next bed, quietly listening to him. It was just between the two of them, and it was a very tender and special moment."

Art was discharged from McGuire in April 1945, nine months after the shrapnel blast and with much broader shoulders (thanks to the exercise he got lifting himself in and out of his wheelchair). He was awarded a Purple Heart for bravery, but he was just thankful to be alive.

Art returned to Jean, Eileen (now three), and his in-laws back in Mount Vernon. Collecting a fifty-five-dollar monthly army disability pension, he set his sights on reclaiming his place in radio.

But the army, apparently, had different plans. Two months after his discharge Art received a cable from Armed Forces Radio—they were still working on getting him transferred from behind enemy lines. Art, appreciating the irony, framed the letter.

5

"That's Right, Mr. Morgan"

B y mid-1945, with victory over the Axis powers assured, America entered a new phase of self-confidence. Riding the coattails of its economic boom were newly minted ex-GIs like Art Carney, hungry to forget the war, reenter society, and recharge their interrupted careers.

Unlike his first foray into radio in the early 1940s, Art found the business more receptive to him when he returned to New York in 1945. Having already paid his dues, established his vocal dexterity, and worked on hundreds of programs, Art was well known in the radio community yet virtually unknown to the general public. He didn't need to impress radio executives and sponsors, and he still preferred to remain somewhat anonymous, working steadily but taking secondary radio roles that wouldn't pigeonhole his talents or, more important, put him in the spotlight.

That would all change soon enough, but for the time being Art returned to the familiar confines of *Gangbusters* and appeared on a number of similar programs (*This Is Your FBI, Counterspy*). He also acted in *Aunt Jenny's Kitchen;* in the pilot episode of CBS's

Escape (an adaptation of the movie *Dead of Night*); and in Mutual Radio's *Mysterious Traveler* series (in an episode entitled "I Won't Die Alone").

Art appeared in NBC's *The Big Story* and impersonated all the male Aldrich Family characters in *Henry Aldrich*. A 1948 newspaper blurb about Art said he "claims to be one of the few Fred Allen impersonators who can sound like the famous comedian without pinching his nose, and on several occasions has done a solo dialogue—a trick involving lightning voice changes, with Mr. Carney actually being two men at the same time."

Monty Woolley's *The Magnificent Montague,* on which Art played Woolley's father, followed, as did a stint with good old Colonel Lemuel Q. Stoopnagle (Frederick Chase Taylor) and Budd, whose act Art had imitated back in A. B. Davis High School.

"The Colonel was delighted to have me. The word had gone around that I was available—cheap," Art recalled. Art and Stoopnagle ad-libbed and improvised, largely making the show up as they went along, which was just fine with the easygoing Stoopnagle. "Sometimes it was terrible," Art said, but whatever it was, the Stoopnagle show was a harbinger of the second-banana roles that soon were offered to Art with increasing regularity.

CBS signed Art to an exclusive contract—paying him even if he *didn't* work—and assigned him to "stooge" roles that teamed him with radio's biggest names: Bert Lahr, Milton Berle, Bea Lillie, Jack Haley, Goodman Ace, Robert Q. Lewis (Art played a night watchman in love with Abby Lewis's scrubwoman), Ethel Merman, Abe Burrows, Bobby Clark, Herb Shriner, and Edgar Bergen.

"The stars always know that I'm not trying to top them," Art once explained about his supporting radio roles. "If they're capable, they know they have to have people around them who work well—people they can trust and rely on. I'm easygoing—not quick to make suggestions or blow up in rehearsal, although I never take a job if I have any doubts about the character being for me.

"Bert Lahr once hired me for a baseball sketch. I was a

sports announcer interviewing him as a player. To me the script was a perfect takeoff on [sports announcer] Bill Stern and I read it that way, but Lahr didn't like it. He wanted the comedy to be broader. When I read it his way I didn't feel comfortable and told him I'd have to step out of the role. Finally, we compromised. Even if his original interpretation was right and mine was wrong, I still couldn't do it that way."

In February 1946 another addition to the Carney family arrived: a son, Brian. Art's higher-profile radio work and CBS contract now translated into a financial stability that allowed Art to move Jean, Eileen, and Brian from the Myerses' Mount Vernon house into an eight-room place in Yonkers. It was Art and Jean's first house, after six years of marriage.

By 1947 Art seemed to have everything—a fast-track radio career, an adoring wife, and two beautiful children. He even realized his wartime dream, joining Fred Allen's comedic ensemble for a few radio shows.

But the drinking that had started with Fred Lowery during the Horace Heidt years—those vodka-and-grapefruit breakfasts—resurfaced. Though Art was tasting his most rewarding show business success, it wasn't enough, or simply was too much for him to handle.

Jack Carney—who would later be instrumental in the Alcoholics Anonymous movement, helping to introduce the Serenity Prayer to AA meetings—was dealing with his own drinking. So were two of Art's other brothers. While alcoholism today is treated as a disease, in the late forties boozing wasn't taken very seriously; it was either considered a harmless pasttime or kicked under a rug of denial and ignorance.

Art's drinking began to put a strain on his family life. Jean was left at home in Yonkers with two toddlers, wondering if Art would return after an exhausting day in Manhattan capped off by a visit to the corner bar.

The problem, combined with or caused by his drinking, manifested itself in alarming mood swings. As with alcoholism, little or nothing was known about manic depression in the 1940s. But the way Art describes his drinking and bipolar moods—dizzying highs crash-diving to rock-bottom lows—suggests a manic-depressive condition. Typically, Art didn't burden others with his problems. Never anything but a sweetheart to friends and coworkers, he turned inward and blamed himself rather than reaching out or discussing his worries. Outwardly he was the same loosey-goosey practical joker he'd always been; inwardly, alcohol helped medicate his torment and self-doubt.

"I'd be so elated over things, I wanted to buy everybody a drink in the house," he said of those days. "When I was doing radio work everything would be fine, but I knew I was going to continue drinking when I got through work, call home, and stay in town. Even if I knew I had an early call the next day, I had to go the route. I mean, really get drunk. I said to my brother Jack, 'Why the hell did I go out and get drunk in New York and stay overnight and lie to my wife and tie one on? Why? Everything is OK.' And my brother said, 'People like you and me and the rest of the family have to watch out for those highs.' "

For Art, 1948 was a professional touchstone in several respects. Not only was Milton Berle making phenomenal inroads in a new medium called television, but Art's association that year with Morey Amsterdam would lead, indirectly, to Jackie Gleason.

San Francisco–born comic Morey "Yuk-A-Puck" Amsterdam was an accomplished cellist and comedy writer for just about everyone in the business, including Will Rogers and several presidents. Amsterdam's "Yuk-A-Puck" catchphrase became a popular novelty song often featured on his radio program, which CBS launched in June 1948.

The Morey Amsterdam Show centered around the fictional Golden Goose Café, a popular New York nightclub fronted by emcee Morey Amsterdam, who played his cello and welcomed various celebrities—Vic Damone, Frank Sinatra, Frances Faye, Romo Vincent—who would perform a few numbers. The show was produced by Irving Mansfield, whose wife, future best-selling author Jacqueline Susann, played Lola, the Golden Goose's wide-eyed cigarette girl.

Art's hectic radio schedule left little time for auditions. One audition landed him on a New York theater stage where Mansfield and Amsterdam sat in the darkened seats, scouting talent for *The Morey Amsterdam Show*.

"I had an open call, and some people got up to read, and here comes this guy who picks up the script for a few minutes and puts it down and starts to walk off," Amsterdam recalled. "And I yelled after him, 'What's the matter? Don't you like the script?' He said, 'Yeah, it's funny, but I don't do comedy, I do heavies on *Gangbusters*.' 'Well,' I said, 'it shouldn't be a total loss, read it anyway.' So he read it, and by the time he read four or five lines I said, 'This guy is just what we want. He's funny. He doesn't know he's funny, but he's funny.' "

"When I tried out for this job," Art remembered, "I tried to impress Morey with my by-now slightly creaking impersonations. But he was not completely convulsed."

Amsterdam, however, was impressed enough to hire Art as Charlie the Doorman, the Golden Goose's dim gatekeeper who was yet another variation on the character Ed Norton. "Amsterdam said he needed someone to play a dumb doorman named Charlie. I looked just the type," Art said with typical self-derision.

In December 1948 CBS decided to bring *The Morey Amsterdam Show* to television. Amsterdam, a generous performer quick to nurture talent, took Art and Jacqueline Susann with him to the *Amsterdam* TV show. He also added to his ensemble the Johnny Guarnieri Orchestra, announcer Don Russell, dancers Dottie Dean and Freddie Blair, Boots Orlanis, Libby Blank, and cadaverous, mute, bug-eyed comedian Leo Guarnieri.

On Friday, December 17, 1948, at 8:30 P.M., those Americans with TV sets—they were few and far between—got their first fuzzy, black-and-white glimpse of Art Carney. But Art and the rest of *The Morey Amsterdam Show* crew didn't have much time to enjoy life on CBS. Four months later, in April 1949, the fledgling DuMont Network, which aired in New York on Channel 5, wooed Amsterdam away from CBS. DuMont hoped Amsterdam could establish a signature show around which the network could build a solid programming base for its East Coast outlets in New York, Philadelphia, and Washington, D.C.

When he moved to DuMont in 1949, Amsterdam encountered some of the same "intellectual property" problems faced by David Letterman forty-four years later when he bolted NBC for

CBS. NBC informed Letterman that much of his *Late Night* shtick could not be transplanted to CBS because it was the intellectual property of NBC and therefore fell under some sort of nebulous trademark-infringement clause. Letterman was forced to change the name of his band, his popular top 10 list, and even the moniker of sometime sidekick Larry "Bud" Melman, who on CBS went under his real name, Calvert DeForest.

In 1949 CBS told Amsterdam he couldn't use the Golden Goose name or the names of his ensemble characters on DuMont because they were CBS property. Undaunted, Amsterdam changed the Golden Goose to the Silver Swan and Art's Charlie the Doorman to Newton the Waiter, a goofy table server dressed in a tuxedo with an ever-present white towel draped over his arm. Art emphasized the look by giving Newton a thick, Chaplin-style mustache, dark eyebrows, and slick hair parted straight down the middle.

The Morey Amsterdam Show aired Thursdays at 9 P.M. on DuMont. It opened with a shot of the Silver Swan's interior, nattily dressed patrons dancing slowly to Johnny Guarnieri's soothing tones until announcer Don Russell, clad in white dinner jacket, introduced Amsterdam. Morey would launch into a three-minute monologue ("My girl was accused of stealing the fur but I took the crap") and a quick rendition of "Yuk-A-Puck" before Newton came crashing in from stage left or right.

AMSTERDAM: What are you doing here?

CARNEY (as Newton): I'm catchin' mosquitoes and saving 'em.

AMSTERDAM: What are you saving 'em for?

CARNEY: I got a date with a girl in a while. I told her I'd take her out for a bite!

AMSTERDAM: Oh, come on! Are you out of your mind? You should be taking care of the customers.

CARNEY: No I'm not out of my mind.

AMSTERDAM: Well, you're flipping your lid or something, for heaven's sake! These poor people are sitting around, haven't got anything to eat or drink, and you're sitting here eating mosquitoes. What's the matter with you, old man? We gotta do something to improve business!

CARNEY: Whaddya mean? Business is good. I was here last night, the place was jammed. I couldn't get in.

AMSTERDAM: Last night we were closed.

CARNEY: We were closed? You just gave me an inkling. I got an idea to improve business around this joint. Get a disc jockey, all the other places have 'em. Talk to people over the air, 'Come to the Silver Swan.'

AMSTERDAM: Who can I get for a disc jockey?

CARNEY: I'm your boy. You're barking up my alley! I was practically brought up on spinning records.

AMSTERDAM: What are you talking about?

CARNEY: I want you to know when I was a baby my nurse kept me on a turntable! I had an automatic changer.

Newton usually complained about his hairy landlady, Trooper, while he and Amsterdam engaged in this sort of nonsensical banter. Their conversation was punctuated by Newton's staccato, machine-gun bark of a laugh ("Ha! Ha! Ha!") and his trademark "Va, va, va, voom!"—his way of describing an attractive woman. Newton emphasized his "Va, va, va, voom!" with elaborate hand gestures. Watching kinescopes of Amsterdam's show, it's obvious that Art quite often stole the spotlight from Amsterdam (shades of things to come with Gleason), a situation Amsterdam seemed to welcome.

"People said to me, 'Why did you give Art all those great lines?' and I said, 'Because he was funny,' " Amsterdam recalled. "I didn't care what people said; the thing that was important to me was that someone was making the show popular. People actually thought we were doing a broadcast from a real night-club. They used to call up for reservations."

Art later said that "Morey Amsterdam taught me plenty about humor. Morey's a stand-up gagman. He's not afraid to pass a gag along to another fellow. He's not afraid you're going to steal his act from him."

Art's second-banana work on the Amsterdam show began to attract critical praise, including a full-page feature article in the August 27, 1949, issue of *TV Guide* (then called *Television Guide*). The article included a picture of Art dressed as Newton, posing with Amsterdam sporting a raccoon hat.

Headlined "Va, Va, Va, VOOM!: Art Carney Rates as Top Comedy Stooge on TV," the article called Art "priceless. . . . His catchphrase, 'Va, va, va, voom!' has all the enthusiasm of a male seal greeting a female arctic explorer who used to have a featured spot at Leon & Eddie's. Carney, as the garrulous, mustached waiter of 'The Silver Swan Cafe,' is always good for his quota of laughs. And he comes to life without any of the standard tricks of the trade."

New York Times TV critic Jack Gould was equally enthusiastic. "In the supporting cast, Art Carney almost runs away with the show," Gould wrote on January 16, 1949. "Playing the doorman at the nightclub, he has an excellent sense of timing and, if only by reason of his much greater height, practically overwhelms Mr. Amsterdam. Too, Mr. Carney has the important gift of knowing when to throw away a line and of keeping his clowning always under control. He should have a bright future in TV."

Art's sudden TV acclaim didn't inflate his ego. If anything, his success with Amsterdam only heightened his anxiety. This translated into drinking binges and the occasional bender. Still, Art kept himself somewhat grounded. He had the support of his family and friends, who still numbered most of the Mount Vernon Bedford Boys.

"When I was dating my future wife, I bragged that I knew Art Carney, who was playing a waiter in the Silver Swan Café on *The Morey Amsterdam Show,* filmed in a broken-down old building," recalled boyhood pal Robert Abbatecola. "I sent a note up and a few minutes later Art came running down the stairs zipping up his pants and was very embarrassed and surprised to see me with this lovely young girl. He took us upstairs where we met the director, who put us on the stage as part of the set and told me to face backward while making sure my date looked at the camera. Elliott Roosevelt and his then wife, Faye Emerson, were the guests, and Artie was very relaxed and funny. We were knocked off the air by a football game and never did get to see ourselves, front or back."

The Morey Amsterdam Show ran on DuMont until October 12, 1950. In the meantime, Art returned to radio for a few appearances on NBC's sci-fi program *Dimension X,* one of the first radio shows recorded on tape. *Dimension X* boasted the creative pedigree of writers Ray Bradbury and Earl Hamner Jr. and cast members Jack Lemmon, Santos Ortega, Jackson Beck, Larry Haines, and Jack Grimes, with whom Art had worked on various radio programs in the forties.

"I remember Art and I doing a *Dimension X* in which Art was a robot and I was a golfer and we had a golf tournament," Grimes said. "He had to play the robot in a game of golf. I remember the characters walking down the fairway and Art with this monotone-type voice, but not too phony or mechanical—it had some sort of human inflections."

In the spring of 1950, Art also started working on Henry Morgan's NBC radio show, which began with Morgan's cynical sign-on: "Good evening anybody, here's Morgan."

Henry Morgan, born Henry Von Ost, had made a name for himself on New York's WOR in the early forties as one of radio's original angry young men. His fifteen-minute *Here's Morgan* shows—or diatribes, depending on his mood—dripped with acerbic sarcasm and often included sponsor bashing (unheard of in those days of sponsor-supported shows). Morgan was famous for needling Adler Elevator Shoes and for accusing Life Savers of "mulcting the public" by drilling holes in its candy. Another sponsor, Schick Injector Razors, used the slogan "Push, pull, click, click," which in Morgan's lingo became "Push, pull, nick, nick." When Schick complained that Morgan was harming sales, he responded on the air by chiding the company: "Frankly, I don't think it's my show. I think it's their razor!"

Although Art joined him on radio, Morgan had already tried—and failed—with several TV shows. His *On the Corner* aired Sundays in 1948 on ABC (on DuMont in New York) and jumped around NBC's schedule in 1949 before disappearing in April of that year.

So Morgan returned to NBC Radio with the half-hour *Henry Morgan Show* and a stock company featuring, among others, Arnold Stang, who later worked regularly on Milton Berle's TV show. Art joined the company in 1950 and was somehow able to handle Morgan's stormy moods and barbed wit. Writer Aaron

Ruben—who'd spent fifteen years with Fred Allen and would help create *The Phil Silvers Show* and *The Andy Griffith Show,* among others—introduced the *Morgan Show*'s episodic format before leaving after only three weeks.

"He [Morgan] was a pretty difficult guy; he was very bright and very witty and funny, but there was something absolutely destructive about him," Ruben recalled. "Most of the time he was ornery and would just lash out for really no reason. I was told he went to a party once where Dorothy Parker was present and before the evening was over he had her in tears."

Morgan's surliness had most of his show's ensemble living in constant fear. He could be caustic, cruel, and unpredictable—exactly the type of person from whom Art would have shied away.

But Art wasn't aware of Morgan's temperament. He auditioned for the show and impressed Morgan enough to be accepted into the troupe. Curiously, Morgan's tongue lashings rarely, if ever, were directed at Art, who along with Arnold Stang got along famously with the boss.

"Art was a great guy to work with and was never a problem; there was never any controversy over how many jokes he had, nothing like that at all," Ruben remembered.

Art's major recurring *Morgan Show* character was the Athlete, a dim-witted jock (baseball's "Peewee" Carney, wrestling's "Gorgeous" Carney, swimming's "Buster" Carney) who gave nonsensical answers to Morgan's questions. The Athlete always started his answers by mumbling, "That's right, Mr. Morgan."

"I would do a real interview and he would, of course, misunderstand the question," Morgan explained. "I'd say, 'How do you feel today?' And he'd say, 'Yes, I ate the Crunchies for breakfast and I find them very nourishing.' He thought it was a standard endorsement and he was going to get paid for it."

The Athlete was, in essence, a broader version of Ed Norton. The Athlete had Norton's loony spirit.

"I was this punch-drunk guy, Lefty O'Toole, and Morgan would interview me each week," Art remembered. " 'I read in the paper that you've pitched four no-hitters this season, Lefty,' he'd say, and I'd say, 'That's right, Mr. Morgan.' 'So what is your favorite ball, Lefty?' I'd hesitate and then say, 'Is it all right to say "spit" over the radio?' 'Yes,' he'd say, and then I'd say, 'Well, my favorite ball is a curveball—with spit on it.' "

A typical Athlete segment aired on April 4, 1950. It began after Morgan—"Standing on his favorite corner, in front of the cigar store"—engaged Arnold Stang's nebbish Gerard in a comic interlude. Then it was off to the NBC studios and "time now to present the athlete who, in our opinion, made the most impressive showing in his particular sport this week. Our man of the week tonight is that great wrestling champion . . . 'Gorgeous' Carney."

MORGAN: Now, Gorgeous, most of the sports writers seem to agree that you are, without question, the most outstanding wrestler in the country today.

CARNEY (as Gorgeous): Right. That's right, Mr. Morgan.

MORGAN: What did you say?

CARNEY: That's right, Mr. Morgan.

MORGAN: Yes, well, first, tell me, what about your name? Isn't there another wrestler named Gorgeous, Gorgeous George?

CARNEY: I was first.

MORGAN: Oh. You had the name first. Are you sure?

CARNEY: Sure. It's my real name.

MORGAN: Oh, well, I certainly won't argue that with you. Let's get on to some more important lowdown about you. . . .

CARNEY: Ask my mother!

MORGAN: What?

CARNEY: Ask my mother if my name isn't Gorgeous! Why'd she do it! I got a brother named Sam, why'd she name me Gorgeous?!

MORGAN: Well, I really don't know. But, uh, Gorgeous, or do you prefer I call you Mr. Carney?

CARNEY: Either way. As long as you call me for breakfast. (*Laughs idiotically.*)

MORGAN: Well, uh, Gorgeous, tell me, how do you manage to stay in such splendid condition?

CARNEY: Oh, sleepin', workin' on the old barbells, drinkin' sauerkraut juice.

MORGAN: I'll bet your brother tries to follow your lead, doesn't he?

CARNEY: Who, Sam? Nah, he stays out late, drinks, leads a terrible life, never know when he gets home.

MORGAN: Even so, I can imagine what your brother looks like, compared to you.

CARNEY: Yeah, he's bigger than me!

MORGAN: Well, Gorgeous, here's something most wrestling fans are curious about, especially those who've seen it on television. Is wrestling really a fake?

CARNEY: No! I get paid! I would like to invite all the fans that could come and see me wrestle next Tuesday night by the Edgewood Park Arena—my mother's gonna be there, you know, the one who named me Gorgeous. She weighs 175, she's in the semifinals! You come on up too, Mr. Morgan, and watch how I (*grunts like an animal*).

"I'd say Art was the least pushy actor I ever met, as though he wasn't really trying to have a career," Morgan said. "The way I can explain it best is that Arnold Stang used to go around telling the other actors what to do. Carney wouldn't think of doing a thing like that. He's one of the few people about whom I cannot ever think of anything wrong."

6

"A MATCH MADE
IN HEAVEN"

By 1950 Art was making a good living. He wasn't a million-aire, but his work on television and radio with Morey Amsterdam and Henry Morgan was keeping him busier than ever. With his family living in the eight-room Yonkers house, Art decided he needed a professional agent to steer him through a growing myriad of financial and professional concerns.

As always, Art relied heavily on the advice of his oldest brother, Jack, who recommended Art meet his good friend Bill McCaffrey.

William McCaffrey was a former office boy in the Benjamin Keith–Edward Albee theatrical circuit who had worked for NBC and Columbia Pictures. McCaffrey was also a recovering alcoholic who had built a small, loyal client base. Actors like Shirley Booth, James Mason, and Mary Martin and baseball announcer Red Barber all relied on McCaffrey's self-professed "mother hen" nur-turing. McCaffrey established his office at 501 Madison Avenue, directly across the street from CBS. Among his employees were Eleanor Kilgallen, the sister of society columnist Dorothy Kilgallen.

"He'd been in the business as a manager/agent since the early thirties and used to enjoy talking about how at one time he had worked for Joseph P. Kennedy," recalled singer Julius LaRosa, a McCaffrey client. "He was gregarious, outgoing, irascible—he was all those marvelous things, a very colorful Irishman who boasted to a certain extent about not having had much formal training. But he read possibly more than anyone I've ever known."

McCaffrey was the perfect agent for Art; they had much in common. They were Irish, devoted family men, and drinkers, although McCaffrey claimed to have beaten his alcoholism. "He got up one morning [after drinking] and he didn't remember a goddamn thing. It scared the shit out of him and he quit," LaRosa said.

Like Jack Carney, McCaffrey was a lot older than Art and was a steadying, soothing, father-figure presence. Art and McCaffrey bonded instantly and formed a show business and personal friendship that lasted until McCaffrey's death thirty-five years later. When Art won his Oscar in 1975, one of the first people he thanked was McCaffrey—which reduced his longtime agent/confessor to tears.

"McCaffrey was not a bad-tempered guy; he was an outgoing, interesting fellow, kind of a self-made man," said Tom Ryan, a former CBS attorney who knew McCaffrey and later represented Art in various legal matters. "He married [NBC president] John Royal's secretary, Margaret O'Connor, a lady who went to Fordham Law School and had Judge [Joseph] Crater the semester he disappeared. McCaffrey had been a drunk before I knew him, but I never knew him to take a drink. He was known quite extensively in the radio business—and most of the people who came over to television came from radio."

An up-and-coming TV performer named Jackie Gleason was the odd exception. Born in Bensonhurst, Brooklyn, in 1916, Herbert John "Jackie" Gleason's life had been extremely difficult. By the time he was seven, Jackie had lost both an older brother (to sickness) and a hard-drinking father who, morose over his older son's death, abandoned Jackie and Jackie's mother in late 1923. Jackie spent his formative years hanging around Bensonhurst pool halls and eating himself into oblivion. It was biographical fodder he would use in *The Honeymooners*.

In the early forties, after a short-lived career as an insult comic playing clubs in New York and New Jersey, Gleason headed to Hollywood, where he floundered badly. In 1942 he appeared in five movies: *All Through the Night, Larceny, Inc., Navy Blues, Springtime in the Rockies,* and *Orchestra Wives.* None made a lasting impression on an industry already bursting with B-movie comics.

Bitter and angry, Gleason left Hollywood and resumed his nightclub career. This time he was a lot more successful. Chucking his prepared material, Gleason began insulting audience members and discovered he could get laughs through this type of ad-libbed humor. He soon gained a reputation in celebrity-packed joints like Slapsie Maxie's and New York's Club 18, havens for the show business elite where Gleason insulted anyone and everyone— much to their delight.

In 1948 NBC approached Gleason to star as Chester Riley in a television version of the radio hit series *The Life of Riley.* It was Gleason's first big show business break.

"I brought him out to California to do *The Life of Riley,* which he did for six months," said Jack Philbin, Gleason's longtime agent and business partner. "It was an excellent show and won awards from the standpoint of excellence in television, but it wasn't accepted by the public. They really wanted the guy who originally did it, William Bendix, but he couldn't do it because the [radio] studios had rules then that none of their contract players could go on television. After six months, when Jackie wasn't renewed, we were trying to sell him to pictures and various places to keep his career alive."

Around that same time, television's DuMont Network, Art's current home on *The Morey Amsterdam Show,* was launching a show called *Cavalcade of Stars.* A Friday-night variety show filled with blackout sketches and dancing girls, *Cavalcade* used rotating hosts and writers in an effort to keep its material fresh. In 1950 Philbin and his partner, George "Bullets" Durgom, managed to wrangle Gleason a coveted two-week *Cavalcade* hosting stint after emcee Jerry Lester defected to NBC.

Gleason was an instant smash and before long had earned a role as permanent host. During Gleason's early *Cavalcade* days the bulk of the show's sketches were written by Coleman Jacoby and Arnie Rosen, who needed two extra weeks to prepare Gleason's first show. In the interim, Joseph Cates, an assistant to *Cavalcade* producer Milton Douglas, rented sketches from several Broadway revues, a common practice that guaranteed material, good or bad.

Gleason's first show went smoothly; for his second show, Jacoby and Rosen were ready to unveil their original material, including a character named Reggie Van Gleason III, Man of Compunction, a top-hatted, mustached narcissist modeled after a popular series of Calvert Whiskey ads. Those ads featured a suave, debonair man-about-town, the "man of distinction," who, of course, drank Calvert Whiskey.

In the sketch, Reggie is hired by a top ad agency to pose for a series of magazine ads touting a certain "distinguished" whiskey. The sketch called for Reggie to visit the agency's fey photographer, who demonstrates for Reggie the correct way of throwing back a drink...and another drink...and another drink...until the two men are completely sloshed.

The photographer was as important—if not more so—to the sketch as Gleason. As envisioned by Jacoby and Rosen, the photographer would provide a comedic canvas onto which Gleason could paint his caricaturish brush strokes. Jacoby and Rosen had worked with Art on radio's *Robert Q. Lewis Show* and were impressed with his deft touch, even though he was a minor supporting player.

They knew they had their photographer.

"We got to know Art pretty well when Arnie Rosen and I were working at CBS. He was brilliant, and we remembered him," Jacoby recalled. "We brought him in cold and pushed him down Gleason's throat."

Joe Cates, after hearing about Art from Jacoby and Rosen, walked over to *The Morey Amsterdam Show* and asked producer Irving Mansfield for permission to "borrow" Art for the Man of Compunction sketch.

"I called Art and he said, yes, it's fine, call Bill McCaffrey," Cates remembered. "I think we paid Art either $175 or $250. Jackie was getting $750 in the beginning. Art came in during Wednesday afternoon rehearsal and took a seat. There were some other people I'd cast in bit parts. Gleason came in and said, 'Hiya, pal, whatta we got?' I handed him the sketch, and he said, 'Who's gonna play it?' I said, 'The guy sitting over there, Art Carney. I'll introduce you to him.' He said to me, 'How would I know him, pal?' He had no idea who Art was. I said, 'He's on *The Morey Amsterdam Show,* but you may remember he used to do comedy with Horace Heidt and his orchestra.' So I went over and introduced him, and Jackie pretended to know who Art was. And then they went to work. It was a match made in heaven."

"I didn't know Gleason, and Gleason didn't know me," Art said later in typical understatement. "I read the part, and that was it. Nothing sensational."

The Man of Compunction sketch aired, according to Cates, on July 15, 1950, and it soon became apparent to everyone present that the chemistry between Gleason and Carney was dynamite, Art's deft, balletic movements contrasting Gleason's heavy-handed comedy.

Recalled Jacoby, "The idea of the sketch was for Carney, for the sake of realism, to say to Reggie, 'I want you to toss a drink off with the élan of a polo player, heir to millions.' And Gleason says, 'I never drink, I abhor the stuff.' And Carney says, 'You never drink?' And Gleason says he didn't want to toss the drink off because of his father, who drank six barrels of whiskey—on the day he died. Anyway, he becomes terribly drunk as Carney begins telling him how to do it, holding his elbow at a right angle to the bottle . . . and they both get drunk; each one winds up taking the other's picture, and Carney winds up posing for the picture, and Gleason winds up under the old-fashioned camera cloth."

After the show, Gleason told Cates to hire Art for the next week and find something for him to do, even though no material was written.

"The first time I saw the guy act I knew that I'd have to work twice as hard for my laughs," Gleason recalled. "He was funny as hell."

Art was soon appearing regularly with Gleason on *Cavalcade of Stars* while still working for Morey Amsterdam on Thursday nights. After Amsterdam's show was canceled in October 1950, Art heard that Henry Morgan was gearing up for another stab at television. He approached Morgan.

Morgan didn't hire Art immediately. In January 1951 NBC

introduced *Henry Morgan's Great Talent Hunt,* a half-hour takeoff on *The Original Amateur Hour,* in which Morgan introduced people with offbeat "talents," like a man who played the violin with his teeth or a woman who had taught her dog to talk. Arnold Stang rehashed his nerdy Gerard persona from Morgan's radio show, and Kaye Ballard was among the *Talent Hunt* cast members.

But *Henry Morgan's Great Talent Hunt* was short-lived. In April 1951 NBC scratched the talent-search format and transformed the show into a traditional comedy/variety half hour. Art and his future *Honeymooners* costar Pert Kelton were now added to Morgan's ensemble.

"Art came to my house and asked to be part of the show," Morgan recalled. "I said to him, in all sincerity, what I believed. 'Kiddo, you are very good on radio, but this is a different medium, and frankly I don't know how I could possibly use you. You have a funny way of using your voice, sure, but this, well . . .' He didn't beg or plead. He said something quietly about just giving him a crack at it. So, against my better judgment, I did."

Art reprised the Athlete for two months on Morgan's TV show and stayed until the final broadcast on June 1, 1951. Art's commitment to Morgan was more out of loyalty than need. *Cavalcade* was growing in popularity, and Art's role in the show was expanding every week. His partnership with Gleason was transforming Friday-night television into a must-see experience for millions of Americans. Back on Bedford Avenue, they let out a cheer: Mount Vernon's favorite son was a television star.

7

GLEASON

The creative seed that sprouts in a two-man comedy team isn't necessarily planted in compatible soil. Bud Abbott and Lou Costello's on-screen magic transcended their shaky off-screen partnership. Dean Martin and Jerry Lewis were hardly friends while ruling the box office roost as Hollywood's top comedy team.

So it's not surprising that compatibility was in short supply between Art Carney and Jackie Gleason, even at the dawn of their remarkable professional relationship. Gleason was gregarious, Art was introverted; Gleason was a braggart, Art was exceedingly modest; Gleason reveled in Toots Shor's spotlight, Art hid in Yonkers; Gleason was alienated from his wife and two daughters, while Art remained a devoted husband and father. Gleason came from a broken home, Art was nurtured in a supportive, loving atmosphere; Gleason lived in a sterile hotel penthouse, Art lived in a comfortable suburban home; and finally, Gleason battled a persistent weight problem, but Art was pencil-thin.

"Art was not part of [Gleason's] crowd, but the crazy thing about it, when these two guys got on stage, the comedy was almost of cosmic origin—it was so good, so rare," said writer A. J. Russell. "They were strangers on the outside, but the moment they faced each other before the camera, they seemed to create an atmosphere of fun that is very, very difficult to achieve."

Prodigious drinking was about all that Art and Gleason had in common, and even in that respect they handled themselves differently. During the 1950s, Gleason's legendary postshow celebrations almost always unfolded in pal Toots Shor's celebrity-packed bar. It was there that the flamboyant Great One—sporting his ever-present carnation and cigarette—would loudly regale his entourage with outrageous stories while challenging Toots to boisterous, excessive drinking contests.

"Gleason and I would be drinking, and we would say, 'Hey, let's call Carney.' And we'd call him up and talk," remembered Gleason's manager, Jack Philbin. "Gleason really liked Art, but Art and Jackie were not the same kind of guys, not ideal companions for one another. Carney didn't want any of that 'I'm the greatest!' stuff, and he was on the quiet side. He wanted to sneak away somewhere."

Art rarely joined Gleason at Toots Shor's. When he did venture into the smoky watering hole, Art was most comfortable blending into the woodwork adorning the bar's outer fringes. "Carney was a good friend of Toots's—he didn't move in the same circle, but he could have anytime he wanted to," Philbin said. "They would have welcomed him, but he stayed away."

"Jackie loved to give parties over at Toots Shor's, and Art would come, and he was very quiet at these parties until he sat down at the piano," recalled character actor George Petrie, a *Gleason Show* regular during the fifties. "Art expressed himself at the piano. I don't know if he ever took a lesson in his life, but he's a very good piano player. And he'd sit there and just bang away at the songs of the day, and we'd start to sing. I never really saw him sitting close to Jackie and talking to him."

Art's drinking, like Gleason's, rarely interfered with his work; unlike Gleason, Art usually drank alone or with a trusted friend or two. Art and Gleason rarely drank together. Not only did they have little in common outside of work and their Irish roots, but Gleason was the boss—of which Art was keenly aware.

Gleason lorded over his production staff, rarely spoke to his writers, and made it clear that every *Gleason Show* decision emanated from his Park-Sheraton Hotel suite. Gleason had a meaty hand in casting, costumes, and contracts. Not only did Art respect Gleason's power, but the situation was perfect for his non-confrontational nature. Art's outwardly submissive demeanor posed no threat to the insecure, bullying Gleason. To Gleason, Art was the perfect foil—both on screen and off.

"I don't think I'm suited to do something like the Gleason show," Art said at the time. "Not as top man, anyway. Some people are perfectly suited to be in a secondary position, and they do a capable job there, but if they take on too much they're lost. Especially if they don't have the temperament for the top spot. I don't think I have [that temperament], and that's why I want to stay where I am. I'm not geared for it—don't have the drive."

Art and Gleason rarely socialized, and Gleason never once expressed an interest in visiting Art and Jean in Westchester. ("In fairness, I never asked him, because I knew that he'd turn me down," Art later told Gleason biographer William A. Henry III). But it was obvious that the duo's feelings ran deeper than star and second banana. It was the intangible, unspoken emotions that told the real story between these two performers.

Art and Gleason formed a mutual admiration society, voicing their respect for each other in countless print interviews. "Gleason and I never had a cross word with each other," Art repeatedly told interviewers looking for a chink in the duo's show business armor. "We hit it off from the moment we met" was another of Art's familiar refrains. Gleason expressed similar sentiments and was quick to credit Art with his show's success.

From the very beginning of his *Cavalcade* show, Gleason rarely upstaged his second banana, welcoming Art's ability to cover up his miscues—Gleason never rehearsed and often forgot his lines—and to draw his own laughs as Gleason's straight man.

"He was the only star I ever worked with who said, 'Go for more,' Art said. "If you got a laugh, that was fine. If you got two laughs, that was better. He didn't worry about me upstaging him or showing him up—although when it came to being spontaneously funny, he was pretty damn fast on his feet."

Cavalcade producer and Gleason comanager Jack Philbin concurred. "Gleason loved Carney, and anything that Art wanted to do, he could, as far as the show was concerned," Philbin said. "Gleason bent over backwards to give Art good jokes. Many times he would give jokes the writers had allocated for him to Art and he'd say, 'No, Art, you do that and I'll react.' Their relationship was good that way. They weren't what I would say personal, inti- mate friends, but as an artist, Jackie admired Art greatly."

But Henry Morgan remembered a different relationship between Art and Gleason. Art, in fact, had talked to Morgan about Gleason when he returned to Morgan's show in the spring of 1951—just after Art's first *Cavalcade* go-round with Gleason.

"Art came back and said he had more fun on my show, that Gleason wasn't so hot to work with," Morgan said. "I was very pleased, and we went on until my show folded and Art went back to Gleason. Actually, he disliked Gleason, and so did the others who worked with him. But when the book came out they all, loy- ally, refused to say anything against him. Including Art, of course."

The few times that Art and Gleason seemed to connect on a raw level involved alcohol. Getting drunk, especially with each other, seemed to loosen them up just enough to let down their emotional guards.

"If I stayed over in New York the days Gleason was at the Park-Sheraton, the next day when I woke up with a hangover I'd head to, of all places, Gleason's bar, where the Irish bartender there knew me," Art recalled. "By the time I got through I was crocked. One such day I went back to the hotel, went into one of the Gleason offices, and curled up on the bathroom floor.

"But he [Gleason] never forced booze on me. Once when I drank and blew my lines I was furious with myself because I let him down. I was so disgusted, I hit every bar on Eighth Avenue afterward. I tried to work up enough courage to face him." After both men had what Art called an "Irish crying jag" and hugged each other, Gleason told Art, "Now we'll get drunk together. But on my show I'll be the one to do it, not you."

Gleason's attitude, however chivalrous and well intentioned, typified his gargantuan appetite for recognition. Everything the Great One did had to be larger than life, including his art deco house in Peekskill, New York, which Art said "looks like it was made out of peppermint wafers." Gleason demanded that CBS make him the highest-paid performer in television, and he was awarded a million-dollar contract. He had a bevy of beautiful *Gleason Show* dancers, dubbed Glea Girls. And, of course, there was his drinking and carousing. Still, Gleason's enormous pop-culture shadow shielded Art from the pressures of having to sin-glehandedly carry a network television show.

Those pressures, at least for Gleason, began to mount as *Cavalcade* entered its second season. The show was starting to attract a larger audience, and the demand for new material was taking its toll, not only on Gleason but on a *Cavalcade* writing staff growing weary of their high-decibel boss. Gleason's writers were often reduced to sliding their scripts under his door. When and if they did meet with Gleason, he could be aloof, arrogant, and nasty, often dismissing their work with a curt "There's nothing there" before admonishing them to try again. When a sketch suc-ceeded, Gleason took the credit. If it failed, he distanced himself and blamed his writers.

Art, on the other hand, ingratiated himself with the staff with his easygoing demeanor and gentle wit. On Gleason's orders, original *Cavalcade* writers Coleman Jacoby and Arnie Rosen began writing Art into many of their DuMont sketches, the ones in which Gleason began to carve his television legend.

Art played Sedgwick Van Gleason, the goateed, bespectacled father of millionaire ne'er-do-well Reggie Van Gleason. (Zamah Cunningham played Reggie's mother.) He also played Clem Finch, a milquetoast who was verbally abused by Gleason's "Loudmouth" Charlie Bratton, who would give Clem an earful while the poor man tried to quietly eat his lunch. In one memo-rable Charlie Bratton sketch, Clem sits down to eat a bowl of prunes in milk. "My stomach's been actin' up lately," he says. Charlie enters loudly, blows cigar smoke in Clem's face, and then orders smoked eel with a double helping of garlic sauce.

Art played dozens of walk-on roles and character parts (usu-ally authority figures) in sketches featuring Gleason's other *Cavalcade* characters: Rudy the Repairman, Stanley R. Sogg, The Poor Soul, and Fenwick Babbitt. He also created his own charac-ters, like mailman Percy Crumps and Professor James D. Enright, the esteemed world traveler and lecturer.

"If you had to pick TV's top straight man, you couldn't go far wrong with a fellow named Art Carney, who lends his versatile talents almost every Friday night to Jackie Gleason," read one early review of Art's *Cavalcade* work in the Boston *Evening American*.

Even though he was highly visible on *Cavalcade* and was starting to win critical acclaim, Art's role in the first-ever Honeymooners sketch was limited to a brief walk-on part as a flour-covered policeman. This primitive version of *The Honeymooners* was completely different than the show America would soon embrace. It was, after all, missing Ralph Kramden's biggest asset: Ed Norton.

Gleason was envious of the radio and television success of *The Bickersons,* which revolved around a married couple who argued incessantly. Looking for a sketch similar in tone, Gleason implored his writers to devise something that would suit his talents. Writers Joe Bigelow and Harry Crane answered the call, creating harried Brooklyn bus driver and perennial loser Ralph Kramden and his dowdy wife, Alice. The childless, bickering couple lived in a depressing, sparsely furnished Bensonhurst walk-up (icebox, no refrigerator) similar to Gleason's spartan boyhood home.

Gleason, naturally, would play the blustery Ralph. For the role of Alice, Gleason chose veteran stage and screen actress Pert Kelton, who had joined Art on *The Henry Morgan Show.*

On October 5, 1951, the first-ever Honeymooners segment was introduced as a short sketch on *Cavalcade.* In the sketch, Ralph and Alice bicker over bread: Ralph wants it for dinner, but Alice says she doesn't eat it. Their ensuing argument escalates into Ralph heaving a bag of flour out the window, hitting a beat cop played by Art. The cop enters the Kramdens' apartment coated from head to toe in white powder.

But Gleason and his writers knew "The Honeymooners" couldn't survive on the weekly rantings of Ralph and Alice. Other characters were needed to expand the farcical possibilities. Art, with his versatility and growing stature, was the logical choice to join Gleason and Kelton in the role of Ralph's best friend and upstairs neighbor, dim-bulb sewer worker Ed Norton.

"I became Norton, the one guy in the world who was even

dumber than Ralph Kramden, the boob Gleason played," Art recalled. "Norton was a fifth cousin, once removed, to Charlie in Morey Amsterdam's show. I liked it because I could be myself, make mistakes in grammar, and be comfortable."

Art described Norton's voice as "a cross between Maxie Rosenbloom and Marlon Brando" culled from various characters he'd known back in Mount Vernon. He created Norton's wardrobe of pinstriped vest over a T-shirt ("Did you ever see anything jerkier?") and the felt hat that stayed seemingly glued to Norton's head, even indoors. It was the very same hat Art had bought in high school sixteen years earlier.

Ed Norton was everything Art was not—loud, brash, opinionated, and socially at ease. Nearly forty years later, Art would say that Ed Norton was his all-time favorite character.

If Ralph had Alice, the writers reasoned, Norton also needed a wife to be his foil and Alice's best friend. They concocted stripper-turned-housewife Trixie Norton. Elaine Stritch, who had done a television pilot with Gleason and Pat Harrington called *Two a Day,* was hired for the role . . . and promptly fired after only one Honeymooners sketch.

"I can hardly remember [the sketch], but I remember when I first met Art he was grounded," Stritch said. "There was something stable about him, and God knows he was a high ticker. He had enough straight man in him to make him a human being you could really have a relationship with.

"In the Honeymooners sketch, I came on pretty strong as Trixie, and Gleason called me into his office afterward and said, 'You can't do this—you're too much like me.' I knew exactly what he was talking about. Ralph and I were doing another version of Ralph and Alice, and that's not what the series was about. But I was not the least bit hurt."

Stritch's role was inherited by Detroit stage actress Joyce Randolph, who had played bit parts in a few *Cavalcade* sketches after working on *The Colgate Comedy Hour* and other early TV shows.

Art's *Cavalcade* schedule allowed him enough time to freelance elsewhere. His growing reputation as a hardworking, versatile second banana was attracting attention within the young TV industry. And with movie personalities moving to the small screen, work was plentiful. When Art wasn't donning Norton's felt hat or Sedgwick Van Gleason's monocle, he could be found on TV inserting dentist-brother Ned's outlandish false teeth and wigs for shtick with Milton Berle, Dean Martin and Jerry Lewis, Victor Borge, Bert Lahr, and Garry Moore, among others.

But the freedom Art had experienced while *Cavalcade* aired on DuMont changed somewhat in 1952, when Gleason moved the show to CBS for a then-unheard-of two million dollars. CBS renamed it *The Jackie Gleason Show* and announced it would air live, every Saturday night, from the Adelphi Theatre. Contractually, Art had the option of refusing to make the move to CBS. Gleason now offered him $750 a week and shortly thereafter raised it to $1,000. But Art decided to join Gleason's CBS show for reasons other than money.

"There was always a special chemistry between us. We brought out the best in each other," he said of Gleason. "Of all the roles I played with him, and maybe of all the roles I ever played, Ed Norton was my favorite. I developed the costume and movements. I developed a lot of the character's attitudes. If I didn't get quite as many other sketch opportunities as I might have liked, that was Gleason's business. He was the star, and it was his show."

Art's CBS contract also allowed him to appear on two outside shows every thirteen weeks, provided they didn't conflict with Gleason air time or *Gleason Show* sponsors. This gave Art the freedom to explore other avenues, mainly drama, which was a genre he had yet to tackle on television.

Gleason's gargantuan CBS deal created quite a buzz, not only in the television community but throughout the world of show business. CBS, capitalizing on the hype, decided Gleason and crew should embark on a five-week summer tour to publicize *The Jackie Gleason Show,* set for a September 1952 launch before a nationwide TV audience.

The tour took the form of a one-hour show complete with a Reggie sketch, a Honeymooners sketch, and musical numbers. Art and Pert Kelton joined Gleason for the Honeymooners segment, performing the same sketch up to five times a day in different movie houses. Zamah Cunningham came along for the Reggie sketch. Midway through the tour, Kelton developed heart trouble and was sent home. Her spot was taken by radio and stage actress Ginger Jones.

"The plot was something about the Kramdens going to a dance with the Nortons. Trixie was referred to, but she wasn't actually in the show," Jones recalled. "Alice was at the ironing board, ironing something. She wore a long blue satin, very full-skirted evening gown, and I think her hair was in curlers. In these days, 'The Honeymooners' still concentrated on the domestic-argument angle, though Norton was already very, very important. It all took place on the typical *Honeymooners* set."

Jones broke her toe while the show was in Boston. Rather than tell Gleason about the injury and risk losing her job, she called Art, who lent some invaluable assistance.

"He brought me a pair of ballet shoes and cut them up so I could get them on my feet. Then, for each performance, he helped me to the theater," she recalled. "He'd bring a tub of ice into my dressing room so that I could thoroughly numb the toe before each performance. Then he'd help me onto the stage."

Years later, Art told Gleason biographer William A. Henry III that the summer of 1952 was the best time he and Gleason ever had working together. While they kept their emotional distance, the close working confines and grueling pace of touring forced them to socialize outside of work for the first time.

"I didn't really know Gleason. . . . He turned out to be a delightful person," Art said. "We didn't discuss anything serious—no politics, no religion, no philosophy, nothing about our families. When Gleason was partying, it was all frivolous and fun talk, trying to top each other. He was very good at that.

"The other thing I remember was how many people showed up and how enthusiastic they were for the Reggie sketch and the Honeymooners sketch. I really had no idea before how many people loved those Friday-night *Cavalcade* shows. It made me think this CBS job might amount to something and last a little while."

8

THE SECOND
BANANA RIPENS

Jackie Gleason's move from the DuMont Network to CBS was
by no means an immediate success. During its maiden season
on CBS, *The Jackie Gleason Show* failed to crack TV's top 20,
although its audience was relatively large and extremely faithful to
Ralph, Ed, Reggie, Sedgwick, and the June Taylor Dancers.

A change had taken place during the show's network switch.
When *The Jackie Gleason Show* debuted on September 20, 1952, it
had a new Alice: Audrey Meadows, who had worked with comedians Bob and Ray and was currently appearing on Broadway
opposite Phil Silvers in *Top Banana*.

But Pert Kelton hadn't left the *Gleason Show* on her own
accord. In the hysteria of the witch hunts of the early fifties,
Kelton had been blacklisted because of alleged Communist affilia-
tions. Officially, her "heart condition" kept her off the show.

Meadows—along with Art, Joyce Randolph, and the June
Taylor Dancers—would now form the core of the *Gleason Show*
throughout its many incarnations during the fifties.

Unlike Art's relationship with Gleason, his friendship with
Meadows was warm and much more personal. Art would often
drive Audrey and her agent home after the *Gleason Show,* usually

getting lost on the way back to Yonkers and crossing the George Washington Bridge into New Jersey. "I'm sure they think I'm smuggling something," Art said to Meadows about the bridge toll takers, to whom he became a familiar Saturday-night sight.

Art and Meadows shared another common bond, on a professional level: their need to rehearse before the live show, something Gleason loathed (out of laziness more than anything else). Gleason claimed to have a photographic memory, a fact he personally contradicted time and again when he forgot his lines on stage. But Gleason had excellent safety nets in Art and Meadows, with whom he worked out a system of gestures that, when used, meant he'd forgotten a line.

Still, Gleason insisted that comedy had to be spontaneous, and he refused to rehearse. "Just follow me, pal," he'd tell Art, who along with Meadows and Joyce Randolph was frustrated by Gleason's work habits and inattention to detail. But Gleason employees realized their places on the show. They knew that Gleason, for all his arrogant bluster, almost always got the big laugh. His onstage electricity was undeniable.

"At first we used to sit around at rehearsals and shout dialogue back and forth at each other until we got something that really stuck," Art said about the early *Gleason Show* days. "And then sometimes Jackie would throw it all out on Saturday night and we'd improvise on the air. I found this very therapeutic. It kept me awake."

George Petrie was one of Gleason's company of stock actors who played a variety of roles on the *Gleason Show* and in Honeymooners sketches. Petrie was a veteran stage and radio actor who had worked with Art on dozens of radio shows in the forties. He shared a dressing room with Art during the *Gleason Show*'s early days on CBS.

"Art worked very hard on the *Gleason Show*, which was underrehearsed by all standards," Petrie said. "Only with Jackie Gleason could you do that, and you could do it not because you were a good actor, but because you were an adaptable actor. The pressure [on Art] was enormous, and he carried a big load. When he walked off [the stage] every time and came into the dressing room, his shirt was soaking wet. That's not hyperbole—it was soaking wet, and you could see through to his undershirt and to his skin. But he made it look very easy."

Art didn't need Gleason's ad-libbing and high-wire "spontaneous" style to keep alert. He had plenty of practice at home, where Jean had given birth to their second son, Paul, shortly after Gleason's CBS premiere.

It was around this time that Art's agent, Bill McCaffrey, began pushing Art to expand his repertoire, to prove that his range encompassed more than his supporting *Gleason Show* characters. McCaffrey reasoned that Art would eventually leave the Gleason fold and strike out on his own in television. In order to do that and be successful, Art would have to shake his Norton image.

At McCaffrey's urging, Art began exercising his contractual rights, which allowed him the two non-Gleason-competing shows every thirteen weeks. On January 12, 1953, Art starred in a CBS Video Theatre presentation of the drama *Thanks for a Lovely Evening.*

Gleason was also eager to prove his abilities beyond sketch comedy, especially after his *Life of Riley* failure several years earlier. Looking for a meaty, dramatic role, Gleason decided to tackle writer A. J. Russell's *Studio One* television drama "The Laughmaker." To ensure that his dramatic showcase wouldn't backfire, Gleason looked close to home for support: He asked Art to costar in "The Laughmaker." In the live drama, Art would play a *New Yorker*–type magazine writer profiling Jerry Giles (Gleason), a self-destructive television comic who is eventually destroyed by his unchecked, childish egomania and glaring insecurities.

"Artie is a wonderful guy, but he was sort of removed, if you know what I mean," said Russell, whom Gleason later hired as a *Honeymooners* writer. "It was always quite amazing to me that this guy was credited with the talent of a clown, because he was nothing of the sort. I believe Artie viewed the human condition and he responded to it. He knew people, and he seemed to know what would make them laugh because he was empathetic to their faults and anything else that might have flawed their reputation."

When *The Jackie Gleason Show* ended its first season on CBS, it was obvious Art had impressed both viewers and critics alike. With the increasing popularity of "The Honeymooners"—still only a small part of the overall show—and his freelance-TV exposure away from the Adelphi Theatre, Art was one of TV's biggest stars. In August 1953 he followed "The Laughmaker" with a dramatic role as a hotel detective on an episode of *Danger,* and he tuned up for the *Gleason Show*'s second season by appearing on NBC's *Campbell Sound Stage* on September 4, 1953.

By the middle of its second season on CBS, *The Jackie Gleason Show*'s ratings had improved dramatically from the previous year. The show was ranked sixth in Nielsen's rating index, sandwiched between NBC's *Colgate Comedy Hour* and CBS's *Arthur Godfrey's Talent Scouts.* Trendex, another ratings company at the time, ranked Gleason's show third between Godfrey and NBC's *Dragnet.*

Art's work on the *Gleason Show* had much to do with its rising popularity, and none other than *Newsweek* noted his contribution in a March 8, 1954, feature, "Art Carney Weighs In."

> There was a real lemon of a show on TV a while back, something sour and flat called "Burlesque." . . . It was the kind of show you might switch off in a hurry except that one thing in it grabbed you and held you—the guy playing the burlesque comic. He was warm and wonderful. He took those dead lines of dialogue and filled them with such a tone and meaning that you sat through the stupid stuff simply to see him, just to feel what he was feeling, just to sense his great gift of comic sympathy. The comic's name is Art Carney and his growing gift has pushed him fast and close to the top TV talent class. . . . [Carney has] the talent of a scene-stealer, the talent of a natural comic with a face of pure rubber.

Still, the second-banana label generously applied to him proved an endless source of irritation to Art. He didn't begrudge Gleason the spotlight—he certainly didn't think of himself as an Oscar-caliber actor—but he began to resent his public image as a loopy supporting player.

"I don't consider myself a comedian at all," he said in 1954. "I don't tell jokes, and if I tried, I couldn't hold an audience's attention for five minutes. I'm an actor, playing a comic role in a situation comedy. If I happen to be funny as Ed Norton in 'The Honeymooners' or as Clem Finch in 'The Loudmouth' or as Reggie Van Gleason's father, it's because I'm doing a job of acting."

Art's rising prominence wasn't lost on the egomaniacal Gleason, and rumors began circulating that Gleason had forbidden Art to make solo entrances during the show because he was too raucously welcomed by the studio audience. Whether or not the rumors were true was never proven; Art, for the record, denied any knowledge of Gleason's alleged dictum.

"Nothing to these stories," he said at the time. "Gleason has been good to me, and I never forget he's the star of the show. Once, during rehearsal, he did say something about not letting me make an entrance alone, because I got too big a hand the week before, but it was just a gag. I'm perfectly happy with our setup. We respect each other, and I think Gleason is the best sketch comic in the business."

But Gleason apparently *was* jealous of Art, telling Orson Welles at the time: "It's like on my show when they laugh at my subordinate, Art Carney, that dirty so-and-so. I smile when Carney gets those laughs, but you should see my insides."

Art's work on the *Gleason Show* wasn't only a public and critical success. Professionally, his TV peers were taking notice of his work, and on February 11, 1954, in a star-studded celebration at the Hollywood Palladium, Art won his first Emmy Award, for Best Series, Supporting Actor. He beat Ben Alexander (*Dragnet*), William Frawley (*I Love Lucy*), Tony Randall (*Mr. Peepers*), and Carl Reiner (*Your Show of Shows*). Art's response to winning the Emmy was a typically understated, "Who, me?"

Gleason was also nominated—as Best Male Star, Regular Series—but he lost to Donald O'Connor in NBC's *Colgate Comedy Hour.*

Publicly, Gleason celebrated Art's victory. Privately, he couldn't have been too happy at being ignored for the second straight year (he was also nominated in 1952) while his unassuming employee grabbed top honors.

In early 1954 Art's professional faith in Gleason was severely tested by two related events.

Gleason had never quite accepted his movie failures a decade before and still yearned to be accepted in Hollywood. In early

January he announced his plans to move *The Jackie Gleason Show* from New York to Los Angeles.

Art's agent, Bill McCaffrey, had wisely inserted an escape clause into Art's contract, stipulating that Art only had to remain with Gleason for thirteen weeks if the show moved to California. After that, Art had the option of remaining with Gleason or leaving the show. "We're East Coast people and neither my wife nor I like the idea of leaving our home, taking the kids out of school and all the rest of it," Art said at the time.

Gleason himself inadvertently solved Art's dilemma. On January 30, just weeks after announcing the planned move to California, Gleason tripped and fell during a live sketch. He dislocated his right foot, tearing ligaments, breaking several bones, and putting his Los Angeles plans on hold.

That took care of problem number one. The severity of Gleason's injuries forced him to miss nearly two months of work. Vowing brashly to return the following week, Gleason lived up to his promise by appearing in the show's final five minutes. He quickly realized he wasn't up to the physical rigors of live television, and he didn't return to the show until late March. But he wasn't about to fade into the background. Discharged from Doctors Hospital, he tooled around the Adelphi Theatre in a wheelchair, barking orders and running the show with his right leg immobilized in a cast.

Although Art shunned the spotlight, Gleason's injury should have meant Art's (albeit temporary) promotion as the *Gleason Show*'s star. But Gleason, for reasons he never publicly discussed, insisted on hiring guest hosts for the first five weeks after his accident. Gleason biographer William A. Henry III later attributed this to Gleason's subtle attempts to sabotage Art's career and keep his second banana from ripening into a major star. (Art denied this.) Gleason knew Art was integral to the success of *The Jackie Gleason Show*. If Art became too hot a commodity in Gleason's absence and left the show, it would be a severe blow, not only for the Honeymooners sketches, but for the versatility and range that Art provided.

Gleason finally relented and allowed Art to host the *Gleason Show* on March 6, 1954. Years later, several people close to

Gleason would insist the Great One gave Art inferior material designed to generate a critical drubbing that would keep Art at bay. In one sketch Art played a pet-shop proprietor speaking to empty birdcages; another sketch cast him as a teacher dealing with a classroom of hoodlums. "It was the worst thing I've ever seen in half a century in show business," said one anonymous insider. "It was the next thing to a willful attempt to murder a man's career."

But Gleason writer A. J. Russell, on staff at the time, discounts that notion.

"I don't believe that existed, and I would deny that most vigorously," he said. "I wasn't aware of it at the time, and it didn't circulate with the cast or the writers. It was just hearsay."

As the March 6 date drew closer, Art ran into boyhood friend Robert Abbatecola, who lived near Art in Yonkers and often took the same train into New York. Art gave Abbatecola four tickets, asking him to come to the show to lend some moral support.

"He was pretty nervous because he was so used to playing second banana and didn't think he could carry the whole show on his own," Abbatecola said. "It would be unfair to say [the show] was the same without Gleason, but it was good in a different way."

If Gleason was trying to sabotage Art's career, he didn't quite succeed, although Art's night in the spotlight was less than memorable. Reviewers said he was ill at ease and gently scolded him for trying to fill Gleason's large shoes, especially in sketches that were obviously more suited to Gleason's blustery TV personality.

"Mr. Carney never has been and, pray, never will be, a comic who exists chiefly on his own personality. . . . Rather he is first and foremost a performer who extracts his humor from the effectiveness of his characterizations," Jack Gould wrote in the *New York Times*. "Had Mr. Carney, the performer, been starred Saturday evening, all would have been well. But unhappily, he was cast in perhaps the one part he never could play: The part of Mr. Gleason. Instead of being himself, he tried to do the things Jackie does—the opening monologue, the 'away we go' dance, etc. To the viewer the effect was neither true Gleason nor true Carney."

However large the setback seemed at the time, it was short-lived. Art's moment in the *Gleason Show* spotlight was forgotten once Gleason returned.

But Art didn't have to wait much longer for his shot at the limelight. Unlike Gleason, his versatility enabled him to perform in numerous outside projects. And as the American television audience was about to discover, Art's meek facade masked the appetite of a ferociously ambitious actor.

9

SAD GOOD-BYES

If Art resented the way Gleason treated him on the March 6, 1954, show, it wasn't apparent to coworkers or in any of the interviews Art gave at the time. He stressed his happiness at remaining in Gleason's shadow and emphasized his loyalty to the *Gleason Show*.

But outside of Gleason's immediate sphere of influence, Art slowly began to build an impressive television résumé, boasting appearances on some of the industry's most critically acclaimed shows. In a short period of time Art was being spotlighted with stars like Ethel Merman, Hans Conried, Dinah Shore, Beatrice Lillie, Alfred Lunt, and Marion Lorne.

Still, Art was having a tough time ridding himself of the Ed Norton image. By the 1955–56 TV season, when *The Honeymooners* debuted as a series, Art's role opposite Gleason and the popularity of his Norton had grown enormously. Art won his second and third consecutive Emmys in 1954 and 1955 for his portrayal of Norton; Gleason again was shunned. Art was no longer simply Jackie Gleason's costar. Aided by Gleason's talented stable of writers—Leonard Stern, Marvin Marx, A. J. Russell, Sid Zelinka, Herbert Finn, and Walter Stone—he had forever emblazoned Ed Norton into America's pop-culture consciousness.

Ed Norton was such a popular figure that by 1955 Art had recorded several Nortonesque novelty songs, including something called "The Sewer Song." Written by George Lee and "sung" by Art in what one wag termed Norton's "mashed potato" voice, "The Sewer Song" was a corny, reflective tribute to life as a subterranean sanitation engineer (the term Norton used to define his job):

> I work in the sewer, it's a very hard job
> You know they won't hire just any old slob
> You don't have to wear a tie or a coat
> You just have to know how to float
> We sing the song of the sewer
> Of the sewer, we sing this song
> Together we stand, with shovel in hand
> To keep things rolling along

> I work down a manhole with a guy named Bruce
> And we are in charge of all the refuse
> He lets me go first while he holds the lid
> I'm telling ya, sheesh, what a sweet kid!

For the 1955 TV season Gleason decided to chuck his established variety format and concentrate solely on the escapades of Ralph, Alice, Ed, and Trixie. He also decided that the thirty-nine half-hour *Honeymooners* episodes would be filmed before a live audience, which meant a huge improvement in the show's visual quality. Like most other TV shows, the *Gleason Show* had aired live. But repeats and West Coast shows were seen on kinescope, a process in which the live action was filmed off a monitor. This translated into a fuzzy picture and poor sound.

The 1955–56 *Honeymooners* series was underwritten in part by Gleason's new sponsor, Buick, which had given Gleason a three-year, eleven-million-dollar contract (worth probably thirty-five million by today's standards). More important, to Gleason anyway, the Buick contract allowed him to keep his title as TV's highest-paid entertainer.

Looking back now on these so-called Classic Thirty-nine *Honeymooners* episodes—watching their brilliant comedy and priceless moments—it's hard to imagine that America largely ignored Gleason and crew when the series debuted on October 1, 1955. But it's true. From October through the following September, *The Honeymooners* was filmed before a live Adelphi Theatre audience every Tuesday and Friday. The TV public, however, wasn't embracing this new format; at season's end, Gleason had dropped from second to twentieth in the Nielsen ratings.

But a funny thing happened on the way to a *Honeymooners* one-season run. While no one watched it the first time around, the show attained legendary stature once it began circulating in reruns. The Classic Thirty-nine are still running, night after night, day after day, in hundreds of TV markets around the country. Even now, more than forty years after their initial broadcast, those 1955–56 *Honeymooners* reruns frequently score higher ratings on New York's independent WPIX, Channel 11, than newer network programming. Perhaps Gleason best summed up the show's timeless appeal with this simple explanation: "It's funny."

Disappointed by the initial *Honeymooners* ratings, Gleason decided to return to his variety format for the 1956–57 season. By this time Art was earning about a thousand dollars a week. But more than the money, Art yearned for different challenges.

No longer the stooge who had supported Bert Lahr, Garry Moore, Martin and Lewis, and Victor Borge in the early fifties, Art's *Gleason Show* success allowed him to pick and choose among the many entertainment projects that were now being sent almost daily to agent Bill McCaffrey's office.

Among the offers Art received were deals to make his Broadway debut in *The Seven-Year Itch* and *Oh Men! Oh Women!,* both of which he declined. Art was offered several movie roles too, which he also turned down. One enterprising agent offered Art between $5,000 and $10,000 a week to tour with a dance band, sing novelty songs, and tell jokes. Art declined, although it was quite a raise from the $150 a week he'd earned with Horace Heidt doing the same act. He had rocketed to stardom on television, and he wasn't yet ready to leave its comfortable black-and-white confines.

He was ready, however, to act in something other than the *Gleason Show,* and beginning with his supporting role in "The

Laughmaker" (1953), Art reeled off a string of starring roles on all three networks in shows like *Suspense, Kraft Theatre, Studio One,* and *Playhouse 90.* With few exceptions, his performances were critically acclaimed.

"Art Carney got top billing last night and rose to the occasion with a splendid performance in an unusual and fascinating play," the *New York Times* said about Art's performance in *The Incredible World of Horace Ford,* a 1955 CBS production in which he costarred with Jason Robards. "Obviously, the portrayal of a complex character like Ford required superior acting. Mr. Carney was so good that he almost made the fantasy credible."

Art's appearances ran the gamut from comedy, like his *Studio One* role in "Confessions of a Nervous Man," to drama (a *Suspense* episode called "The Return Journey"). He costarred with Ethel Merman and Jack Leonard in a rare color presentation of "Panama Hattie" on *Best of Broadway,* and after starring in "Burlesque" (*Kraft Television Theatre*) was described by legendary stage actor Alfred Lunt, who watched the performance with wife Lynn Fontanne in Boston. "This man is a really remarkable comedian," Lunt said. "There is practically nothing he couldn't do on the stage."

Art put Lunt's declaration to the test in 1956, when he decided to perform in a summer-stock production of *The Seven-Year Itch,* his first legitimate stage experience. He starred in the play as Richard Sherman, the role immortalized on Broadway by Tom Ewell. The tour took Art to Dennis and Falmouth, Massachusetts, and to Ogunquit, Maine. Art's costars were television actress Brett Somers—newly married to actor Jack Klugman—and a young unknown named Lee Remick, who left the production halfway through its run to film Elia Kazan's *A Face in the Crowd.*

"I had gotten married on June 20 and the following Monday went to Dennis and we started rehearsing," Somers said. "The first night we were in rehearsal we all went out for dinner and everybody ordered drinks, including Art, who ordered a ginger ale. Of course, at the time I didn't know he had a drinking problem, and I looked at him and said, 'My God, who ever heard of an Irishman who doesn't drink?'

"One thing that just used to piss him off was when people would come up and say, 'Hi, Norton, how are things down in the sewer?' And when his father, who was hard of hearing, came to see the play, his wife would tell him what the line was, and then we'd get a laugh in the back from him. People just loved Art because there was something endearing about him. But you felt he was a man who most of the time was in a lot of pain but never showed it, never said anything about it. He had a lot of demons."

Those demons were beginning to affect Art's marriage. Although he had bought a house in the serene Connecticut shore town of Saybrook, where the family retreated every summer, Art's home life was on the rocks. Both Somers and Jack Smight, who directed Art in *The Seven-Year Itch,* sensed trouble between Art and Jean during the summer of 1956.

"He had some marital problems that were going on at that time, but he never really talked much about his problems," Smight said. "He's got that old keep-everything-under-the-rug Irishness. But Art provided so much humor along the way, and the audience just loved him."

Art's professional achievements did little to stop his drinking, which continued to play a huge role in his life. Gleason was also drinking heavily, but he never hid this fact and actually reveled in his garish public image. Art, on the other hand, was quiet and reflective. He brooded from one project to the next and constantly worried about his career. Unable to accept that he brought joy to millions of people, he felt unworthy of his talent. It all came too easily.

"He certainly wasn't a sloppy drunk, but he loved the sauce, like all of us did in those days," said Elaine Stritch, the first Trixie Norton, who kept in touch with Art and worked with him several times after her brief *Cavalcade* stint. "I remember going to lunch with him one day on a break when we were in rehearsal. We were sitting and having a drink, and Art looked at me and said, 'You know, I can't make it out. I am absolutely loving every minute of doing this play with you, and it's so exciting and I'm interested in it and want to express myself, but what I really would like to do is to go and get a hotel room and a couple bottles of Dewar's and you and I sit down and talk about what the hell this world is all about.' Generally, most people who have a drinking problem in this business are fearful about their talent, their own identity, and whether they're attractive or unattractive."

Art's drinking didn't seem to affect his work, but it was obvious to his colleagues something was amiss. While in rehearsals for a 1955 *Climax* show, in which he played private eye Donald Lam in "The Bigger They Come," Art showed up late and was stopped by costar Jane Darwell.

"She hadn't had a drink in years, but I was drinking, definitely drinking," he said. "On New Year's Eve, they dismissed us early, and most of us partied it up. When I came back on the morning of January 2, I said, 'Hi, Miss Darwell.' She looked at me and said, 'Hi, Artie. Did you have a speeder on the way to work?' Only another drinker or ex-drinker would know that word 'speeder'—a quick drink in the morning to help see you through the day."

Another witness to Art's drinking was Joan Reichman Canale, who was Gleason's secretary from 1953 to 1957. Canale was Gleason's typist and gal Friday; one of her duties was locating Art when he occasionally missed a *Gleason Show* rehearsal because of his drinking.

"I was the one who had to go get him out of his different little haunts," Canale said. "I was sitting with him once in a place called Downey's on Eighth Avenue. Art had been into the juice pretty heavily, and somebody came over and kept saying, 'Oh, you're so wonderful, you're so marvelous, you're so terrific!' And he never thought he was [because] he never had much of an opinion of himself. And when they left, Art looked at me and started to cry. He really felt like, 'Gee, why are they saying this to me?' I wasn't trying to psychoanalyze him or anything, but as I look back, I think he really didn't have a very high opinion of himself."

Besides Art's parents and immediate family, his lifelines to emotional stability remained his agent, Bill McCaffrey, and his big brother Jack. McCaffrey was an ex-drinker who certainly understood the morass into which Art occasionally plunged, but he seemed unable to really help his client when it came to alcohol. Jack Carney had a drinking problem and had joined Alcoholics Anonymous. He urged Art to attend some AA meetings, but Art found the experience horrifying: When word spread of his appearance at a Westchester AA meeting, people showed up, with their children in tow, to gawk at the famous television star. "Geez, can you imagine what that did to me?" Art said.

On November 28, 1956, Jack Carney was found dead in his King Edward Hotel room near Times Square. Wearing a T-shirt and undershorts, Jack was clutching a telephone; the police surmised he had died while trying to call for help. Jack was only fifty, and he left behind a wife and two children. He had been producing *Arthur Godfrey's Talent Scouts* when he was granted a medical leave of absence the previous May; he had returned to the show in September.

An autopsy revealed that Jack was killed by a massive heart attack. Art identified the body, a shattering experience he would later incorporate into his Oscar-winning role in *Harry and Tonto*. In the movie, Harry (Art) goes to the morgue to identify the body of his talkative friend (played by Herbert Berghof). Art drew parallels to Jack's death when talking about that scene.

"There [Jack] was, one day, dead in a hotel room, all by himself, the phone off the hook, and I had to identify him," Art said. "I had to go to the morgue to identify my brother, who had made it all possible for me. So you see, I was there. I know all about it."

Jack's death was a shattering blow. Art had lost not just a brother he loved dearly, but one of the few people he trusted for personal and career advice. It was Jack who had introduced Art to Horace Heidt in 1937 and to Bill McCaffrey in 1950, and Jack who helped get Art into radio and television. It was Jack—a fellow alcoholic—to whom Art turned when his drinking demons reared their ugly heads, and Jack who warned his kid brother to beware the "highs" that usually meant an emotional crash wasn't far behind.

With Jack gone, Art began turning more and more to Bill McCaffrey for guidance. And shortly after Jack's death, Art faced his toughest career decision.

The Jackie Gleason Show, back in its sketch/variety format for the 1956–57 season, wasn't doing much better than *The Honeymooners* had the season before. The *Gleason Show* was up against the ninth-place *Perry Como Show* on Saturday nights and was failing to break the top 20. A gloomy Gleason began talking about retiring when the TV season ended in May.

Gleason's apparent disinterest in weekly television sparked rumors that Art would leave Gleason after his contract expired, that he would become a "free agent" if Gleason chose not to return for the 1957–58 TV season.

Gleason's manager, George "Bullets" Durgom, told the press Gleason would return with limited TV appearances. But the skeptics doubted that Gleason's huge ego could recover so quickly after having been beaten badly by Perry Como and knocked out of television's ratings elite.

In January 1957 Art and Gleason held a joint press conference to discuss their future together. They sounded, as one typical headline said, like the "Honeymoon Not Over for Gleason and Carney."

"Even if Jackie doesn't do a weekly show next year, I may still be with him on another show," Art said. "But if nothing good comes along, and I'm offered the right Broadway script, I may do that." McCaffrey added, "If at the end of the season Jackie wants to talk to Art about the following year, Art will not only sit down to discuss it but will bend over backward to work it out."

Art echoed McCaffrey's sentiments in a conversation he had three months later with Hollywood gossip columnist Sheila Graham. But perhaps sensing Gleason wouldn't return in September, Art now sketched a more concrete career plan.

"Jackie has stated publicly that he doesn't want to do a weekly show. So, whether I do any more shows with him next season depends on where I sign," Art said. "I've had offers from NBC, CBS, and ABC, and right now I'm trying to make up my mind. If I sign with NBC, I can't work with Jackie, because he has one of those lifelong contracts with CBS. But if I'm with the same network, we can work together again.

"I've been offered three series of my own, but I've turned them down. I'd rather be the second banana with a big show than carry the burden all by myself. I'd rather not have the full load of responsibility."

Art didn't have much choice in the matter. CBS, disappointed in Gleason's ratings, politely showed him the door, exiling the Great One for the 1957–58 season. Ostensibly, Gleason was to recharge his batteries, get his creative house in order, and return a little further down the road. With Gleason's shadow finally—albeit grudgingly—lifted, it was Art's turn to stand in the spotlight.

═══ 10 ═══

BROADWAY BOUND

The absence of both Jackie Gleason and the grind of a weekly TV series seemed to revivify Art. He now busied himself with a flurry of projects that pushed him further into the public spotlight.

Art's first post-Gleason TV showcase was his most notable work to date: a live *Playhouse 90* episode called "The Fabulous Irishman." Aired by CBS in June 1957, "Irishman" told the remarkable story of Robert Briscoe, the first Jewish Lord Mayor of Dublin. It was a starring role Art at first declined because of its dramatic importance. Simply put, Art didn't think he could handle the role. But under Bill McCaffrey's gentle prodding, he finally relented.

"I had heard they were going to do Briscoe's life, but it had never occurred to me as a possible part for me," Art said. "Of course, I'm Irish on all sides, and I don't care what they do to me for makeup. Briscoe had a broken nose, so they'll probably give me a hump on the nose and dye my hair black."

Written by Elick Moll and directed by an upstart named John Frankenheimer, "The Fabulous Irishman" pushed Art dramatically further than any of his previous roles. The story spanned several decades, beginning with Briscoe's 1918 role in the Irish Revolution against the British, when he joined the Irish Republican Army and became a follower of Eamon De Valera and a member of the Sinn Féin. The rest of "Irishman" followed Briscoe's life as he evolved into a beloved Irish patriot and politician.

Art had never been to Ireland, but to get into character he perfected his brogue by studying recordings of Briscoe made from a recent U.S. visit. And not wanting to sound foolish or phony, he enlisted a rabbi to teach him Hebrew. The role called for Briscoe to lead a Passover Seder, to chant a Passover song called "Had Gadya," and to recite the Kaddish, the Jewish mourner's prayer. "The greatest compliment I had on the show was when a Jew said to one of my friends, 'I didn't know Art Carney was Jewish,' " Art said afterward.

"The Fabulous Irishman" was a critical success and helped to remove the burdensome sewer-worker stamp from Art's public persona. Although Art's live work in "Charley's Aunt" (*Playhouse 90*) and "The Man Who Was Irresistible to Women" (*Star Stage*) had emphasized his versatility, it wasn't until "The Fabulous Irishman" that critics started taking note of the actor lurking beneath Art's comic image.

"That Mr. Carney is a gifted, intelligent performer nobody ever denied. But the richness of his talent—the quiet skill, the charm, the insight—never before came through as they did last night. . . . By all accounts the most talked-about show of the year," critic Harriet Van Horne wrote. "Whether the scene called for the soft words of love, the fighting words of revolution or the devout words of a Hebrew prayer, Art Carney was sound and true and very touching in his performance. To see him out of his sewer-digging costume—unbuttoned vest over his undershirt—is to realize that he's handsome, too. Plainly, last night was a triumph for him in every sense."

Said the *New York Times*: "Art Carney, who has yet to make a serious misstep in his television career, was ideal in the title role. There can be no question about it. Mr. Carney is a versatile and brilliant actor."

"The Fabulous Irishman" would be Art's last live anthology TV appearance for over a year. Shortly after the show aired, he starred as Elwood P. Dowd in a one-week summer-stock production of *Harvey* at Connecticut's Ivoryton Playhouse. It turned out to be a dry run, of sorts, for his next project.

In the fall of 1957, Bill McCaffrey was approached by Morton Wishengrad, a TV/radio writer for *The Eternal Light* series. Wishengrad had written a three-act play, *The Rope Dancers,* that was headed to Broadway after a tortuous four-year journey. He had seen Art's comic performance in "Charley's Aunt" the previous winter and was suitably impressed to offer Art a starring role in *The Rope Dancers,* as an alcoholic, ineffectual husband and father.

"Morton felt he needed someone with a strong empathy with the public, someone who was, in a sense, an entertainer," said Sir Peter Hall, then twenty-six-year-old Peter Hall making his Broadway directorial debut after establishing himself in his native England. "I remember feeling Art had a quality that is often true of entertainers, especially singers and comedians, of an ability to get to the truth, which was quite startling. I saw some of Art's television work, and then I met with him, and it all worked out."

Unlike his role in "The Fabulous Irishman," Art displayed little trepidation in accepting the *Rope Dancers* role. "I worried would my voice carry in a theater, but aside from that, it didn't bother me," he said. But costar Siobhan McKenna, acclaimed for her stage performance in *Saint Joan,* was another matter. It wasn't that the venerable, Irish-born, classically trained McKenna didn't want to appear in the play. But she had final approval of her costar and was leery of a television actor of whom she'd never heard.

Art Carney and Siobhan McKenna were as different as night and day. McKenna preferred to chat about George Bernard Shaw, while Art did his best to crack her serious facade with his Arthur Godfrey impersonations. Shortly after they met, McKenna took Art to see Christopher Plummer perform in *Hamlet.* Art, who was drinking at the time, fell asleep and snored through the entire show. Before long, he had perfected his Siobhan McKenna impression—performed, naturally, behind her back.

But McKenna finally relented, approving Art after the duo rehearsed a few times. "I OK'd him for the part because he was all the things I could look for in James," she said. "I was so impressed by his simplicity. I would think his future in the theater could be great, but that depends on himself."

Following "The Fabulous Irishman," Art knew that *The Rope Dancers* would be, up to this point, his professional touchstone. Not only was it miles removed from anything he had attempted, but it would thrust him into the Broadway spotlight in a dramatic role (mostly) devoid of laughs. Notwithstanding his summer-stock experience and radio career, *The Rope Dancers* would be Art's first steps outside of television. He was adamant about proving he could prosper without a medium most "serious" actors considered frivolous and unworthy.

"My first play had to be a straight play," he said. "On TV I had done dramatic work, but I wanted to be accepted as a stage actor. I understood *The Rope Dancers* and wanted to do it. When I got on stage, then I found freedom—no mikes, cameras, booms in the way. I was playing only to the audience."

"Art was great fun to be with all the time, but he was laboring under the burden . . . of having to play a serious role with very few laughs in it, which was an unusual situation for him," said costar Theodore Bikel. "But if you master the art of comedy, then you have to be a superb performer."

Art attempted to inject some levity into rehearsals, understandable in light of the play's dark, brooding subject matter. "I wanted him to have warmth and humor, to be likable and sometimes funny," Art said of his character.

The Rope Dancers was set in a turn-of-the-century New York tenement. It told the story of James Hyland (Art), a drinking, womanizing, frustrated poet married to cold, passionless Margaret Hyland (McKenna). She blames the philandering James for their daughter's deformity, a sixth finger Lizzie Hyland (Beverly Lunsford) keeps shamefully hidden with a mitten. Lizzie was conceived the same night James slept with a prostitute, and both Margaret and James feel Lizzie's deformity is God's way of punishing them for James's sins.

During the course of *The Rope Dancers,* Margaret kicks James out of their apartment and tries ignoring the well-intentioned advice of slovenly downstairs neighbor Mrs. Farrow (Joan Blondell), who lives with her daughter, Clementine (Barbara Ellen

Myers). Slowly, Margaret's anger toward James melts away, and she experiences a sexual and emotional reawakening. But the play's resolution is anything but bright: Lizzie's death after a kindly doctor (Bikel) amputates her sixth finger plunges James and Margaret into an impenetrable gloom. (Wishengrad borrowed the play's title from the writings of German philosopher Friedrich Nietzsche: "Man is a cord above an abyss. A perilous arriving, a perilous traveling, a perilous looking backward, a perilous trembling and standing still.")

Before it could open on Broadway, *The Rope Dancers* traveled to several cities—Princeton, Philadelphia, Boston, New Haven—for the traditional out-of-town tryouts. Art was hitting the bottle again, but his drinking never affected his performance, which required tremendous focus on his part. It did, however, result in one particularly eyebrow-raising situation.

"Art had his moments of nervous terror," Peter Hall said. "In one scene, he made his entrance down a fire escape and it necessitated him being loaded, as it were, up in the flies before the play started. He then came down when the play was about fifteen minutes old. When we did the technical rehearsal of the play in New Haven, Art came down the fire escape and fell flat on his face on the floor. He was pissed [drunk] out of his mind. But that was the only dramatic incident for the rest of the run. I put that down to stress and strain."

At first, audiences who came to see *The Rope Dancers* had a difficult time accepting Art as anything but Ed Norton. During one New Haven performance, they laughed inappropriately through two acts; in Boston they greeted his entrance as James Hyland with applause and sustained laughter. It was a fact noted by renowned Boston theater critic Elliot Norton.

"Art Carney is seriously handicapped in this performance. Because he made so many millions of people laugh for seven years as an illiterate sewer worker, . . . audiences naturally expect him to do the same kind of part on the stage," Norton wrote. "The art of Art Carney is that he wins over the television followers, who want him to be uproarious, so that they follow with quiet conviction and sympathy the character James Hyland rather than the actor Art Carney."

Siobhan McKenna, for all her reservations about Art's ability, was also impressed. "I think he will have a great future," she told Norton. "There will be many parts he can play, including a lot of the Eugene O'Neill characters."

On November 20, 1957, Art made his Broadway debut when *The Rope Dancers* opened at the Cort Theatre. The more sophisticated New York audiences checked their laughter at the door, and while *The Rope Dancers* received only mediocre reviews, Art's performance was largely praised.

"In the part of the amiable father, Art Carney may not be speaking all his lines with the subtlety of phrasing that has been written into them," wrote *New York Times* critic Brooks Atkinson. "But his charm, tenderness and homeliness are winning."

Variety's reviewer noted that the show "tends to be rather somber" and "Art Carney's version of the thwarted-writer-turned-worthless-husband stamps him as something considerably more than simply a TV comic. He offers an affecting blend of charm, weakness, paternal love and blarney."

Despite the enthusiastic reviews, Art fell into his familiar behavior when confronted with success: extreme self-doubt. It didn't matter that the esteemed Brooks Atkinson—who would later have a Broadway theater named after him—lavished praise. Wishengrad, Joan Blondell, and McKenna all sensed that Art felt like a failure, that he could never meet the high standards of legitimate theater. Although they repeatedly assured Art his performance was fine, "I don't think he ever believed us," Wishengrad said.

"I think Art is a testament to the fact that finally—when you're talking about actors, entertainers, comedians, singers—they're all dealing with the same thing, which is truth," Hall said. "And if you don't have that truth, you don't communicate. The fact that Art had that wit and warmth and that ability to make people see the ridiculous also made him very moving."

The Rope Dancers proved to be too dark of a ride on the emotional roller coaster. Its lukewarm critical response, which translated into a mediocre box office turnout, forced it to close after 189 performances. (Art had missed only one performance.)

The great Broadway experiment had worked, and while Art

might not have believed in himself, critics and audiences ultimately had little trouble accepting him in this dramatic role. Art, for one, was relieved to shed James Hyland's emotional baggage. "To me, the role was depressing," he said, and he subsequently declined an offer to reprise the role on television.

As 1957 turned into 1958, Art prepared for his return to television—and, perhaps, to Jackie Gleason.

═ 11 ═

SQUEEZING
THE TUBE

B y 1958 Art was earning about two hundred thousand dollars a year. That was enough to afford an eighteen-foot motor-boat, three cars, a mink stole for Jean, the summer house in Saybrook, Connecticut, and a part-time housekeeper. Art indulged his passion for jazz (Art Tatum, Oscar Peterson, André Previn, and Erroll Garner were favorites), photography (no darkroom but plenty of equipment), and sweets, wolfing down milk shakes, Hershey bars, Mallomars, Necco wafers, and hot-fudge sundaes. Combined with the double whammy of his drinking and prodigious appetite, Art's sweet tooth had caused his weight to rise considerably since his *Honeymooners* days. Art wasn't strikingly overweight, but it was enough to flesh out his smooth, scrubbed-pink complexion, his face framed by the familiar widow's peak, and his distinguished, graying temples.

Art's relationships with his children, Eileen, Brian, and Paul—now sixteen, twelve, and six, respectively—was by all accounts close and loving. Brian called his dad "Fats," while Art called Brian "Winchell" and was convinced his son would be a columnist. Both Brian and Paul were exhibiting signs of musical talent, with Paul showing promise on the piano (unlike his dad). Eileen, meanwhile, was involved in various school activities—sorority president, cheerleading squad captain, and vice president of the high school's teen center.

Rollin Myers, Jean's father, with whom Art had played double piano years earlier while romancing Jean, died in March 1958, a few years after moving in with Art and Jean after his wife's death. Art's own parents, Edward and Helen, now seventy-nine and seventy-eight, had moved out of the Bedford Avenue house but were forced to live apart because of Edward's declining physical condition. While Helen lived in a small Mount Vernon apartment, Edward stayed in a convalescent home in nearby Tarrytown, New York.

The Carney brothers—Bob, Ned, Fred, and Phil—all kept in touch with Art, who spent a good deal of his free time helping raise money for various local charities (shades of his father, "Civic Virtue" Carney). Art attended Bedford Boys reunions when his work schedule permitted, and he would sometimes drive through the old Mount Vernon neighborhood. Once he even knocked on the door of his boyhood home at 345 Bedford Avenue and took a tour of the place—after the owners recovered from the shock of seeing Art Carney on their front stoop. It was a Saturday night, and *The Honeymooners* was on. As Art told the story, the old man who answered the door wondered how Mr. Carney could be in two places at once.

But Art's impressive salary and celebrity did little to increase his public exposure, which was just fine with him. Art and Jean attended St. John's Episcopal Church on Sundays and went to PTA meetings for their children, who attended public school in Yonkers. A natural introvert, Art insulated his family as best he could from the spotlight. He rarely permitted newspaper or magazine writers to glimpse his private life, and he even declined an invitation to appear on Edward R. Murrow's *Person to Person* television show. Jean, who described herself as "a homemaker," was even more leery of the spotlight. Her one hands-on brush with fame came during a typically loud Gleason party at Toots Shor's, when she removed a wooden splinter from Marilyn Monroe's backside in the ladies' room.

Art's social circle, with few exceptions, consisted of old

Mount Vernon friends and Yonkers neighbors like Edward and Mary Orsenigo, who lived next door on Westchester Avenue. In the early 1950s, Art and Ed Orsenigo had torn down a fence separating their yards so they could make a baseball field on which their children could play.

Art's old radio and TV boss, Henry Morgan, also kept in touch. "Once I was playing in summer theater and Carney came to see the show. His beachfront house wasn't too far away, and he invited me to spend an afternoon there," Morgan said. "As I sat on the beach, he ran back into the house and came out with a little bag of pebbles he'd collected. Didn't seem like much. 'Wait,' he said. Then he ran down to the shore, dunked them in the sea, and showed me the result. He had a bag of beautiful, shining jewels. Sort of the introspective Carney."

Singer Peggy Lee was one of Art's few show business friends during this time. They had met backstage on *Cavalcade of Stars* in 1950; Lee recalled that Art was wearing a fancy raccoon coat. They struck up an immediate friendship based on their mutual shyness. It was a friendship strengthened even further when Art discovered that Lee's husband was a drinker who attended Alcoholics Anonymous meetings.

"We loved to play games on each other," Lee said. "I still have some notes that Art would write me, like he was a seven-year-old boy writing to a six-year-old girl. I found he had a childlike quality. When I was playing in Basin Street, he would send me things like Jujubes and candy on a strip and Milk Duds—every kind of old-fashioned, little-child candy.

"I was trying in my own way to get him interested [in AA] because I worried about him a lot," Lee said. "But I would sit there and talk to him and keep him from drinking, and I think that's why he would come up and see me once in a while—so he wouldn't be tempted."

While Art's friendship with Lee prospered, his professional relationship with Gleason took a detour. After a year away from television, Gleason was ready to return. In June 1958 he announced he would be back in September for the new TV season. He voiced a desire to work with Art.

Whatever questions the public had about a Gleason-Carney

reunion, however, were answered shortly thereafter. Gleason, with great fanfare, unveiled his new weekly sketch-comedy format—featuring Buddy Hackett as his sidekick. It would be a short TV marriage doomed from the start, and it left industry insiders wondering why Gleason had chosen Hackett over Art.

But Art and agent Bill McCaffrey appeared unconcerned about Gleason's decision. They felt Art needed to distance himself from his Ed Norton image, to build on his *Rope Dancers* success and seek new areas in which to display his talents. Although McCaffrey had met with Gleason's agents to discuss a possible Gleason-Carney reteaming, the negotiations went nowhere. To the surprise of no one who knew their offstage relationship, Art and Gleason hadn't spoken in months, choosing to declare their mutual respect for one another only through the press.

"Professionally, I had no alternative. My manager and I kicked the thing around, talked about the really good offers I've received for the fall, and when we added it all up there seemed to be no doubt that I'd be taking a backward step if I resumed with Jackie on a weekly basis," Art said after Gleason's Buddy Hackett announcement. "I'd be going back to where I started, to being a second banana, if you know what I mean. I'm no different from all other actors. I take pride in moving forward. . . . I hope Gleason will invite me on his show occasionally. He's fun to work with. I like the guy. I think he's big enough to realize the way I feel about not going back with him. In all the time I've worked with Gleason, I've never known him to be small about anything."

Whether Gleason was jealous, angry over Art's three Emmys, or had a true desire to try something different, his decision proved best for Art. Although Art still shied away from headlining his own series ("No guts, I guess," he told a *Newsweek* reporter), he could now undertake a variety of comic and dramatic roles while pondering a return to the stage.

"We've had a lot of offers from the movies and the networks, but Bill and I aren't rushing into anything," Art said. "I'm not interested in a weekly series of my own, and I'm not interested in signing an exclusive contract with a network unless I know what the specific property is. I don't want to get hung up with a dog of a show just to sign a contract. I'd like to have some flexibility on television, to take advantage of my versatility."

Gearing up for his run as a television freelancer, Art appeared on several shows in the summer of 1958, most notably NBC's *Dinah Shore Chevy Show.* Television journalists, meanwhile, were trumpeting his upcoming role in CBS's *DuPont Show of the Month* adaptation of *Harvey,* the 1944 Broadway smash and the TV season's first big live play.

Art was no stranger to *Harvey,* having played drunken Elwood P. Dowd—who communicates with a huge white rabbit—the previous summer at the Ivoryton Playhouse in Connecticut. And Art was no stranger to these types of roles. Battling an off-stage drinking problem, he seemed to gravitate toward stage and screen characters that mirrored, to some degree, the private wars he waged with his own personal demons. Not only had Art already played alcoholic James Hyland in *The Rope Dancers,* but he would subsequently star as an alcoholic in the one-man drama *Call Me Back,* and in a *Twilight Zone* episode as a soused Santa Claus.

Television criticism in the medium's early days suffered from a time lag. By the time reviews appeared in daily newspapers, the shows they were reviewing had already aired (unlike today, when critics routinely receive review tapes weeks ahead of time). But for "Harvey" the show's producer, Talent Associates, had invited critics to watch a dress rehearsal on closed-circuit television in a cramped CBS office.

It's interesting to note that critic Jack O'Brian, writing in the *New York Journal-American* after viewing the closed-circuit broadcast, found the show had a "bustling, let's-git-it-finished-on-time feeling, which doesn't do its best by such an airy whimsy. . . . Elwood here doesn't ever quite convince us he sees the pooka; and if he does, it actually is only a hallucination. A gentle, harmless crack in his attitude, but a crack nonetheless."

But New York *Daily News* critic Kay Gardella watched both the closed-circuit rehearsal and the finished product and was inclined to give Art and costars Marion Lorne, Elizabeth Montgomery, and Larry Blyden a thumbs-up. She noted how "Harvey" progressed from its rough form to the polished show that subsequently aired live.

"As Elwood P. Dowd, the kindly, middle-aged bachelor who likes to go down to Charlie's place and hoist a few—he never gets drunk, mind you—Art Carney turned in a fine, sensitive performance," Gardella wrote. "He was just as natural in the role of Harvey's pal as he was as Jackie Gleason's sidekick Ed Norton; he even managed to cause his sister as much embarrassment as he did Ralph Kramden."

"Harvey" aired in September 1958. After flying out to Hollywood for a guest spot on the *Dinah Shore Chevy Show* and an appearance on a Sid Caesar TV special, Art quickly began preparing for his next role: As a gun shop owner who witnesses a mob rubout and becomes a murderer himself in "Safety for the Witness," an episode of the popular *Alfred Hitchcock Presents* series.

Tragedy once again struck the Carney family shortly after Art completed taping the *Alfred Hitchcock* segment. On October 29, 1958, almost two years after Jack's death, Art's nephew Kevin Carney (Ned's son) was killed in Ithaca, New York. A truck carrying Kevin and thirteen fellow Ithaca College students, retaliating for an earlier campus prank, overturned on its way to Cortland State Teachers College. Kevin, an eighteen-year-old physical education major, was the only fatality.

Kevin's death cast a shadow over the final two months of 1958. Art's final television project of the year was an hour-long ABC production, *Art Carney Meets Peter and the Wolf,* which aired in November. Art costarred with thirty of Bil and Cora Baird's marionettes, with whom he would reappear ten months later in *The Sorcerer's Apprentice.* As usual, Art's performance was greeted warmly by critics and television journalists, who by now were shifting the focus of their reviews and profiles away from the Gleason relationship and concentrating on Art's versatility.

But old journalistic habits were hard to break, and the cursed "second banana" phrase inevitably reared its ugly head. In the eighteen months since Art and Gleason had parted company, Art occasionally voiced his desire to reprise Ed Norton, should Gleason come calling. But he and Bill McCaffrey now rejected the opportunity outright when Gleason—looking for a quick ratings fix—floated the possibility of a *Honeymooners* reunion.

"There's a danger in becoming identified with Norton,"

McCaffrey said. "Going back to it now would be a tactical error."

As the decade neared its end, Art could look back on a career that had grown remarkably since he crossed Morey Amsterdam's radio bridge into television. The fruitful professional relationship with Gleason, three Emmy Awards, a Broadway triumph, and a critically acclaimed post–*Gleason Show* career balanced the low points—drinking, depression, Jack's death, marital woes—that marked Art's rise into the public spotlight.

The new year would bring Art a slew of professional successes, including a lucrative TV contract and a new home for Jean and the kids. "You know, everything seems to have fallen into place this season," Art said late in 1958. "I couldn't be happier."

══ 12 ══

ENTER DAVID
SUSSKIND

Although *The Twilight Zone* wouldn't hit the air for another ten months, its creator, Rod Serling, had carved quite a name for himself among the pantheon of early television writers. His *Playhouse 90* episode "Requiem for a Heavyweight" was an instant classic, and an actor's value increased if his résumé included a role in a Serling-scripted program.

Art's chance to work with Serling arrived when he was cast in Serling's "The Velvet Alley," another *Playhouse 90* production that CBS aired live in January 1959. It was Art's first dramatic television role since "The Fabulous Irishman" in 1957, and it costarred Jack Klugman, with whom Art had become friendly during the *Seven-Year Itch* summer-stock tour in 1956.

In "The Velvet Alley," Art played struggling New York freelance writer Ernie Pandish, who finally lands a big Hollywood contract after years of struggle and self-doubt. Since this was written by the moralistic Serling, it contained his trademark preachiness. Ernie's success, naturally, comes with a price: He begins moving in the Hollywood fast lane, and before long he has become an arrogant lout. Ernie fires his longtime agent (played by

Klugman, who then suffers a heart attack), divorces his wife, and loses the respect of his father.

"We got two weeks of live rehearsal before we did 'Alley' live before an audience, and Art would come in, take off his trousers, and he'd have little hearts on his shorts saying, 'I love you,' " Klugman said. "There was a scene in the show—the morning after the wonderful reviews of Ernie's TV show—when we're in the bedroom of a hotel and I'm packing to go back home to New York. And there was a lot of good dialogue there. Ernie and me, as his agent, were very, very hot, we were high, so we started to laugh. And as a result, Art and I would go into convulsions of laughter and not say the lines. And [director] Frank Schaffner loved it and said, 'Do it that way.' So he called Rod Serling and told him what we were doing, and Rod said, 'No, no. Those lines are very important, let me come down and see it.' So he came down and we did a run-through of it, and he just fell on the floor laughing. Rod said, 'I don't care if I don't hear a fucking word.' He just loved it."

So did the critics, who applauded Art and Klugman's "Velvet Alley" performances. The *New York Times* noted that Art "gave a sympathetic and straightforward interpretation of the writer."

Shortly thereafter, Art and agent Bill McCaffrey were approached by independent producer David Susskind. Susskind was the president of Talent Associates, a company that packaged entertainment specials for television. He was impressed with the ratings for ABC's *Art Carney Meets Peter and the Wolf* (which were nearly double the ratings of its nearest competitor) and with the 30 rating Art had notched with "Harvey." Susskind was also impressed with Art's performance as Robert Briscoe in "The Fabulous Irishman." That special had been one of the highest-rated shows in CBS history.

"In our business, it's common knowledge that Milton Berle wants to play Othello," Susskind said at the time. "With Art, it's something different and much more reasonable. He doesn't talk Hamlet. He simply had an actor's ambition to get out of a narrow corner, which is what Norton got to be."

In May 1959 Susskind sold eight specials—all to be headlined by Art—to General Motors for two million dollars. Sponsored by

GM's AC spark plug and Delco-Remy divisions, the specials would air on NBC every month during the 1959–60 TV season. There would be four ninety-minute specials and four sixty-minute shows, ranging from variety to dramatic "reviews"—from Thornton Wilder's *Our Town* to *Man in the Dog Suit,* which had been a success on Broadway with Jessica Tandy and Hume Cronyn. It also called for Art to star as a suicidal drunk in the harrowing one-man drama *Call Me Back.* As an added perk, Art would be able to pick and choose his costars.

"I'm still sticking with comedy because I think the public thinks of me first and foremost as a funnyman," Art said shortly after signing the contract. "I'm afraid they won't go for it if I do all dramatic shows. The third ninety-minute dramatic presentation will be two or three one-act plays. I'm reading now for them but haven't decided which to do. Somerset Maugham properties are under consideration and there's a one-act original I'm keenly interested in, which would be practically a monologue. The big catch, if we can get it, is *The Informer.* I can't understand why it hasn't been done before on television."

After signing the deal with Susskind, Art sold his eight-room Yonkers house. In the fall he moved Jean, the kids, and cats Charcoal and Butterball into a six-bedroom, four-bathroom brick-and-shingle colonial on Wrexham Road in the Bronxville section of Yonkers.

After a quiet summer and a May guest spot with Sid Caesar that reunited him with Audrey Meadows, Art launched the first of his eight specials. In October, *Small World, Isn't It?* debuted on NBC. It was a comedy sketch/revue show costarring Hans Conried, Gloria Vanderbilt, and Hermione Gingold, the veteran British actress. Gingold was extremely difficult, throwing frequent temper tantrums and literally spitting on scripts she didn't like. Susskind approached Art and offered to fire Gingold, but Art politely declined.

Gingold joined Art in a memorable parody of the movie *Separate Tables,* a sketch that was reminiscent of a Sid Caesar–Imogene Coca *Your Show of Shows*–type skit. It was written by Sheldon Keller and former *Show of Shows* and *Caesar's Hour* writer Larry Gelbart.

"Art played a drunk in that *Separate Tables* sketch, and he was brilliant, walking into a couch and just folding over onto it," Keller said. "He played the suave, David Niven part, and he had those great moves. The sketch was hip. There was nothing like that going on in television at that time."

Keller didn't know Art very well while working on *Small World,* yet he sensed a sadness lurking beneath Art's sunny exterior. Even while Art spent rehearsal breaks performing his "celebrity farts" routine for Keller, the writer suspected that something was amiss.

"His guilt was overwhelming," Keller said. "You think Jews have guilt? That man invented it."

Gelbart also noted a sadness in Art's personality. "The thing I thought was very special about Art was that he had a lot of physical pain and problems in his life," Gelbart said. "But people really felt terribly affectionate about him because he had an incredibly sweet nature. Art was especially good because he's got this ability with accents and with characterizations, and he had that wonderful bag of gifts that let him be whoever you wanted him to be. He has a tremendous internal gyroscope. He only picks what's right for him to do, then he does it right."

Art also had the opportunity in *Small World* to show the American TV audience his impersonation of Edward R. Murrow. As Murrow, Art ended his interviews of a Riviera party hostess (Gingold), a Hollywood starlet (Edie Adams), and a Greek shipowner (Conried) by engulfing himself in cigarette smoke while puffing away with three hands.

Art was working on the third of his eight specials when his face appeared on the cover of *Newsweek* magazine, a spot usually reserved for politicians and world leaders. The November 30, 1959, *Newsweek* cover featured two shots of Art—sporting identical suit jacket and tie—in pensive and comical poses. The photos were placed over the headline "The Art of Art Carney." The magazine's feature story was headlined "Artful Art: Up from the Sewer" and began with this italicized editor's note:

> At a moment when the critical bombardment of television has become fairly deafening and blinding, fireworks of

an entirely different sort are popping around a one-man show named Art Carney.

Never before in television history has one performer undertaken the wide variety of roles that Carney will play in nine sparkling specials this season. . . . What sort of man is this immensely talented Carney?

The *Newsweek* feature skirted Art's drinking with a few colorful, unattributed quotes. "Carney's limit is one sniff of half a Martini on a cork," one person joked. The article also rehashed Art's career, and while it was well written and researched and informative, "Artful Art" still neglected to answer the question it posed. A *TV Guide* feature that ran the same week ("A New Perspective for Art Carney") did a better job, in less space, of highlighting Art's attitude: "He talks easily above a veneer of reserve. But Ed Norton wears a necktie now. And the pre-Gleason Art Carney has grown up."

Through his association with David Susskind, Art also met Barbara Isaacs, a Talent Associates production assistant who would become his second wife several years later. Isaacs had worked with Art on several of his 1959 and 1960 specials, and the two struck up a close friendship. Though their backgrounds were vastly different—his Irish Catholicism versus her Jewish heritage—Art and Barbara began a friendly relationship that would turn more serious in the future.

Art's next project was a live television adaptation of Thornton Wilder's *Our Town,* which was codirected by noted film director Jose Quintero. Art played the philosophical Stage Manager, commenting on life in Grover's Corners, New Hampshire, and the tragedy of Emily Webb (Kathleen Widdoes). She marries the boy next door (Clinton Kimbrough), dies in childbirth, and briefly returns from the dead to observe life in the small town.

New York Times critic Jack Gould called Art's performance "becomingly straightforward" but questioned whether Art's affectation was "a shade too crisp and a little wanting in philosophical overtones."

Art's saturating television presence during this period (1959–60) exposed him to mild criticism, which never really became vicious or mean-spirited. Art's good-guy reputation usually shielded him from pointed critical barbs. When someone did criticize Art in print, it was like the anonymous director who scolded him for being *too* easygoing.

"Art's got to learn to fight for what he wants," the director told Roger Kahn, profiling Art ("Actor Without an Ego") for the *Saturday Evening Post.* "After all, a good actor has to be more than a puppet, moving when someone else pulls the strings."

Almost without exception, in-depth magazine and newspaper articles all promised to deliver the goods on the "real" Art Carney, but they never succeeded. "There's no *there* there," writer Gertrude Stein once said of Oakland, California, and Art's public probably felt the same way about him. Art hated giving interviews and was visibly uncomfortable talking about himself and/or his performances. He preferred to talk about his war wound, compliment a costar, or reminisce about the good days working in radio.

Although Art was one of TV's biggest stars and a proven Broadway talent, he didn't seem to mind that Hollywood wasn't flooding agent Bill McCaffrey with movie offers. Only occasionally would he talk about unspecified screen offers he'd turned down.

But if Art was content to remain in television, Jackie Gleason had abandoned the medium for now, storming Broadway in the hit musical *Take Me Along* and winning a Tony Award. Gleason had also resumed the movie career he had aborted in the midforties, and talked casually of returning to television somewhere down the road.

Revisionist television historians might point to Art's drinking as the real reason he never "climbed out of the sewer" to star in a TV series after his mid-fifties *Gleason Show* success. Art himself offered a slew of contradictions: While he insisted he craved neither the attention nor the weighty responsibilities of starring in a series, he agreed to the high-profile Susskind specials.

In January 1960 Art took a dramatic leap into uncharted territory with a one-man performance in Tony Webster's *Call Me Back,* a sixty-minute dramatic monologue. Art played pathetic drunk

Tom O'Neill, whose emotional palette is colored by booze and pills. Sitting alone in his stark apartment with a telephone and a liquor bottle, Tom begins phoning friends and loved ones. While the calls grow progressively incoherent, Tom reveals the sad story of his life.

"I want to call anybody, anywhere," he tells the operator. "You mean I must have a name? Is that a new policy?"

Divorced and unemployed—and missing his young daughter and his girlfriend—Tom becomes more and more depressed when no one returns his phone calls. He eventually swallows a handful of pills, washes them down with booze, and dies.

"He's alone in a room with his only connection to the outside world his telephone," Art said, describing Tom. "Like a lot of alcoholics, they get telephonitis. They think, 'Gee, they'll be glad to hear from me,' and at three in the morning call California. 'Hello, what time is it out there?' A very common thing. I've had experience with both, the pills and the booze, and so had the author, Tony Webster. So when I read it I said, 'I don't want anybody else to do it.' "

Tensions on the set of *Call Me Back* ran high, because of the show's serious subject matter and its outcome. Art tried breaking the mood by clowning around with *Call Me Back*'s director, Tom Donovan. At one point Donovan called for a five-minute break. Art, speaking in a little girl's voice, said, "Good evening, Mr. Murrow. I'm Franny O'Neill and that drunk, lying down there on the floor, that's my daddy, Tom O'Neill."

Art's performance in *Call Me Back* received rave reviews. "Carney pulled off a towering tour-de-force. . . . His progression from a clear-eyed sober citizen though a half-dozen phases of drunkenness to thick-tongued (but always comprehensible) drunken stupor was a model of surefooted acting," noted the *New York Herald Tribune*.

Time magazine noted that "an ex-alcoholic, [Carney] has solved the problem himself. . . . Actor Art Carney kept dialing telephone numbers, bugging long-distance operators, playing the sole part in a TV play about a sinking alcoholic. . . . Gagwriter Tony Webster helped Art Carney add a superbly handled tour de force to his impressive list of acting credits."

After *Call Me Back,* Art returned to light sketch comedy that included several more specials written by Sheldon Keller, Larry Gelbart, and a dazzling young writer named Woody Allen. As a teenager, Allen had worked as a staff writer for Sid Caesar.

"Art played everything from an Edward R. Murrow character to a beatnik," Gelbart recalled of *Hooray for Love,* which was written by Gelbart, Keller, and Allen and costarred Tony Randall and Janis Paige. "I remember a joke Woody wrote. Art and Janis Paige played a couple of '60s [Greenwich] Village people, and she had taken him back to her apartment after a date. He said, 'Do you live alone?' and she said, 'I've got two roommates.' He said, 'Where are they?' And she said, 'When they found out I was on a date they went to Europe.' And Art was wonderful in a *Wild Strawberries* [the Ingmar Bergman film] parody where he played a kind of Max von Sydow character with the double-talk Swedish, of course."

In early 1960 Art headlined a special called *Three In One.* It was Art's ultimate showcase of versatility, spotlighting him in three one-act plays. In the first he played a drunken Irishman in Sean O'Casey's *Pound on Demand*; in the second, a crippled, insane seaman in Eugene O'Neill's *Where the Cross Is Made*; and in the third, a music hall song-and-dance man in Noël Coward's *Red Peppers.* Old friend and drinking partner Elaine Stritch joined Art in *Peppers.*

"I remember we were rehearsing downtown on Second Avenue, and there was an awards dinner the night before and we had a 10 A.M. call," Stritch said. "A picture of Art kissing Dinah Shore was on the front page of every newspaper that morning. So we're all sitting in rehearsal and it's 10:30, and there's no Art Carney. My heart was breaking because I didn't want him to get in trouble and I knew he'd been out. So we're sitting around waiting, and about 11 A.M. Art walks in and says, 'Those fucking answering services!' Well, I mean, he did a number about how unreliable his hotel was, and how they hadn't awakened him, and how he was moving out of the fucking hotel and who needs this kind of shit. It was a beautiful monologue. And of course we're all sitting there with the *Daily News* in our lap and he's just all over the place with such bravura. His last line was, 'Let's go to work.' I'll always remember that. That was typical of him."

Art's series of eight specials ended in the fall of 1960. He now talked of starring in a TV version of *Come Back, Little Sheba* that would be adapted by William Inge and would costar Shirley Booth, a fellow McCaffrey client.

Art was also back at CBS, working with Rod Serling on an episode of Serling's eerie show *The Twilight Zone*. In the episode "Night of the Meek," Art played Henry Corwin, an alcoholic department-store Santa. After being fired for drinking on the job, Henry discovers that he has magical powers—that he really *is* Santa Claus. The show aired on December 23, 1960, and is noteworthy for being one of the few (relatively) lighthearted *Twilight Zone* episodes. Also, it was shot on videotape, which at that time was a relatively new technological development.

Art spent six days at CBS, working in the network's studios in Culver City, California. He rehearsed "Night of the Meek" with director Jack Smight, who had directed Art in *The Seven-Year Itch* in 1956.

"It was one of the first times I had worked with Art in a dramatic sense, and I thought he did a wonderful job," Smight said. "He certainly was able to identify with the guy."

In November 1960, John Fitzgerald Kennedy was elected President. Kennedy's election led, indirectly, to Art's first brush with the network censors.

Art's first 1961 special was NBC's *Everybody's Doin' It*, which aired on January 17, three days before Kennedy's inauguration. *Everybody's Doin' It* included an eight-minute sketch in which writer Herb Sargent lampooned the incoming Kennedys, poking fun at their zest for touch football and Jackie Kennedy's expensive taste in clothing.

In the sketch, Art played JFK on his first day in office, talking to wife Jackie (played by Lee Remick). The skit included such scandalous material as the following exchange:

Remick: "I removed a horrible eagle from behind your desk."

Art: "That's the seal of the President; I'm not sure you should have done that." (Remick then tells him she replaced the eagle with a picture of the Kennedy clan.) "How could you?" Art says. "The wall's only twenty feet wide."

NBC, walking on eggshells around the new President,

ordered the sketch to be cut from the show. "We have never shied away from spoofing political figures, but we thought it would have been improper to have performers actually portraying the President and his wife," was NBC's official response. "Our decision was based on a matter of good taste."

Art followed *Everybody's Doin' It* with another special, *Fads and Foibles,* which he taped in 1961 for a 1962 airdate. But he was growing tired of the TV routine; he feared he was overexposing himself on television. So Art decided to leave television for the time being and concentrate on other projects. At McCaffrey's urging he turned down numerous offers to headline variety series and sitcoms. He also declined various movie offers, including a chance to appear opposite John Wayne in *Hatari,* which would have meant leaving his family for four months to shoot on location in Africa.

"Bill [McCaffrey] and I think it's good for me to get a change of pace from television," he said. "I'm not going to grab anything unless I think it's absolutely right for me, and that goes for Broadway, television, or the movies—unless things ever get to such a standstill for me that I need a part just for the paycheck."

Even though Art publicly announced his intentions to shy away from television, CBS had other ideas. During the summer of 1961, the network began planning two specials, both of which would reunite Art and Jackie Gleason. One special would be a one-hour *Honeymooners* show, the other an hour-long drama about the life and times of Stan Laurel and Oliver Hardy, with Art playing Laurel and Gleason as Hardy. Neither special, however, went beyond the discussion stage.

"I don't know why [the Laurel and Hardy project] didn't happen, but I wish that it had," Art said. "Undoubtedly it would have been a great script and a great project. Gleason and I were great Laurel and Hardy fans to begin with."

═══ 13 ═══

"You Have to Be
Happy to Play
Comedy"

In September 1960 Art's daughter, Eileen, entered college, something her famous father had never attained. Eileen enrolled as a freshman in Endicott Junior College, a traditional, old-line school located in Beverly, Massachusetts. Art and Jean were naturally proud of their daughter's accomplishments, which would ironically parallel Art's return to Broadway.

Age of Consent was an autobiographical stage comedy written by Henry and Phoebe Ephron. *Consent* documented the trials and tribulations of Frank Michaelson, a doting California father who finds it hard to cope after his oldest daughter leaves for college in New England. The Ephrons based the play on their daughters Nora and Delia, both of whom would later become successful writers.

Art had expressed an interest in returning to Broadway, perhaps in a light comedy, and the Ephrons offered him the lead role. It was perfect casting, especially with Eileen off at college and away from home for the first time.

"I turned it down the first time around," Art said. "I was looking eagerly for a good comedy, and this one had a lot of appeal, but I still felt that it wasn't quite right. I said no and kept on looking. But the play was revised, as nearly all plays are . . . and they asked me to look at it again. I was happy to be able to go along with the new version."

Probably the biggest factor in Art's changing his mind about starring in *Age of Consent* was George Abbott, the seventy-five-year-old Broadway legend, who agreed to direct the Ephrons' play (now called *Take Her, She's Mine*). Abbott also reminded Art of one of Jean's uncles.

"This time I most definitely wanted a comedy, one that had some heart and truth in it, not just a script full of gags and slapstick situations," Art said. "And I think I found the right one."

Art believed in the project enough to invest some money in the production. "Not a lot, a little," he said. "Just to see what happens."

Harold Prince was brought on board to produce *Take Her, She's Mine,* and Teresa Wright was mentioned as Art's possible costar. The role eventually went to veteran stage actress Phyllis Thaxter, who was in the process of divorcing CBS president James Aubrey.

Take Her, She's Mine was originally scheduled to open on Broadway in January 1962. But Prince was confident in Abbott's ability to work his magic and moved the show's Biltmore Theatre premiere up about three weeks, to December 21, 1961.

Relative newcomer Elizabeth Ashley was chosen to play the pivotal role of Mollie, the Michaelsons' oldest daughter, who is the play's primary catalyst. Both Ashley and Art's daughter, Eileen, had suffered severe kidney infections, a parallel that immediately endeared Ashley to Art.

Rehearsals for *Take Her, She's Mine* got under way in the fall of 1961, with tryouts scheduled for Boston, New Haven, Philadelphia, and Washington, D.C.

While Art's previous Broadway performance, in *The Rope Dancers,* was a success, his acting here would be even more closely scrutinized, especially by George Abbott. *The Rope Dancers* had been Peter Hall's first Broadway directing experience, but Abbott was a larger-than-life theatrical icon, equally revered and feared by colleagues and actors. Anyone who didn't address him as "Mr. Abbott" risked incurring the great director's wrath.

"Mr. Abbott was always running down the aisle and jumping up on the stage, and he was always after Art because Art had innumerable false faces," said sportswriter/actor Heywood Hale Broun, cast in *Take Her, She's Mine* as Art's archrival.

"To get to the real Art Carney is almost impossible," Broun said. "Art was either doing an imitation of somebody or he was doing his Norton character. And he had another character, which Mr. Abbott called 'Art Carney.' During rehearsals every now and then, from the back of the theater, Mr. Abbott would say, 'Art, you're being Art Carney again—I don't want you to be Art Carney, I want you to be Frank Michaelson.' "

Costar Louise Sorel recalled Abbott as "a sort of sergeant at arms with a big soft heart. Basically, his philosophy was get on the stage, say your lines, and get off. And he was right—we were in a show that required precision, and he really understood that medium. We did what he told us to do, and it worked."

But it wasn't that easy. *Take Her, She's Mine* underwent a handful of revisions during its out-of-town tryouts. Sorel remembered that even on the train to New Haven the Ephrons sat in the rear car passing notes to cast members with revised lines of dialogue. "We always thought we were being fired," Sorel said. "[The Ephrons] would do little cuts on the train as they were thinking things through, and there were some changes made in New Haven. But it was basically a very simple concept, and the changes were minor. There were a lot of light comedies on Broadway then."

The revised show, which was a little more daring, focused on the relationship between the unconventional Frank and his flaky daughter Mollie. It was a close bond, mirrored in the off-stage friendship that developed between Art and Elizabeth Ashley.

"Mr. Abbott understood he had a treasure in Art Carney and understood that Art could give this show the soul and sort of universal human condition that would make it translate," Ashley said. "Mr. Abbott kept rewriting, setting me up as the foil for Art. Without Art there would have been no play."

But for whatever reasons—nerves about being on Broadway, problems with the part, marital strife—Art was drinking heavily again during the play's run. And this time it began to creep into his work.

"Clearly [the drinking] was present, and it worried us enormously," Sorel said. "I had never been in a Broadway show, and there were some times when he missed performances. He knew that everyone knew [about the drinking]. It was always like, 'I wonder if he'll show up today.' But we were so used to it, and I just remember being upset more than anything. Everybody just fell in love with Art, and I think all the females felt very protective of him. We just wanted to take care of him because there's something very childlike about him. He was a man with a lot of pain, and I think we were so enamored of him that we would have done anything for him—anything."

While the show was still in New Haven, Ashley was in her hotel room memorizing her lines when the phone rang. It was Art, obviously drunk, calling from a bar down the street. He asked Ashley if he could come up to her room, and she said yes, wondering what she would do if Art made a pass at her. Ashley had grown up surrounded by alcoholics and knew their personalities sometimes changed when they were drunk.

But making a pass "was the farthest thing from his mind," Ashley wrote in her memoirs. "All he wanted was someone to talk to. He just didn't want to be alone. I didn't know it then, but he was at that point in his life where he was having to make the choice of do or die, and that one is as hard and lonely as it gets.

"Without even taking off his overcoat and hat, he sat down in this bleak room in the Taft Hotel, pulled a brown paper bag from his pocket, and began regaling me with stories and routines from the old days when he worked as an entertainer in Horace Heidt's band."

After draining his liquor bottle, Art passed out on one of the beds, still wearing his hat and coat, which Ashley gingerly removed before moving into the other room. The next morning, Art was struck by incredible remorse. He was ashamed and couldn't bring himself to face Ashley, instead keeping his back to her as he stared out the window. All he could say was "I'm sorry, I'm sorry" before finally turning toward Ashley with tears in his eyes.

"I'm sorry I imposed on you," he said. "And I'm sorry I made a fool of myself. Please forgive me." When Art and Ashley saw each other at rehearsal later that day, Art acted as if nothing had happened.

"He was up and wonderful and funny and supported everyone else with his strength," Ashley said. "He was the Rock of Gibraltar. . . . I got just a little hint of what it cost him every waking moment of his life to be that wonderful, funny, soft, vulnerable, sweet man. I began to have a sense of the price."

But it wasn't all sturm und drang. Art's ability to separate his offstage drinking from his work routine had been finely tuned during the Gleason years, and there were some enjoyable moments during rehearsal.

"In the play, Art and I were supposed to have a wrestling match, the question arising as to whether my son had endeavored to seduce his daughter," Broun recalled. "Mr. Abbott, very quickly, choreographed two minutes of wrestling, then he jumped off the stage, ran up the aisle, and we started to rehearse it. Art made the first mistake, and he whispered in my ear, 'Hope the old sonofabitch didn't notice,' and from the back of the theater a voice said, 'Art, Art,' and Art said, 'The old sonofabitch noticed.' "

If his past track record was any indication, Art privately fretted over how the play would be received. His statement to *Newsweek* a week before the play opened—"I feel comfortable in this play. I'm not sticking my neck out. Whatever happens it can't hurt me"—was more bravado than anything else.

When *Take Her, She's Mine* opened at the Biltmore on December 21, Art surprised each and every cast member with expensive opening-night gifts: gold-banded watches for the older, more established actors and steel-banded watches for the younger actors. It was a generous act that only further endeared Art to the troupe.

"When I thanked him, he kind of grinned and said, 'I'm too

shy to go around and wish people luck, so it just seemed easier to give all of you a watch,' " Broun said.

The offstage problems—namely drinking—persisted, though Art managed to hold it together well enough to miss only half of one matinee, when old-timer John Beale filled in for the first act.

"John was on for the first act and then Art showed up and took over the second act," Sorel recalled. "He just came out and the audience went crazy because they didn't really care; they loved the vulnerability. When he came on, the audience was thrilled, and Art just said, 'Well, I seem to be a little late.' They loved it."

But as loved and admired as he was by his *Take Her, She's Mine* colleagues, Art still hid behind a facade, rarely allowing anyone a glimpse into whatever private hell he was enduring. One night, on his way up to his dressing room, Heywood Hale Broun passed by Art's dressing room and heard an unfamiliar sound.

"From Art's room came this rather strange voice saying, 'Hello, Woody.' I went in and I realized it was just a moment I was getting to talk to the actual Art Carney. He said to me, rather seriously, 'Do you like poetry?' I said, 'Yes, I do.' And he produced a little book of children's poems by a woman named Joan Walsh Englund, who was a well-known, popular poet. And he said, 'These are some of my favorites,' and he read me a couple, again in this kind of strange, rather pleasant voice which I'd never heard before. At that point someone else coming upstairs said, 'Hello, Art,' and he said, 'Hello, glad to see you,' and he was back to doing one of his voices. It was very rare ever to get to talk to who he was; it was either one of his imitations or the sort of show business 'Hi, there, how are you?' kind of thing."

The show's lukewarm critical response failed to deter box office business, and *Take Her, She's Mine* settled in for a profitable, yearlong Broadway run before its evolution into a 1963 Hollywood movie starring Jimmy Stewart.

It didn't seem to matter that critics labeled the play "a rambling affair" that "suffers from its authors' inability ever quite to reconcile a generally spoofing manner with occasional attempts to have their matter taken seriously." Both Art and Abbott—along with Thaxter and (particularly) cast member Richard Jordan—received excellent notices, while Ashley established herself as a major star, winning a Tony Award for her role as Mollie.

"Art Carney and George Abbott made me a star," Ashley said later. "I really think that working with Art Carney eight shows a week laid the foundation for my ability to play comedy. Working with Art, actually getting your hands around those moments, you smell them and feel how it actually works at the bottom line. It's the kind of miracle that can occasionally happen to somebody in this racket, that you can be that young and run into Art Carney in a play that's not very good but that because he was phenomenal became a hit. He was the most organically 'in the moment' artist I've ever worked with."

If Art experienced any joy over his second Broadway success in as many outings, it was short-lived. On February 27, 1962, his father, Edward Carney, died at the age of eighty-two in Tarrytown Hall, the nursing home to which he'd been moved three years earlier. Art's mother, Helen, who had already outlived her oldest son, now was forced to bury her husband. Edward was honored with a two-page obituary in the local newspaper, a testament to the indelible mark "Civic Virtue" Carney had left on Mount Vernon over the previous forty-five years.

The drinking continued. Art admitted as much in a March 1962 newspaper article written "By Art Carney, Star of Stage and Television," in which he discussed "How Faith Changed My Life," vis-à-vis his relationship with Uncle Rich, the kindly older man who had lived with the Carneys in Mount Vernon and had made such an impact on Art and his brothers. It was one of the rare times Art would publicly reveal his religious beliefs.

> He was there, out of sight, when I drank. When I got older and had real responsibility, the remorse was worse than the hangover. I told myself I was headed for that endless lost weekend. I tried to quit. It wasn't easy. But when you talk to yourself or to Rich you have to tell the truth. He was gone when I dropped to the depths as a drinker. But at the lowest point I heard him remind me: "Just ask, 'Lord, Jesus, help me,' and He will—if you really mean it." I try hard to beat the temptation every time but, whenever I say, "Lord Jesus, help me," and I mean it, I win, and the drink loses.

Apparently Art didn't "mean it" much over the course of that year, and he made headlines on November 8, 1962, when he was arrested for drunk driving and missed an evening performance of *Take Her, She's Mine.*

The scenario played itself out in midtown Manhattan when Art, driving his sports car on Broadway around 11:50 A.M., hit the back of a cab that had stopped for a red light, causing minor damage to both vehicles. The cab driver testified that he exchanged some words with Art—"who talked slurrish-like, and his walk was a little unsteady"—before calling out to a policeman, who arrested Art after "a light hassle." Art was taken to the West Sixty-eighth Street station, where he refused a blood-alcohol test, telling the cops he'd had "a couple of beers," was being treated for nervous tension, and had gotten no sleep the night before.

The arresting policeman filed a complaint, telling the assistant district attorney, "I believe he [Art] was under the influence of liquor, but not to a great extent. . . . I say he was intoxicated, but, unlike a dead drunk, he could manipulate on his own."

Art appeared at his November 9 court hearing in dark sunglasses and driving cap and was visibly relieved when his case was dismissed for lack of evidence. "I'm a married man with three children," he told reporters afterward without removing his sunglasses. "This is one of those unfortunate things that happen."

Why it happened only Art knew for sure. At forty-four he was in the midst of a successful Broadway run, was being wooed with movie and TV offers, and once again was considering a reunion with Jackie Gleason (Hollywood executives were floating the idea of a *Honeymooners* movie). The entertainment world was his oyster. Art had demonstrated his ability on television and on the Broadway stage. Earlier in the year he had, ironically, talked at length about *Take Her, She's Mine,* about a state of mind he shared—perhaps falsely—with the outside world.

"I don't go all the way with 'The Show Must Go On,'" he said. "No one is irreplaceable. If something happened to my family, I don't think I'd go on. Being a human being comes first. Besides, you have to be happy to play comedy."

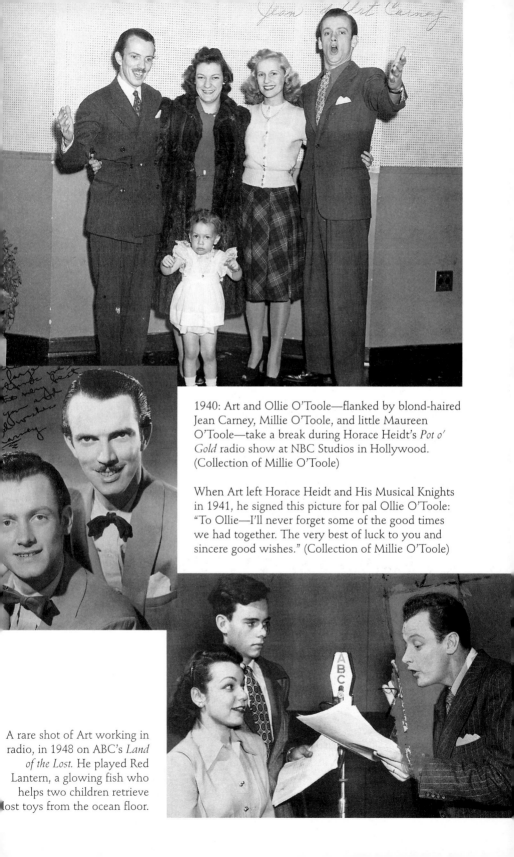

1940: Art and Ollie O'Toole—flanked by blond-haired Jean Carney, Millie O'Toole, and little Maureen O'Toole—take a break during Horace Heidt's *Pot o' Gold* radio show at NBC Studios in Hollywood. (Collection of Millie O'Toole)

When Art left Horace Heidt and His Musical Knights in 1941, he signed this picture for pal Ollie O'Toole: "To Ollie—I'll never forget some of the good times we had together. The very best of luck to you and sincere good wishes." (Collection of Millie O'Toole)

A rare shot of Art working in radio, in 1948 on ABC's *Land of the Lost*. He played Red Lantern, a glowing fish who helps two children retrieve lost toys from the ocean floor.

The big break: In 1948 Art made his TV debut, as Newton the Waiter on *The Morey Amsterdam Show*. In 1949 Milton Berle *(left)*, announcer Don Russell, and Art (dressed as Newton, right) helped Amsterdam celebrate the show's one-year anniversary. (Collection of Morey Amsterdam)

Jackie Gleason, Art, and Audrey Meadows share a laugh during a 1952 read-through for *The Jackie Gleason Show*. (CBS)

An early-1950s publicity photo. The familiar widow's peak was already visible.

The role for which Art will be immortalized: dim-bulb sewer worker Ed Norton on *The Honeymooners* (with costar Joyce "Trixie" Randolph). Art bought the battered felt hat in high school back in Mount Vernon.

Art gets a peck from Audrey Meadows after winning his third consecutive Emmy in March 1955. Wife Jean looks on. (CBS)

Art with his oldest brother Jack in 1956, shortly before Jack's untimely death. Art relied heavily on Jack for personal and professional guidance. (CBS)

In 1957 Art made his critically acclaimed Broadway debut, as a drunken philanderer in Morton Wishengrad's searing drama *The Rope Dancers.* That's director Peter Hall (now Sir Peter Hall) instructing Art, Joan Blondell, and Barbara Ellen Meyers

Onstage during *The Rope Dancers,* with Siobhan McKenna.

On the set of a Rexall TV special in 1959: Art, Audrey Meadows, and Sid Caesar hamming it up.

"Big Mouth" Martha Raye gets close with Art and ex-boxer Rocky Graziano for NBC's *Martha Raye Show.*

Art returned to the big screen in 1964's *The Yellow Rolls-Royce*, directed by Anthony Asquith and stacked with an all-star cast. Art played a loyal chauffeur trying to keep mob moll Shirley MacLaine out of trouble. (PhotoFest)

On March 10, 1965, Neil Simon's *The Odd Couple* opened on Broadway with Art in the role of "lint-picker" neatnick Felix Unger and Walter Matthau as slovenly sportswriter Oscar Madison. Art disliked Matthau intensely; this, coupled with heavy drinking, depression, and marital strife, forced Art to leave the show seven months later after suffering a nervous breakdown. (PhotoFest)

Art with wife Jean and daughter Eileen a few days after *The Odd Couple* opened to rave reviews and standing-room-only crowds. (PhotoFest)

The Odd Couple was a hot ticket, and celebrities like Robert and Ethel Kennedy often dropped by to congratulate Art and Walter Matthau, who later won the Tony Award for his brilliant *Odd Couple* work.

Art as the villainous Archer in a two-part 1966 episode of ABC's *Batman,* the first prime-time TV series shot in color. Barbara Nichols played his partner in crime.

Art and Jackie Gleason discarded their *Honeymooners* roles in this 1966 CBS musical satire, "The Politician."

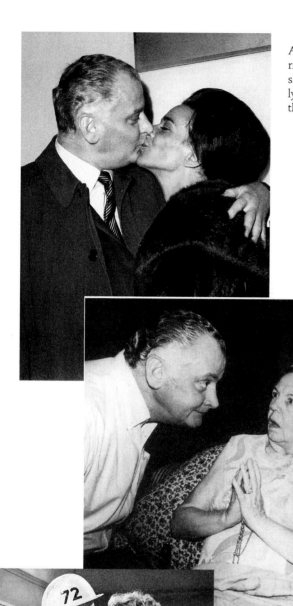

Art surprised everyone when he married Barbara Isaacs in December 1966, shortly after divorcing Jean. The newlyweds first met in the late fifties through producer David Susskind.

Broadway, Part IV: Art received a Tony nomination for his work in Brian Friel's *Lovers.* Costars included *(left to right)* Grania O'Malley, Anna Manahan, and Beulah Garrick.

Art's onetime CBS stablemate Lucille Ball refused to appear in the 1967 big-screen feature *A Guide for the Married Man* unless Art agreed to costar with her.

Broadway, Part V: In 1972 Art and Barbara Barrie took over for Peter Falk and Lee Grant in Neil Simon's *The Prisoner of Second Avenue.* Art's role as a stressed-out Manhattanite riddled with drink and depression mirrored his own life.

Art capped his remarkable personal and professional comeback by winning an Oscar for *Harry and Tonto,* his first starring movie role. Writer/director Paul Mazursky approached Art after James Cagney, Cary Grant, Laurence Olivier, Jimmy Stewart, and Frank Sinatra all turned the role down.

Hard-boiled detective Ira Wells and ditzy Margo Sperling (Lily Tomlin), the perfect odd couple, in Robert Benton's 1977 gumshoe homage *The Late Show.*

Art as senile Dr. Amos Willoughby in *House Calls* (1978), a romantic comedy in which he costarred with old adversary Walter Matthau.

iple threat: George Burns, Lee Strasberg, and "the kid" played lifelong friends who decide rob a bank in 1979's *Going in Style*.

orpus C. Redfish is reunited with son Travis (Meat Loaf) and daughter Alice Poo (Rhonda ates) in *Roadie* (1980).

Lucille Ball and Joyce Randolph joined Art in paying tribute to the late Jackie Gleason at a Museum of Broadcasting gala in September 1987. (*New York Post*)

ft, top) Art finally got the chance to act with boyhood idol James Cagney in 1984's *Terrible Joe 'oran,* Cagney's final on-screen appearance. Art won his sixth and final Emmy for the role.

rare moment of levity with Jackie Gleason during the filming of *Izzy and Moe* in 1985. :hind the scenes Gleason was morose and belligerent. He and Art got together only for pub-:ity purposes and rarely spoke to each other. (*New York Post*)

:levision's greatest comedy team, together for the last time in *Izzy and Moe.*

Pop goes the Weasel: In 1989 Art had a recurring role as look-alike Barnard Hughes's annoying brother on *The Cavanaughs,* a CBS sitcom.

Art as Grandpa Vanderhof with Jean Stapleton (as daughter Penny) in a CBS production of *You Can't Take It With You.*

=== 14 ===

TRANSITIONS

In the five years since Art and Jackie Gleason parted company, both men had proven that their professional survival was not mutually exclusive. Art, of course, had won acclaim for *The Rope Dancers*, his eight-special NBC package (including *Call Me Back*), and *Take Her, She's Mine*. Gleason, too, had been busy, winning a 1959 Tony Award for *Take Me Along* and receiving an Oscar nomination for his role as pool shark Minnesota Fats in Robert Rossen's 1961 movie, *The Hustler*. While Art had peeled away his second-banana image, the Great One only added to his larger-than-life public persona.

Yet both men still felt the onstage attraction to each other, the electricity they had first generated on *Cavalcade of Stars* and later on *The Jackie Gleason Show*, the chemistry that had people comparing them to Laurel and Hardy (much to Gleason's irritation). The thirty-nine *Honeymooners* episodes that Art, Gleason, Audrey Meadows, and Joyce Randolph had filmed during the 1955–56 season were now hits as reruns, having finally found an appreciative audience.

In early 1962 Gleason announced he was returning to CBS in September with a new variety show, *The American Scene Magazine*. Art made it clear as early as February that he had no problem returning to the Gleason fold—at least on a limited, as-needed basis befitting Art's stature.

That was fine, except for one major sticking point: Bill McCaffrey and Gleason's agents had failed to reach an agreement. "Bill McCaffrey, speaking for me, wanted certain things," Art told *New York Post* columnist Earl Wilson, without elaborating. "After all, what are we working for? But I know Jackie'd do anything for me and I hope he knows he's got the same kind of friend in me." The situation didn't seem any clearer that July, with Art firmly entrenched in *Take Her, She's Mine* and anticipating a long Broadway run.

"I know people seem to think I'm signed up [with Gleason]. I haven't. I'm going to stay with this [play]," he said. "I will appear from time to time, if possible, but Gleason is taping his Saturday-night show in the middle of the week. And Wednesday I have two shows to do."

A Gleason-Carney reunion was finally negotiated but turned out to be only a one-shot deal, on the *American Scene Magazine* premiere in September 1962. Art and Gleason revived Ralph Kramden and Ed Norton for a Honeymooners sketch, with Sue Ann Langdon playing Alice (there was no Trixie in the sketch). The scenario was typical *Honeymooners* fodder: Ralph had finally broken down and bought a TV set, and he invited Norton over to watch a Saturday-afternoon college football game. But everything goes awry when the TV set dies during the opening kickoff. Norton disassembles the television, relying on what he'd learned while watching the radio-room guys during his navy days. Naturally, he can't figure out how to put the TV set back together again, and Ralph does his classic slow burn when the boys discover the TV wasn't broken at all: There was a power blackout in the neighborhood.

Physically, Art appeared gaunt and haggard during the sketch, but he slipped back easily into Norton's goofy skin and appeared to be having fun. It was the show's finale; immediately afterward, a sweaty Gleason—still wearing his bus-driver's uniform—came out to address the audience. But rather than say his usual good-byes and introduce his costars, Gleason took the time to praise Art and thank him for coming on the show. It was a touching, warm gesture that Gleason obviously meant from his heart.

"I want you to know how much of a kick it is for me to work with a guy like Art Carney," Gleason said. "I've been in show business about thirty years now, and in all the time I've been appearing in shows all over the country, I have never worked with a comedian who has as great a comic sensitivity, as fine a delivery, as Art Carney. People ask me, 'How is it to work with Art? We notice he gets an awful lot of laughs.' Well, that's true—I'm delighted that he does. . . . And besides being a great comedian, he's also one of the finest dramatic actors I've ever seen. In other words, what I am trying to say is, to me, Art Carney is one of the great performers in show business."

They were kind words, yet Gleason had already decided to move *American Scene Magazine* in a different (and subsequently disastrous) direction. He would eschew previous material like "The Honeymooners" for more dramatic bits and solo turns, aiming the spotlight mostly on himself with a supporting cast featuring Frank Fontaine (as Crazy Guggenheim), Alice Ghostley, and Langdon.

Gleason's decision to change the direction of *American Scene* was news to Art, who might have thought about returning to the show intermittently.

"I don't know anything about it; I wasn't involved in the show," Art said. "I wasn't even in contact with [Gleason] then. I can't say I cared much for the show. It had no Honeymooners and very few comedy sketches of any kind. It was mostly monologues and musical numbers, as I recall it. But [Gleason and I] had no cross words about that or anything else at the time."

Art's busy theatrical schedule made frequent television appearances impossible, though he was glad to return to TV whenever he could. Notwithstanding his *American Scene* appearance, Art's TV audience had to make do with *Honeymooners* reruns or Art's occasional talk-show appearances or guest-star roles. *Take Her, She's Mine* was already locked in to a steady run and was doing brisk business at the box office. When Elizabeth Ashley won a Tony Award for her role in the show, it assured that *Take Her, She's Mine* would run through the winter of 1963, when it finally closed after more than four hundred Broadway performances.

But Art didn't rush headlong back to television after the final curtain dropped on *Take Her, She's Mine.* For starters, the timing, as far as TV was concerned, wasn't advantageous. The 1962–63 TV season had already reached its midway point, with series and specials locked in to the schedule.

So Art took a step back. He recharged his batteries and dropped out of public view for a few months, savoring daughter Eileen's upcoming August 1963 wedding. He guest-starred with Andy Williams and Danny Kaye on their respective TV specials and resurfaced in June to star in NBC's *DuPont Show of the Week* "The Triumph of Gerald Q. Wert."

For his summer performing plans, Art settled on a two-week summer-stock production of *Time Out for Ginger* encompassing the same New England circuit—Dennis, Massachusetts, to Ogunquit, Maine—that Art had traveled seven years earlier in *The Seven-Year Itch.*

Time Out for Ginger was a fluffy, no-brainer comedy written by Ronald Alexander. Art was cast in the role of Howard Carol, a small-town banker and father of three teenage girls. Howard believes in letting his daughters do their own thing yet still wishes his youngest daughter, Ginger, had been a boy. Ginger takes daddy's seize-the-day philosophy to the extreme. She tries out for the high school football team, makes the squad, and even scores a game-winning touchdown that drives Daddy into seventh-heaven histrionics (a showstopping scene in which Art, as Howard, colorfully reenacts the touchdown). In between, Howard and his wife, Agnes, deal with the usual parental difficulties of boys, boys, and more boys courting their daughters.

Time Out for Ginger had been critically pummeled yet had enjoyed a modicum of success in its previous incarnations, including a musical television adaptation starring Jack Benny. The show certainly wasn't much of a stretch for Art, who was now playing his third "father" stage role and floating from easygoing Frank Michaelson in *Take Her, She's Mine* to easygoing Howard Carol. *Time Out for Ginger* required only two weeks' rehearsal, indicating that everyone involved in the production wasn't too concerned with their cardboard-thin stage roles. As an added bonus, Phyllis Thaxter, who had costarred with Art in *Take Her, She's Mine,* agreed to play Art's *Time Out* wife, Agnes. *Ginger's* cast also included up-and-coming actors Rosemary Forsyth, Lisa Richards, Susan Tyrrell, Tom Ligon, and Will Mackenzie, with veterans Emory Bass and John Cecil Holm rounding out the ensemble. New York stage director Porter Van Zandt led the group through rehearsals, preparing them for the July 1 opening in Dennis's Cape Playhouse.

No one connected with *Time Out for Ginger* remembers Art having any noticeable problems with alcohol during the run of the play. Ginger ale seems to have been Art's choice of drink that summer, but he could have been excused for slipping back into his old habits when he received grim news just two days before opening night.

Art's mother, Helen Carney, died on June 29 in Tarrytown Hall Nursing Home, in the very same room and very same bed as her husband. She was eighty-four. A strong woman, Helen had lived alone in her Mount Vernon apartment until she was too ill to care for herself. In death, as in life, she took a backseat to her husband. A good portion of Helen's obituary in Mount Vernon's daily newspaper detailed husband Edward's career and civic achievements, with only a few paragraphs devoted to Helen's accomplishments as a renowned violinist. A requiem mass for Helen was held on July 2, 1963, in Mount Vernon's St. Ursula's Church.

Although naturally grief-stricken over his mother's death, Art pulled himself together for the opening night of *Time Out for Ginger,* somehow transforming himself from a mourning son into a jocular father engaged in a four-sided stage farce.

"All I remember was that his mom died and it was like, God, is he going to make it?" Will Mackenzie recalled. "We thought he was going to start drinking again, but he got through the show and never missed a performance. We'd go into restaurants, but he palled around with all of us; I think because of his mom's death he just loved hanging around with the kids. Art played jazz piano, and I remember we'd go to these hangouts, and he would sit down and play the piano, and, of course, he'd pick up the tab for everybody."

Said Emory Bass: "When we heard [about his mother's

death], we thought that would close the show instantly. But Art was an old pro about it. He stayed on and did the show."

Art, as usual, didn't want to burden anyone else with his problems. His mother's death had obviously taken its emotional toll, but Art kept his feelings to himself. One night, while sitting with Emory Bass on the dark porch of Dune Lawn, the fashionable inn near Ogunquit, Art finally shared some of his feelings.

"He came and sat with me for a long time and kind of told me the story of his life," Bass said. "He needed to unwind and get it off his chest. I think he wanted the lights off because I think he had tears in his eyes. And that was unusual for Art; I don't think he talked easily to people, but he kind of unburdened himself." Art later repaid Bass for his emotional support by offering to drive an unwieldy framed print Bass had purchased back to New York.

Despite his mother's death, Art had reason to smile a little. *Time Out for Ginger* was generating ecstatic reviews, like this glowing assessment from renowned Boston theater critic Elliot Norton: "Art Carney is creating more than a fair share of innocent merriment in a comedy that wasn't very much until he undertook to play it and will surely cease to please when he abandons it. . . . Carney is almost heroic in the way in which he allows the younger ones to use him as a foil. As an expert technician, he could upstage any one of them, but he stands his ground mutely, while they bounce the funny lines off his chest. Is there any other comedian who would do this?"

Art was obviously having fun away from the pressures of television and Broadway. Although the *Time Out* reviews understandably focused on Art, the show's young cast, especially Susan Tyrrell, was also receiving quite a bit of attention. Tyrrell, who had just graduated from high school, was the daughter of a well-known television executive and was acting in her first show. Her performance in *Time Out for Ginger* spurred intense interest, so much so that *Look* magazine assigned a reporter to follow her throughout the two-week summer tour for a feature article devoted to Tyrrell.

"There was a feeling like maybe three or four of us were going to go off and do lots of things; there were lots of people— agents and managers and bullshit like that—buzzing around that production," said Tom Ligon. "But Art was just this sweet clown who would share the stage and have this ball with you while you were on. I remember the first night I ever went on, I was supposed to come on and say, 'Hiya, Mr. Carol,' and he'd say, 'Hiya, Eddie.' And I was so green that I came on and right away said, 'Hiya, Mr. Carney,' and he looked at me and said, 'Hi, Tom. You want to do it again?' He would take anything in stride. He wasn't this tough bird."

When the troupe moved from Dennis to Ogunquit, Art asked Ligon to drive his car while Art napped in the backseat. Somewhere in New Hampshire, Ligon, driving with an expired license, was pulled over for speeding by a state trooper.

"Art gets out of the car and says to me, 'Let me handle this whole thing.' He walks over to the trooper—I see him talking to him for a few minutes—then he comes back and says, 'Just follow him to the courthouse,' " Ligon recalled. "We drive in, Art pays the fine, and he continues the drive up.

"About twenty years later I was playing in *The Young and the Restless* at CBS in Los Angeles, and I could see on the in-studio monitor that Art was going to be on *The Mike Douglas Show*. So I go out of my dressing room and go across into the other studio, go backstage, and I see this figure sitting on this bucket in the shadows. And I could see by his white hair that it's Mr. Carney. So I walk over to him, and no sooner do I get out a 'Hello' than he kind of glances up at me and says, 'You got the license yet?' He didn't miss a beat. I fell on the floor screaming with laughter."

Time Out for Ginger ended in mid-July. In August, Art's daughter, Eileen, now twenty-one and working at the CBS office, was married in Bronxville's St. John's Episcopal Church. After the ceremony, in which younger brother Brian served as an usher, the newlyweds returned to Yonkers, where Art and Jean held a backyard reception.

While Eileen and her new husband flew off to Saint Thomas for their honeymoon, Art prepared for his return to Europe. It would be the first time he had traveled overseas since taking a Nazi bullet on Saint-Lô, but this time it was MGM, not Uncle Sam, who was footing the bill.

After years of rejecting movie offers, Art and Bill McCaffrey finally decided on a project that would put Art back in the movies for the first time since 1940's *Pot o' Gold.* Television, for now, could wait; if Art and McCaffrey played their cards right, the upcoming European trip could be the beginning of a new career: Art Carney, movie star.

══ 15 ══

THE BIG SCREEN

In February 1964 Ed Sullivan welcomed the Beatles into America's living rooms and, from there, into its collective consciousness. The TV landscape was changing: Even with the Vietnam War still in its infancy and the specter of draft dodgers, hippies, flower power, and the Generation Gap several years away, television executives began skewing their network programming toward a younger audience. Gone were the salad days of early TV giants Sid Caesar, Milton Berle, Red Skelton, Jack Benny, and George Burns. Of the sketch/variety television performers popular throughout the 1950s, only Jackie Gleason still registered on television's pop cultural radar screen—and just barely.

The ratings for Gleason's *American Scene Magazine* were good enough to justify its yearly renewal by CBS. But younger TV viewers discovering *The Honeymooners* magic for the first time were watching reruns already a decade old.

Gleason continued to resist the temptation to revive Ralph Kramden and Ed Norton, stubbornly sticking with Frankie Fontaine and Gleason's own solo characters. Art said at the time that he and Gleason spoke on the phone and kept in touch, but they hadn't worked together in nearly two years and had no plans to continue their professional relationship in the foreseeable future. Although they appeared together in January 1964—Art hosted a

CBS special celebrating Gleason's thirty-five years in show business—when or if they would ever reunite was anyone's guess.

Art had cemented the foundations of his television legacy in the fifties and early sixties, and at forty-five he now seemed apathetic about reaching a new generation in these changing times. Gleason's waning popularity might have given Art pause to reconsider his own TV durability. Both he and Gleason had come of age during the relatively serene Eisenhower era, light-years removed from the anger and turmoil following John F. Kennedy's assassination and the daily dinnertime news reports now chronicling the carnage in Southeast Asia.

After hosting the CBS Gleason special, Art made only a handful of TV appearances in 1964. He guest-starred on pal Jonathan Winters's special (in which Art "had a terrible off night," according to the *New York Times*) and starred in an episode of NBC's *DuPont Show of the Month* ("A Day Like Today"). In the fall he costarred in NBC's "The Timothy Heist" (*Bob Hope Presents Chrysler Theater*) and CBS's "Smelling Like a Rose" (*Mr. Broadway*).

By that time Art had already completed his part in his second movie and first since 1940: MGM's *The Yellow Rolls-Royce*. The movie was filmed in May 1964 on location in Europe, with Art's segment shot in Italy and featuring Shirley MacLaine, George C. Scott, and Alain Delon.

Art played a loyal chauffeur named Joey who drives a mobster (Scott) and his moll (MacLaine) around Italy in the yellow Rolls-Royce of the movie's title. Joey wasn't too far removed from Ed Norton; a little brighter and perceptive perhaps, but if Art wanted to stretch his talents, this certainly was a strange choice. Television viewers loved Ed Norton, but this was an expensive movie financed by a major Hollywood studio.

The Yellow Rolls-Royce was typical of the bloated, internationally flavored movies of that era—*The Pink Panther, What's New, Pussycat?*—and featured an all-star cast, including Rex Harrison, Jeanne Moreau, Ingrid Bergman, Omar Sharif, and Wally Cox, who were left with a dull script and Anthony Asquith's lackadaisical direction. Written by Terence Rattigan, the screenplay stitched together three vignettes, each linked by the 1932 Rolls-Royce that always figured prominently in its owners' lives. Art's vignette was sandwiched between a Harrison–Moreau–Edmund Purdom love triangle, in which a British gentleman (Harrison) discovers that his wife (Moreau) is having an affair (with Purdom). The other story revolved around a rich American (Bergman) who smuggles her lover (Sharif) into Yugoslavia to fight the Nazis.

Art wore an ever-present bow tie and straw boater as Joey, the gum-chewing chauffeur working for Miami mobster Paolo Maltese (Scott). Maltese is visiting Italy with his dizzy fiancée, Mae Jenkins (MacLaine), who's more interested in grabbing a hamburger than in seeing the country's historic sights.

Maltese, looking for a way to travel the countryside, buys the yellow Rolls-Royce and tries explaining Italian history to the flighty, diamond-encrusted Mae. When Maltese is called back to Miami to oversee a gangland murder, he entrusts Mae to Joey, instructing his chauffeur to keep Mae occupied until his return the following week.

Soon after Maltese leaves, Mae catches the eye of a young Italian photographer, Stefano (Delon). Before long, she's fallen in love with Stefano and hopes to dump the abusive, unromantic Paolo.

Italy's breathtaking scenery turned out to be the vignette's only memorable aspect. Although Art spent most of his screen time alongside MacLaine and shared a good deal of his dialogue with her, he was given very little to do besides talk tough (sounding like Ed Norton), explaining the difference between "amoral" and "immoral" to Mae, and, in one scene, don a one-piece, striped bathing suit. Although Art was in almost every scene within the forty-eight-minute vignette, his work was forgettable and went largely unnoticed. In May 1965 *The Yellow Rolls-Royce* opened to generally bad reviews and subsequently performed poorly at the box office.

By that time, however, Art was back on Broadway and teetering on the edge of a nervous breakdown, his drinking at full throttle and his marriage to Jean disintegrating. What had started as the theatrical role of a lifetime was quickly turning into a living nightmare. Art, abusing both alcohol and pills, had another reason to fret: a troublesome costar named Walter Matthau.

$=== 16 ===$

THE ODD COUPLE

In the fall of 1964, Art had received a script from Neil Simon
for a play called *The Odd Couple*. Simon was formerly part of
Sid Caesar's legendary *Show of Shows* and *Caesar's Hour* stable
of comedy writers. He had also written, briefly, for *The Jackie
Gleason Show* (an experience he detested) before moving into
theater. Simon already had several Broadway hits under his belt
(*Barefoot in the Park, Come Blow Your Horn*) when he began writing
The Odd Couple, a semiautobiographical, three-act comedy.

Danny Simon, Neil's brother, was a fellow comedy writer
whose slovenly appearance and almost subhuman living conditions became the basis for *The Odd Couple*. In Neil Simon's fertile
imagination, Danny was transformed into crusty Oscar Madison,
a cigar-smoking New York sportswriter. Oscar, happily divorced
from his wife, lived in a fetid bachelor pad. He was at his best
playing poker with buddies Vinnie, Speed, Roy, and Murray and
betting on the horses. In his spare time Oscar chased the twitter-
ing Pigeon sisters, Cicely and Gwendolyn, British neighbors who
lived upstairs.

But Oscar's utopian existence screeches to a halt when he's
visited by boyhood friend Felix Unger, a CBS newswriter who's
suicidal after the breakup of his marriage. Felix has come to

Oscar's apartment seeking refuge. Grudgingly, Oscar lets his old pal move in, unaware that he's an anal-retentive roommate from hell, a pathological neat freak who disinfects playing cards and severely cramps Oscar's slobbish style.

Art accepted the role of Felix, aware that *The Odd Couple* was headed for Broadway. Renowned comic improvisationalist Mike Nichols had agreed to direct the show, which would be backed by Broadway financier/producer Saint Subber.

According to Simon, it was no coincidence that he had sent the *Odd Couple* script to Art. Simon had known Art slightly from *The Jackie Gleason Show* and pictured Art as the perfect Felix Unger.

"I can't remember anybody else that we had gone to," Simon said. "I don't remember if I had seen him do it somewhere else before or he did it for me in rehearsal, but Art started to show me how his father would sign his report card: It took him about ten minutes to do it, with the hands, looking the card over and over and over, getting ready, pushing things away. And I said, That is Felix Unger, so prissy with the details and all. Art was sensational."

Art dubbed Felix "the lint picker" and viewed the role as a natural for his style of comedy. Unlike the gregarious Ed Norton or Frank Michaelson in *Take Her, She's Mine,* Felix was more spiritually and emotionally attuned to James Hyland, the failed alcoholic father Art had portrayed in *The Rope Dancers.* On the surface, Felix was played for laughs, but his underlying persona was a morose, pathetic, confused man-child trying to cope with a harsh reality check he can't quite cash.

"Art was wonderful as Felix, because if you don't have faith in the character of Felix, there is no play," said Sidney Armus, who costarred in the role of Oscar's poker-playing buddy Roy. "You've got to have faith with the trouble that Felix is going through. The drama is the breakup of the family, with Felix Unger representing the divorced person, estranged from his wife, a guy who loves to give his kids breakfast in the morning. This is a father! And that's what the audience sees first. And if you don't accept that, then the play is nothing. The audience had to trust Felix Unger before they could absorb Oscar, the poker players, and the Pigeon sisters."

Art certainly had a lot in common with Felix Unger: They were both depressives, both obsessively hygienic. (Art feared perspiration and was constantly dousing his face with water. This became a running in-joke on the *Gleason Show* in the fifties.) Both men shared certain anal-retentive qualities, like Art's insistence on stacking his change in neat piles every night before going to bed. More ominous, they were both dealing with irreparable problems at home.

Art and Jean, married for twenty-five years, had been through some tough times, mainly due to Art's drinking. As *The Odd Couple* began rehearsals, their marital problems were becoming worse. While Jean hadn't kicked Art out of their Yonkers house, the situation was tenuous, and Art spent many nights in a downtown Manhattan hotel. At night, after everyone else went home, he would often stroll over to the Cort Theatre—where he'd starred in *Take Her, She's Mine*—and chat with the doorman. Someone who dearly loved his family and always prided himself on maintaining a tranquil domestic life away from show business, Art was undergoing a painful transition.

"When I went into rehearsal for *The Odd Couple* I was under strain and stress," Art said. "I found it difficult to memorize my lines. I was having marital problems and the part itself was not an easy part. Felix wasn't just the guy who came out and said funny things."

Said Simon, "Art is a sweet and wonderful man, but he was having troubles during the rehearsals and run of the show you wouldn't believe."

If Art was beginning to crack under the strain, it didn't get much better when Simon and Nichols cast Walter Matthau in the role of Oscar Madison. When he entered *The Odd Couple,* Matthau was largely unknown outside of Broadway circles. He had played several small movie roles (including in 1964's *Fail Safe*) and was known for his laconic demeanor and his hangdog, world-weary expression. He also carried the reputation of being a mischievous onstage grandstander, which some theater people considered obnoxious.

Art and Matthau had never worked together and seemed, by all appearances and first-person accounts, to get along famously during the play's rehearsals. Matthau, however, sounded an early alarm.

"I remember sending the script to Walter, who said he wanted to play Felix," Simon said. "I said, 'Why do you want to play Felix?' And he said, 'Because that's acting. Oscar I can phone in.' "

Matthau insisted on playing Felix and constantly browbeat Nichols, urging the rookie director to reconsider his decision. Matthau even talked in print about switching roles with Art, who had remained characteristically mute on the issue.

"Listen, don't give me the bit about we're a comedy team," Matthau told one reporter. "I don't care what Neil Simon told you. He's a playwriter, not an actor. Hell, Art and I, we don't shoot gags. We don't push the laughs. We play it as a story of two guys in a whacked-up situation. If the audience decides something is funny—let them laugh. If they don't laugh, the hell with them. And I'll prove to everybody I can play Felix. After we've run a year, Carney and I are going to exchange parts. He liked the idea, too. It'll be great."

But Nichols wasn't so sure. "Oh, Walter has wanted to play Felix all along," he said. "I think it is a bad idea. I have thought it was a bad idea the first time he broached it. I will continue to think it is a bad idea, and by no means will I allow them to change around and switch roles next year."

Before it could open on Broadway in March 1965, *The Odd Couple* needed to work out its kinks in the usual out-of-town venues: Wilmington, New Haven, Washington, D.C., Boston. Simon and Nichols both needed to fine-tune the play's comedic engine, to test, discard, and/or add new material while gauging the chemistry between their two stars.

"They are really and truly unselfish men," Nichols said of Art and Matthau. "And they cared about the play and not about their own parts or their own importance in a scene. And they adjusted their tempo of remembering lines and learning moves so beautifully to each other, as if they'd been doing it for years."

Behind the scenes, however, things weren't going so smoothly. Art's old-school methods were to learn his lines and stick to Simon's script, never changing a syllable or phrase. Matthau, however, was the exact opposite. He loved to ad-lib and add his own "stage business," and much to Nichols's growing irritation, he refused to heed Nichols's instructions. When Matthau continued to ignore the playwright's verbal directions, Nichols began relaying his thoughts to Matthau in the form of scribbled, handwritten notes that were usually ignored.

The biggest fight for control between Nichols and Matthau occurred during one particular *Odd Couple* scene in which Oscar is trying to interrupt Felix, who's raving hysterically. In the scene, Oscar looks up to the ceiling and says, ostensibly to God, "Why doesn't he hear me? I know I'm talking. I recognize my voice!"

Art and Matthau always rehearsed the scene this same way, until opening night in Wilmington. Without warning, Matthau, instead of looking up to the ceiling, decided to pick someone out of the audience and speak to this person directly with his "Why doesn't he hear me?" line. An angry Nichols sent Matthau a note asking him to perform the line as written, fearing that Matthau would break the play's sense of staged reality and risk losing the audience's attention.

"The next night Matthau did it again, and the night after that, and the night after that, and he never did the show without doing it that way," said one cast member. "And after a few nights Mike continued to give him notes that said things like, 'I know you're never going to change this, Walter.' It just became a company joke."

Matthau found other ways to express his unhappiness over scenes or bits of dialogue he thought irrelevant. Even Art agreed with Matthau that a line Felix yells to Oscar in the second act—"Hey, Yogi, you're getting too old for doubleheaders!"—was out of character for the prissy Felix. But Art kept his mouth shut and performed the line as written. Matthau, however, took a different tack, sending a letter to Simon under the guise of "Dr. Irving Blane," who had seen the play and wanted to share a few thoughts with the playwright. "I would like to congratulate you on your new play—a masterpiece of talent, humor, and artistry," wrote Dr. Blane. "But there is one line in it which is wrong for Mr. Carney and my wife and I hope you won't mind if we tell you about it." It was, of course, the "Hey, Yogi" line. Unbelievably, Matthau's ruse worked: Simon, unaware of Dr.

Blane's real identity, deleted the "Hey, Yogi" line before the next performance.

Nichols also faced a (much less combative) struggle with Art, who couldn't seem to nail the role of Felix and was frustrated with Nichols's direction. "Who do you see me as?" Art asked Nichols during one rehearsal. "Hume Cronyn? Who?"

Art gave little indication—at least during the show's out-of-town tryouts—that Matthau's shenanigans were bothering him. He didn't miss a single out-of-town performance, a remarkable feat considering he was drinking heavily while trying to hold together his tattered marriage. "I remember going to lunch with Art and we sat for over an hour and he hardly spoke," Simon said. "So I knew he was going through some problems."

Art's obvious distraction was also apparent to *Odd Couple* stage manager Harvey Medlinsky. "He kept to himself and everybody respected that because we sort of knew he was working through his problems," Medlinsky said. "One thing that encapsulates my memory of Art in the show was when we were staying at the Ritz-Carlton in Boston. Late one night, at one or two in the morning, I was coming back across the [Boston] Common. It was winter, and it was cold, and there was snow on the ground. And I came across a figure I recognized. It was Art, bundled up, and my recollection was of him wandering through the Common dealing with what was bothering him. Seeing the solitude, late in the night . . . there was Art, obviously disturbed and upset."

The Odd Couple was an out-of-town success, which boded well for its upcoming Broadway debut. Television legend Art Carney was considered the show's major drawing card. One cast member remembered a daily sight: "a line of people backstage, waiting to see Ed Norton."

While Nichols wrestled with Matthau and tried helping Art "get" the part of Felix, Simon was dealing with his own monumental, behind-the-scenes crisis. He didn't know how to end the play.

"We were all going through problems in doing the play because I kept rewriting it so much," Simon said. "The third act was always a problem because the first two acts worked so enormously well. So there was a great deal of tension because two days before we opened in Wilmington I brought in a whole new third act. Walter was really up in arms about that, saying there was no way he could do it." Art, of course, said nothing.

Simon, searching for an ending, took his cue from Boston theater critic Eliot Norton, who liked the show. Norton wrote a review headlined "Oh, But for a Third Act" in which he suggested Simon end the play with Felix overcoming his grief and romantically conquering the Pigeon sisters.

"Eliot Norton's idea was a lousy ending," said cast member Sidney Armus. "Here we have this father coming back with these two chicks and saying, 'I'm going upstairs and fuck my brains out.' That's not Felix Unger. But who knows, I think Norton convinced Simon that the audience loved the girls and that he needed to bring them back. So he brought the girls back and patched something together. Felix wins when he's not supposed to, and the audience goes home happy. That's an ending that has nothing to do with the theme of the play. It's a showbiz ending."

It might have been a showbiz ending, but *The Odd Couple* was a sleek, finely crafted play by the time it opened in Broadway's Plymouth Theatre on March 10, 1965.

"Oddly enough, on opening night in New York—in the days when they had critics come on opening night and take up 250 seats—suddenly it dampened the amount of laughter," Simon recalled. "Critics, for some reason, don't laugh very much, and I thought, Oh my God, we're not doing well, because it seemed like such a subdued audience. But then the reviews were unbelievably spectacular for the play, for Mike Nichols, and for the two stars."

Simon isn't exaggerating. The day after its opening, *The Odd Couple* was already being hailed by critics as the season's smash hit, and by the weekend the show was setting box office records.

"About the only sure conclusion reached by *The Odd Couple*, Neil Simon's new comedy at the Plymouth, is that it's impossible to keep a poker game going with Art Carney around," exclaimed the *Christian Science Monitor*. "The first act specimen, a disheveled glut of bad tempers, stale sandwiches and squirting beer cans, is hung up by the threatened suicide of Felix Unger, in whose person Mr. Carney twitches from complex to complex."

But whatever joy Art was deriving from the ecstatic reviews

was muted by his continuing marital problems. "He was sort of going through what Felix was going through, so he had a tough time dealing in real life," Simon said.

Art was also growing more and more disenchanted with Matthau's onstage behavior. The "stage business" Matthau had injected into his out-of-town performances was now magnified under the Broadway microscope, where Matthau could play to the critics and sold-out audiences getting their first real look at this veteran performer. Art, who never liked to improvise on stage, was thrown off-kilter by Matthau's nightly improvisations. Although Art never confronted Matthau directly, it was apparent to the rest of the cast that he was extremely unhappy with his mugging, "look at me" costar.

"Walter had a way of milking things, of making [the audience] continue laughing by doing all kinds of tricks," one cast member recalled. "He used to do all kinds of things on laughs, and since Art's real discipline wasn't theater, he was treading. Art was a guy who knew he was a good sketch comic and a good comedian, but in plays he would have to focus on the acting and let the comedy be part of it so people wouldn't say, 'Oh, he's just Ed Norton.' Well, the more Walter did these things, the more it got on Art's nerves. But Art wasn't the kind of guy who brought it up and talked about it. It was generally the gossip backstage that isn't it a shame that Matthau's making Art's life even harder, because we knew Art was having some personal difficulties. But he would sort of suffer in silence."

The one scene in which Matthau particularly irritated Art was the infamous "I know I'm talking" scene, where Matthau had made a habit of talking to an audience member instead of addressing the heavens. Matthau continued doing this once the show reached Broadway, Nichols by this time having given up sending his notes. In the scene, Matthau's lines were followed by Art's Felix launching into a diatribe. "Are you through?" Felix asks Oscar. "Because now I've got something to say." It was a moment when the audience was supposed to be riveted on Felix, for the momentum to shift from Oscar to Felix—from Matthau to Carney.

Said one cast member, "Sometimes [Matthau] would go

back downstage three times, just play [the scene] with old-fashioned milking, or else he'd turn his head away as if he was going to move and then look back again. It was something that would be fine in vaudeville but that was out of tempo with this play, because under all the jokes there's a dramatic scene going on. I would look at Art when [Matthau] was down there doing his shtick and I got the feeling Art didn't like this very much. He was there with egg on his face."

Arnold Stang, Art's former *Henry Morgan Show* colleague and Yonkers neighbor, saw *The Odd Couple* on opening night. He immediately sensed a problem.

"At the end of the first act I was furious because Matthau was really upstaging Art," Stang said. "[Matthau] was busying himself doing things, and he was great and very effective, but he was screwing Art. And I think it affected Art very deeply, and I think that emotionally it took him a while to get over it. It really threw him."

According to one *Odd Couple* insider, Art's allies in his silent war with Matthau included the poker players, Paul Dooley, Sidney Armus, Nathaniel Frey, and John Fiedler. Like Art, they were becoming increasingly irritated with Matthau's onstage shenanigans, which not only disrupted Art's timing but also jangled their nerves.

"The poker players took to sniping a little bit onstage, sort of saying things under the laugh or saying things in a way that said to Matthau, Oh, you want to play games? We can play games, too!"

With tensions reaching a boiling point, stage manager Harvey Medlinsky called a meeting to discuss the cast's declining morale. One cast member accused Matthau of "fucking up" the play every night, but Art remained silent. He still refused to confront his costar, and even in interviews conducted years later would only talk about Matthau's *Odd Couple* behavior off the record.

"I spoke to Art a couple times about it backstage," said boyhood friend Larry Haines, who was also appearing on Broadway at that time. "Our curtain came down a little ahead of his, and I went backstage to chat with him and he said, 'I can't catch [Matthau's] eye onstage' or 'He never looks at me.' So I guess there was that kind of feeling with Art. He was a perfectionist, and if things didn't work out the way he wanted them to it could be very upsetting."

However much Matthau had complained about having to play Oscar, he was getting all the *Odd Couple* laughs and would later win a Tony Award, launching him on the road to a successful film career. Art, critically praised, didn't even merit a Tony nomination.

But it would have been surprising if Art had even noticed this snub. At the time, he was in two Broadway shows; while *The Odd Couple* was being staged in the Plymouth, Art's voice—in the guise of Franklin Delano Roosevelt—could be heard in *Flora the Red Menace,* which opened in May with leads Liza Minnelli and Bob Dishy. Also, his drinking had reached critical mass, spurred by his crumbling marriage.

Art and Jean's attempts to save their marriage were dealt a severe blow when Art moved out of the Yonkers house and into a Manhattan hotel. He was drinking heavily—"I needed a shot of Scotch the minute I opened my eyes in the morning"—and his off-stage problems began creeping into his *Odd Couple* performance.

"There were so many parallels to my own life in that role," he said. "The character carries around pictures of his kids and his house and shows them to visitors. During one performance, when I was doing that onstage I broke down and cried. The parallel was too painful. The marriage problem was affecting me emotionally, mentally, and physically."

On another night, Felix was supposed to enter the beginning of the second act with a tray piled high with sandwiches for Oscar and his poker-playing buddies. As scripted by Simon, Felix would walk across the stage and place the tray on a table. As Art got halfway across the stage, he slipped and dropped the tray, horrifying Dooley, Armus, Fiedler, and Frey, who quickly ran over to help. "No, no, just leave it," Art said in character, "the cat will get it."

It was obvious to those in the play that Art's concentration was dimming. He began to miss so many shows that his understudy, Paul Dooley, grew accustomed to getting the last-minute call to drop his role as Speed and assume the part of Felix Unger. In mid-September alone Art missed twelve *Odd Couple* performances. By early October, after only seven months in the role of Felix, Art reached his emotional breaking point after a Saturday-night show.

"I got in the car and told my wife, 'I'm driving up to Connecticut,'" Art said. "So I went up there to our summer place, had some drinks, and went to bed. The next morning I called my doctor in New York and the doctor called the Institute for Living in Hartford to see if they could take care of me. I had decided, I'm not going back to the play. I want to try to save my life and my marriage and my health and everything else, and *that* to New York and the successful play and everything!"

"It was a breakdown, mentally and physically," Art told *TV Guide*. "Thank God I made the decision that 'I've had it.' I couldn't have gone back to that play. I was defeated. I had the sense to realize I was cracking up."

Art's abrupt departure shocked the show business community and thrust Paul Dooley into the spotlight until a Felix Unger replacement could be found (Eddie Bracken took over after about a month). Ironically, Matthau was scheduled to leave the show a month later to begin shooting a movie for seventeen weeks.

Art's Saturday-night breakdown and subsequent withdrawal from *The Odd Couple* wasn't announced publicly until the following Tuesday. "There are a lot of reasons I won't go into," Bill McCaffrey told the press tersely. "It will probably take a month or two in a hospital for [Art] to get back a little security of mind." McCaffrey told reporters that Art had been "building up tension for some time" and was fretting about his performance. "He is an introverted person and he is not used to giving eight performances a week," McCaffrey said. "He is used to radio and television, when you can get a break from time to time. He was getting himself into a state."

Art retreated to the Institute for Living in Hartford, Connecticut, a sanitarium that had once been known as the Asylum and the Hartford Retreat. It was a well-known, inpatient psychiatric center with a solid reputation for providing clinical care. (Silent actress Clara Bow had once been a patient.) Art stayed in the Institute for Living for three months, drying out and undergoing psychiatric counseling.

"Everything sort of tumbled down on me at once and I didn't want to work anymore," he said about leaving *The Odd Couple*. "I wanted to get away from everything and everybody and see if I couldn't get myself into a better physical shape and mental attitude. I used to meet other people who had had—call them breakdowns, if you want—emotional disturbances, and they said, 'It will work out, you'll adjust.' But you think you'll never be a working member of society again, never be able to function. You think, You don't understand. I'm sicker than you were."

═ 17 ═

GLEASON REDUX

Although Hartford was hundreds of miles and an entire lifestyle removed from Miami, the two cities shared a common denominator in January 1966: Each laid claim to half of television's greatest comedy team.

While Art recuperated in the Institute for Living, Jackie Gleason was thinking of ways to revive his flagging television career. In 1964 Gleason had moved *The American Scene Magazine* and his entire operation—including most of his loyal staff—from New York to Miami. Gleason loved Miami's year-round warm weather, which allowed him to indulge his newfound appetite for golf. More important, he could lord over a city that welcomed him with open arms and pocketbooks—a situation that no longer existed for him in New York. Gleason built himself a huge house adjacent to a golf course and promised to revitalize Miami's nonexistent show business community by airing *American Scene* from downtown. For his efforts, Gleason was treated like royalty. Miami was instantly smitten with their imported celebrity and showed their gratitude by giving Gleason his own state-of-the-art auditorium to use for *American Scene.*

CBS, however, was far from pleased with Gleason's on-air performance. *American Scene* had finished the 1962 and 1963 TV seasons ranked seventeenth and fifteenth, respectively, and the show fared even worse when Gleason moved it to Miami. By the end of 1965 *American Scene* had dropped below the Nielsen top 20. Nervous CBS executives were wondering why they were paying Gleason a reported six million dollars per year for his uninspired mediocrity.

Gleason was too shrewd a businessman and performer not to realize he had big problems. He knew he needed a spark to pull *American Scene* out of its doldrums, and he knew that spark was hunkered down in a Connecticut psychiatric hospital worlds removed from the show business spotlight.

Gleason seemed to sense, almost instinctively, that he needed the old *Honeymooners* format to pump new life into his stale show. So, near the end of 1965, he sent word to Art—through Bill McCaffrey—that he wanted to bring *The Honeymooners* back in January 1966 for a one-shot, one-hour show. If that show was successful, he told Art, it could mean a Kramden-Norton resurrection.

"It made me feel just wonderful, the exuberance and joy that he expressed that I could come out of the hospital and work with him again," Art said. "It seemed particularly right for me then, because one of the reasons I enjoyed doing Norton was that he was an extrovert and gregarious, which I'm not, and I was a little down in that period."

By this point, Art had been at the Institute for Living for three months. It was enough time, or so he thought, to check himself out of the clinic and fly down to Miami for his *Honeymooners* reunion with Gleason, Audrey Meadows, and Joyce Randolph. The *Honeymooners* episode would be an expanded version of a show that aired in the fifties, a plot revolving around Ralph and Alice temporarily becoming adoptive parents. But there was one important difference in this sixties adaptation: It would be a musical, with Art, Gleason, Meadows, and Randolph having to learn new songs.

After his silent war with Matthau and his nervous breakdown, Art was looking forward to stepping back into Ed Norton's comfortable vest and T-shirt. It had been nearly three and a half years since he last played the role, on the inaugural season of *American Scene Magazine*.

Gleason, showing true class, went to extraordinary lengths to make sure Art was comfortable when he arrived in Miami (knowing full well that Art hated the warm weather). Not only did he install Art in a fancy Miami apartment and give his pal a brand-new set of golf clubs, but he even tried playing marriage counselor, flying Jean down to Miami to reconcile with Art.

Arnold Stang had worked with Art on *The Henry Morgan Show* and was in Miami the week Art arrived. "When Art came into his new apartment, he opened the refrigerator and it was filled from bottom to top—there wasn't an inch of space—with ice cream," Stang said. "Gleason knew Art liked ice cream, and that was OK for both of them. I don't know what Art thought of it, because he wouldn't say."

The Honeymooners reunion proved to be a critical success and notched impressive ratings. CBS, hungering for more of the proven *Honeymooners* formula, targeted the 1966–67 TV season to reprise *The Honeymooners* as a weekly series in its new musical format.

This great news, however, proved to be emotional poison for Art, who lapsed back into a deep depression just weeks after his joyous *Honeymooners* return. Before long, he had reverted back to the nervous-breakdown behavior that had forced him into the Institute for Living.

"One day, for no reason at all, I thought I'd like to get some of those Seconals or Nembutals—I don't know, I took them all," he said. "Without even thinking, I'd call up the drugstore. I had four or five drugstores that I'd alternate so they wouldn't get suspicious. I'd call up and say, 'Uh, gimme some shaving cream, some blades—I'll pick 'em up—uh, some aftershave lotion. And—oh, yes, uh, would you give me thirty of the Seconals, thirty of the Dexamyls?' 'Right, Mr. Carney, I'll have them for you,' he'd say. And with no doctor's prescription!"

After his return from Miami, Art had moved back into the Yonkers house with Jean as they tried to work out their problems. But one night, while reading the newspaper, Art passed out and fell on the floor. This terrified Jean, who thought he'd suffered a heart attack, and after an ensuing argument Art left home and went on a days-long bender. When he finally returned to

Yonkers, Art packed his bags and headed straight back to the Institute for Living.

"I knew my marriage was over, because when I woke up the next morning I had a cut on my chin, and a ripped shirt and slacks," he said. "I was a basket case, because I was loaded when I got [to the Institute] and they had to give me sedation that night. I just looked up at the doctor and said, 'Is it all over?' It was all over. He had talked to my wife. So I had a good cry for myself and then I just had to go on from there."

After nearly twenty-six years, Art and Jean—now expecting a grandchild—made plans to obtain a Mexican divorce. Shortly after leaving the Institute for Living a second time, Art moved out of his comfortable Yonkers house—away from Jean, Brian, and Paul—and into Manhattan's Warwick Hotel. It would be his lonely home for the next few months. "I was a prisoner of myself," he said. "I worked very little and didn't leave the room much." Art began to wander the streets at night, sometimes unable to sleep because of his severe depression.

"I couldn't *wait* to start drinking again," he said. "Here I was, a nice guy for twenty-five years with three kids and a house in Bronxville, sittin' in my bathrobe staring at the walls. The room had twin beds in it. The suitcase was on the other twin bed. I didn't even completely unpack it. I left it there."

While Art was self-destructing in New York, down in Miami a rejuvenated Gleason was signing a deal with CBS that called for Gleason and Art to star in ten one-hour musical *Honeymooners* shows. This would mean that Art would have to move down to Florida for part of the upcoming TV season. Although he hated to travel outside of New York, especially to hot climates, at least the move to Miami would give Art the chance to leave behind some bad memories in New York.

The CBS contract and upcoming reunion with Gleason, however, did little to appease Art's emotional problems. Still drinking, Art was now barraged by a slew of physical ailments, including a diaphragmatic hernia or "upside-down stomach," that were aggravated by his alcoholism. It was a no-win situation for Art, with the alcohol dulling his intense stomach pain.

"I'd develop a routine. I'd go across the street to this Chinese restaurant—my hangout—have a Seagrams V.O. and water, and sip it very slowly," he said. "Then another one, then another one—I'd get four or five. Then I'd order Chinese food and a bottle of beer and get the paper, and by that time—late afternoon—I'd be ready to go back to my room and go to bed for the night. The booze was irritating my condition, but it anesthetized me so I could eat."

In July 1966, two months before he needed to be in Miami, Art flew to Los Angeles for his next project: a guest-starring role on ABC's hit TV series *Batman,* a touchstone of sixties kitsch and the first prime-time series shot completely in color (reportedly costing a million dollars per episode).

Batman, which debuted in 1965, was immediately embraced as a pop-cultural phenomenon. Armed with their sleek, shiny Batmobile and skintight leotards, series stars Adam West and Burt Ward battled cartoonish villains played by some of Hollywood's most notable personalities: Otto Preminger, Victor Buono, Cesar Romero, Cliff Robertson, Milton Berle, and Burgess Meredith. *Batman* was Hollywood's flavor of the season, with celebrities fighting for a guest-starring role or a cameo.

By September 1966 *Batman* had lost some of its luster but still ranked as one of television's highest-rated shows. (A *Batman* movie was filmed between the series' first and second seasons.) With stars clamoring for a hammy, villainous *Batman* lead part, Art was fortunate to be offered a role as the Archer. At the very least he'd be working again and, hopefully, demonstrating he could handle the rigors of performing after a long layoff. "It's an opportunity, basically, to overact and have some fun," he said at the time. "It's not limited."

Art's *Batman* episodes were entitled "Shoot a Crooked Arrow" and "Walk the Straight and Narrow." The Archer was an anti–Robin Hood who traveled with his entourage—Barbara Nichols as Maid Marilyn and Doodles Weaver as Crier Tuck—robbing from everyone in sight. The Archer also carried a tape recorder that played continuous applause—a good thing, since Art's wan, uninspired performance didn't draw any applause from critics or viewers.

Stanley Ralph Ross had written Art's *Batman* episodes. "For some reason he had something troubling him. I never knew what his problems were, but the show didn't come out as well as I would have liked," Ross said. "I was disappointed in the show and its whole pacing. It just didn't work. It should have had Howard Hawksian tones and zipped along really fast, but it was really draggy. The interesting thing for me was that if you told Art you wanted him to imitate Cary Grant, it didn't sound like Cary Grant, but in his mind it was Cary Grant. And in his mind it was very funny."

As the Archer, Art had to recite Damon Runyonesque dialogue and wear green tights and other medieval garb. When the shows aired in September, it was obvious that Art was terribly miscast. The Archer appeared uncomfortable. Art was flabby and out of shape, having gained about twenty-five pounds since checking into the Institute for Living the previous year. Unlike the villains played by Meredith, Romero, and Frank Gorshin, who were asked back several times, the Archer would be Art's first and last *Batman* appearance.

Art was excited to be joining Gleason in Miami to begin taping the musical *Honeymooners* episodes that would fall under the umbrella of *The Jackie Gleason Show.* CBS had increased its order from ten to twenty shows and added new costars Sheila MacRae (as Alice) and Jane Kean (as Trixie). Pert Kelton, the original Alice Kramden, who was blacklisted from the old DuMont Network show, returned as Ralph's pesky mother-in-law. It was Gleason's way of repaying Kelton for the way she had been treated.

"That [show] was a tremendous lift," Art said. "I had thought I was through, that I was washed up. But I was so relieved and so elated at the prospect of working again. Gleason knew what I was going through. We never once had a fight or a cross word."

As he had done the previous January, Gleason once again graciously welcomed Art back into the fold, revealing more of his feelings toward Art than he had ever done before. "You do better working with good people," he told one journalist. "It's like I want to think I'm as good as he is. No, not better—you can't get better than Carney. But the competition is good. It's a funny thing to say, but I love this man."

Art hated Miami Beach and its oppressive heat. Although he tried, he couldn't learn to share Gleason's feverish enthusiasm for golf. Upon arriving in Miami Beach, Art was asked by journalists what he liked best about the city. "The planes going back to New York," he retorted only half jokingly.

Art soon fled the golf-course condominium that Gleason had picked out for him. Instead, he settled into an oceanfront apartment near the city's downtown district.

"Jackie said he made one of the biggest mistakes of his life by putting Art up in a suite with maid service overlooking a golf course out on the flat plains of South Florida," said Pete McGovern, Gleason's longtime publicity agent. "That was not for Art. He didn't like golf and didn't like to be with people. He liked to walk the streets, and he would escape every once in a while and go on a toot. He used to walk on the street with his hat in a certain way and would change it so people wouldn't recognize him."

At the jam-packed *Jackie Gleason Show* press conference welcoming Art, MacRae, and Kean, Art was "pale, baggy-eyed, tight-lipped and silent," said one report.

Although he was, next to Gleason, the new show's centerpiece, Art wasn't required to work every week. The one-hour musical *Honeymooners* aired randomly, sometimes twice in a row, sometimes every other week. While Art, Gleason, Kean, and MacRae had to learn new songs for each episode, the actual *Honeymooners* plots were, for the most part, musical rehashes of the fifties version. Occasionally, a non-*Honeymooners* show was plugged into the formula.

"Frankly, I think Art would have been a lot happier staying on Broadway, but Gleason offered us lots of money," MacRae said. "The point is, Art could do what he liked, which was to define the role [of Norton]. He and Jackie would just step foot on the stage. They didn't have to do anything to prepare. But Art certainly knew what was funny, and so did Jackie."

For years television viewers had been clamoring for a Gleason-Carney reunion, and they quickly showed their appreciation. Within a few months of its premiere, *The Jackie Gleason Show* was one of the season's highest-rated shows. It finished the season in fifth place, Gleason's highest-rated season since 1954–55. Garry Moore and Milton Berle, on the other hand, had recently failed in their television comebacks.

"The artful Jackie Gleason and Art Carney still bounce one another in a way that creates comedic sparks," *Variety* gushed after the show's September debut. "For video, the frame of bus driver and sewer dweller in bleak tenement digs is still an imaginative and audacious premise, and Gleason and Carney still know how to make the best of it."

Gleason was once again TV's reigning king, but there was a difference this time. "I'm not a stooge anymore," Art proclaimed that season. "I used to be."

Said Jane Kean, "It's too bad I didn't tape some of the rehearsals because they would ad-lib and it was just so funny, they just knew how to work off each other. Gleason was not like Milton Berle—he wanted everybody around him to be good, and he let Art just go as far as he could, never clamping down on him in any way. He always encouraged Art to do anything he wanted."

But while their professional relationship remained one of boss (Gleason) and employee (Art), it was obvious that Art's reemergence into the *Honeymooners* spotlight was the driving force behind *The Jackie Gleason Show*'s resurgence. Art's usual modesty—"All I care about is doing my part the way I think it should be done. It's Jackie's show"—contrasted starkly with the media's spin on Gleason's newfound popularity. Proclaimed one headline, "How Carney Put Gleason Back on Top."

Art's visibility ironically coincided with a reunion of sorts with his *Odd Couple* nemesis, Walter Matthau. In early December 1966, Art flew to Los Angeles to film a cameo with Lucille Ball in Twentieth Century-Fox's *A Guide for the Married Man,* a comedy slated for spring 1967 release. In the movie, Matthau starred as a bored husband who was instructed in the art of marital infidelity by his pal, played by Robert Morse. While Morse instructed Matthau, an all-star cast of cameo performers acted out Morse's instructions in short vignettes.

Ball refused to commit to the project until Art came aboard, and they joined a cameo cast including Jack Benny, Carl Reiner,

Sid Caesar, Phil Silvers, Ben Blue, Polly Bergen, Terry-Thomas, and Jayne Mansfield.

Art's stay in Los Angeles amounted to about a week, and he probably never even saw Matthau. In their four-minute vignette, Art and Ball played a long-married couple, Art a hard-hat construction worker named Joe, and Ball his long-suffering wife, forever slaving over a hot stove.

Joe returns home from work and purposely insults his wife's dinner selection, thereby insuring what Morse's character labels "the bust-up scene": Joe is now free to leave the house, wine and dine his mistress, and then call his wife and apologize, playing on her sympathy—"I caught a hamburger in some joint," Joe says forlornly.

Around this time Art, now forty-eight, renewed his friendship with forty-one-year-old Barbara Isaacs, whom he'd met through his association with David Susskind in the late fifties and early sixties. Art was now legally separated from Jean, and his friendship with Isaacs quickly evolved into a loving relationship. Art and Jean's marriage legally ended in early December when they finally obtained their Mexican divorce. After twenty-six years, three children, and a grandson (born the previous June), Art and Jean were no longer a couple. Art's son Brian was now a twenty-one-year-old aspiring musician and had already moved out of the house. Jean retained custody of fourteen-year-old Paul.

Ronald Biscow, brother of Art's boyhood friend Vic Biscow, recalled: "At the time Art and Jean were divorced, Vic tried to maintain a relationship with both of them and went to visit Jean one day. Vic had a phone call to make, and while he was on the phone he noticed Jean had a memo pad that said, 'Mrs. Art Carney.' Vic asked Jean why she still had that out, and she said, 'Because some day in the future I'll be using it again.' "

Barbara Schanzer Isaacs was a native New Yorker and Brooklyn College graduate with a grown daughter, Shelley, seventeen, and son Douglas, fifteen, from her first marriage, to furniture executive Arthur Isaacs. In addition to working for Susskind, Barbara, a brunette, had been a sometime actress and dancer who retained her lithe, slender figure.

Art was rebounding wildly from his divorce and didn't waste any time filling the void created by Jean's departure. The thought of being alone, especially in Miami, was not a pleasant one. Jane Kean, meanwhile, tried calling Jean to persuade her to reconsider the divorce. "Art was very depressed after that, because Jean turned him down," Kean said.

On December 20, 1966, Art obtained a New York marriage license, and on December 22 he and Barbara were married in the chapel of the Marriage License Bureau in Manhattan's Municipal Building. Art wore a dark suit, blue shirt, and blue-striped tie; Barbara wore a mink coat over a shocking-pink dress.

The marriage ceremony lasted five minutes and was witnessed by Art's business manager, Robert Grimaldi, who served as best man. Barbara's children and mother were also there. In their vows, Barbara substituted "cherish" for "obey," while Art substituted "keep." After the ceremony Art joked with reporters and photographers, telling them Barbara was "only twenty-two" and asking them if they'd like the newlyweds to "shake hands" when he was asked to kiss Barbara on the cheek.

"He was still hung up on his first wife and he married on the rebound," Kean said. "Art was Catholic, and the belief is that they're married to the one they married in the church. When Art came back [to Miami], he was sort of in a funk, but he recovered. The first we ever knew about Barbara was when he came back married to her."

Art and Barbara appeared happy when they returned to Miami in January after a short New York honeymoon. Art's yearly salary by this time had reached about four hundred thousand dollars, and he and Barbara planned on settling in Manhattan with Barbara's two children once the TV season ended later that spring. Being in Manhattan would keep Art close to his children and to Jean, with whom he remained on good terms.

Back in Miami this new Odd Couple—the introverted, Irish-Catholic Art and bubbly, Jewish Barbara—struck up a close friendship with Sheila MacRae and her new husband, *Gleason Show* producer Ronald Wayne. Although he probably didn't remember, Art had once helped Sheila get a radio job as a *March of Time* geisha girl back in the forties.

"Art was still struggling with his [drinking] problem during that first year [in Miami], so Ronnie and I gave him the first vitamin treatment he'd ever had," MacRae said. "We brought the vitamins over and forced him to take them, and he got to love them. He'd say to Ronnie, 'Whaddya mean, you choke down forty vitamins a day with water?' and we all laughed. He and Barbara were great together."

Art joined MacRae in helping to raise money for the Children's Center, a Miami day school that specialized in treating autistic children. But his drinking continued, fueled perhaps by his guilt over his divorce and remarriage.

"Art would start on ginger ale and go to beer, then go to the hard stuff," Pete McGovern said. "Jackie was a big boozer who could go until two or three in the morning, but then he'd go home and would be up at six-thirty calling people. But Art would keep going and we'd find him days later."

During one particularly bad stretch, Art went on a bender for several days. With the Friday-night *Gleason Show* taping quickly approaching, a worried Gleason summoned his top aides to the Hialeah Country Club and ordered them to find Art. Although Gleason had made it clear he was not to be interrupted, a waiter approached: There was an urgent telephone call for Mr. Gleason.

Said McGovern: "The guy on the other end says, 'Mr. Gleason, this is so-and-so, I own a bar in Hollywood [Florida] and I just came to work and looked in the cash register and there's a wristwatch in there. My night man left a note saying a fellow in here named Art Carney is asleep in a booth.' Art had left his watch because he needed $2.50 for another drink. And Jackie says, 'Describe the watch—take the band off and read to me what it says in there.' And the guy says, 'To my pal, Art, from his pal, Jackie.' So we went and got him, and when we got there Art was sleeping.

"They filled Art full of coffee and he showered and changed and went out to the theater," McGovern said. "And he went in to see Jackie and said, 'I can't do it, Jackie.' So Jackie talked to him and said, 'Do this for me, we'll make it together. We'll just wing it like we used to.' They went out, and as soon as the lights went up and the curtain opened, Art was sensational, like nothing had happened. Being in front of an audience changed his whole complexion."

Years of drinking, combined with his advancing age, had lessened Art's tolerance. As a younger man it had been easier to shake off the effects of a bender and perform in public. Gleason's Miami-based cast and crew expected the occasional absence now, knowing Art was drinking someplace. And it didn't help that Gleason turned a blind eye toward the lapses of his "pal."

"We figured we would lose Art for at least a show a season," said Gleason's agent, Sam Cohn. "But what he did the rest of the time made it worth it."

"There were a couple of times when he went off and we had to cancel one or two shows," Kean said. "There's a difference between an alcoholic and a heavy drinker. Gleason was a heavy drinker, but he could stop. Art, if he took one drink, he couldn't do that, and it would be sometimes several days to get him back on track, and he would have to go into the hospital."

Art experienced one particularly frightening episode that was fueled by alcohol, pills, or a combination of both. It occurred during a *Honeymooners* rehearsal, when Art suffered what appeared to be a sudden fit of paranoid, delusional behavior while setting up a camera shot with Gleason and MacRae.

"Art and I had this scene in the kitchen and all of a sudden Art said to me, 'You know, they're coming to get us.' And I thought he was joking," MacRae said. "And I said, 'Oh, yeah?' And then suddenly he just grabbed my arm and said, 'Don't move.' Before I knew it Ron Wayne had rushed down because he had been observing Art's behavior. And the thing was, Jackie went right out the back [kitchen] door, walking straight past us. Art was all right in a couple of days."

Art's drinking was also affecting his reputation within the show business community. In 1967 Hollywood producers began laying the groundwork to bring *The Odd Couple* to the big screen. Art thought he and Gleason would be the perfect team, this time Art playing the role of Oscar and Gleason as lint-picking Felix. Gleason was enthusiastic about the prospect of costarring with Art in an *Odd Couple* movie. But after Art's nervous breakdown and continued drinking problems, he was viewed as a liability. Unlike on Broadway, there were no understudies in Hollywood, where a missing or ill star could mean potential financial disaster.

Recalled one insider: "We were getting a lot of pressure to use the guys from the Broadway play, but people said, 'You can't. If you have a lot of money you can do it, but it's too much. Art misses half the cues all the time.' So that was fifty percent of it. The rest of it was that Jack Lemmon and Walter Matthau had made a picture together ['The Fortune Cookie'] not too long before. So we went with the two of them."

Art lobbied strongly for a Carney-Gleason *Odd Couple* movie, but Matthau and Lemmon—a comedy team with proven box office clout and fantastic chemistry—were eventually chosen (with Matthau once again forced to play the slovenly Oscar). Art was bitterly disappointed.

But there were also some good times down in Miami. Much to her credit, Barbara had brought Art out of his shell, persuading him to go dancing at Miami night spots like the Diplomat Hotel, the Jockey Club, and the Tennis Club. Although Art still hated being asked for autographs and hearing the inevitable "Hey, Norton, how are things down in the sewer?," he loosened up in Barbara's company, sometimes even sidling up to a piano and banging out a tune or two in a crowded room—no mean feat for this noted introvert.

"Barbara was good for him because he seemed pretty happy and she was very protective of him," said actress Mitzi Gaynor, a close friend. "She was very aware of who Art was. Of course, she worked with David Susskind, knew all about actors, so this was nothing new to her."

Despite his battles with the bottle, Art's television colleagues embraced his return to the medium he had helped define. In 1967 and 1968 Art won his fourth and fifth Emmy Awards for his work on *The Jackie Gleason Show.* Gleason, once again, was ignored in his quest for the elusive Emmy. He could only watch from the sidelines while his sidekick garnered accolades.

In January 1968 Art, Barbara, and her two children moved into a luxurious, tastefully furnished three-bedroom/three-bath co-op on Seventy-third Street in Manhattan. The place was big enough to include a room for the nonexistent live-in maid—Art used it as an office—and to accommodate Art's upright piano. The Carneys employed a cleaning woman who also cooked dinner, "And we always cook big—whether it's a roast of beef or pork, it's a sizable one, for extra servings," Barbara told a reporter telling New Yorkers about "Mrs. Art Carney's Roast Pork" recipe.

Sheila MacRae and Ron Wayne had moved to New York and lived a few blocks away on Sixty-fourth Street. As they had done in Miami, the Carneys and Waynes socialized often, going to plays and movies together and dining at each other's apartments.

But Art saw less of his Miami cohorts during the 1968–69 TV season, when Gleason decided to scale back his work schedule and the *Honeymooners* segments. During that season, Art and Gleason appeared together only seven times. Not surprisingly, *The Jackie Gleason Show's* ratings began to slip, with too many reruns filling the familiar Saturday-night time slot.

"Basically, Jackie was almost lazy," Kean said. "It would be a challenge for him to become number one, and then when he would, he would sort of relax. And then that drive wasn't there anymore."

Gleason's decision to lighten his workload allowed Art to spend more time in New York, eating Barbara's roast pork and, somewhat reluctantly, preparing for his return to the Broadway stage.

BROADWAY, ACT 3

B y spring 1968 Art, now forty-nine and paunchy, was two and a half years removed from the emotional turmoil he'd undergone during *The Odd Couple*. Working with Gleason in Miami had resurrected Art's career and had proven professionally invigorating. He now looked forward to continuing his work on *The Jackie Gleason Show* while making the occasional talk show appearance and guest shot. Barbara pampered her husband but gently pushed him to stay active and pursue other professional offers. These included a weekly TV comedy-drama series called *The Governor and His Daughter*—in which Art would play a widowed governor—and a movie role opposite Phyllis Diller in *The Adding Machine,* which was scheduled to begin production at London's Shepperton Studios. Neither project panned out. (Milo O'Shea assumed the role Art would have played in *The Adding Machine*.)

"She's a comfort to him, no question about it," Bill McCaffrey said of Barbara. "A year ago, I couldn't get Artie on a TV panel show with a twenty-mule team. But now, he's a little more open, more flexible than he used to be."

The year 1968 also marked the thirtieth anniversary of Thornton Wilder's *Our Town,* the TV production of which Art had starred in a decade before. Once again *Our Town* would, in a roundabout way, affect Art's career.

Morton Gottlieb was a successful Broadway producer who first met Art in 1957, when Gottlieb worked as stage manager for *The Rope Dancers* on Broadway. To commemorate *Our Town's* anniversary, Gottlieb was thinking of staging the play in Lincoln Center's sparkling new Vivian Beaumont Theater; he asked Art to reprise his role as the Narrator.

But Art was in no rush to return to the footlights. *The Odd Couple* debacle was still fresh in his mind, and its emotional scars were just beginning to heal. Gottlieb, to his credit, showed some guts. Art wasn't exactly being inundated with theatrical offers. Many Broadway backers were still nervous about his ability to function in a costly, high-profile stage production.

After mulling over Gottlieb's offer, however, Art agreed that *Our Town* would be his reentry into legitimate theater. There was one major problem.

"Thornton Wilder said it's been done on bare stages, in the round, in the square, in church yards, and in barns, and he said he wanted it done on a typical proscenium stage and not on a projected stage like the Beaumont," Gottlieb said. "I had already started working on renting the Beaumont and here I was without *Our Town.*"

Shortly thereafter, Gottlieb was given the script for Brian Friel's *Lovers,* a bittersweet, two-act comedy that had been staged the previous year in the Dublin Gate Theater with Hilton Edwards directing Irish stage star Anna Manahan. With the Vivian Beaumont already rented, Gottlieb didn't have much time to waste: He agreed to back *Lovers* and once again approached Art to star in what would be two entirely separate performances within the same play.

"I was doubtful, to be honest," said Art, who initially declined Gottlieb's offer but reconsidered after talking it over with Bill McCaffrey. "I thought maybe it was too inside, too Irish, too Catholic, to be successful. But then people said, 'Look at *Fiddler on the Roof*—you don't have to be Jewish.' But I still wasn't confident about myself. I think the very fact that this play came along when it did has helped me, because I had been idle for a while, and for me that's not good. . . . This came at a very good time to give me that little boost, that confidence that I always seem to need."

It wasn't the New York critics who Art feared, since they had always treated him fairly with mostly favorable reviews. It was worse: that all-too-familiar feeling that he was in over his head, that if he succeeded in the play his emotional highs would be followed by the inevitable crash into a drowning depression.

"I remember we looked at his name outside the theater before we opened," Manahan recalled. "It was ART CARNEY IN "LOVERS." And he said, 'Oh, don't mind that. If it's a flop, it will come down tomorrow night.' "

Meanwhile, down in Miami, Gleason agreed to shoot around Art's fall *Honeymooners* schedule once *Lovers* opened. *The Jackie Gleason Show* was taped, and it really wasn't too much of a scheduling problem. But back in New York, Art's anxieties began mounting. Unlike *The Rope Dancers, Take Her, She's Mine,* or *The Odd Couple,* Art would be stepping into a role originated by another actor. And he would be surrounded by an entirely Irish/English cast, all classically trained actors who didn't know what to expect from an American television star, and vice versa.

"Being Irish myself, I wasn't afraid of my brogue in this play, but I've never been to Dublin and I didn't want to sound 'stage Irish' on the pronunciations," Art said. "I wanted to be as legitimate as possible. Hilton Edwards said to me, 'Just speak the nicest English you can and you'll be okay.' The actors helped me with words like 'old,' which is spelled 'aul' in the script and pronounced 'owl.' "

Friel had written *Lovers* as two distinct playlets, one titled "Winners" and the other "Losers." In "Winners" Art played the Narrator, who watched young lovers Joe and Mag (Eamon Morrissey and Fionnuala Flanagan) from a nearby hilltop in the small town of Ballymore, Ireland. The Narrator occasionally commented to the audience about Joe and Mag, who, he immediately informs the audience, will die later that day, just three weeks before their wedding. Mag is two months pregnant with Joe's baby, which lends the vignette its poignancy as they discuss their future. In one scene they roll down a hill, giggling merrily.

Art's role in "Losers" was more active and gave him a lot more stage presence. In "Losers," he played fortyish bachelor Andy Tracey, who meets Hanna (Manahan), a hot-blooded spinster ripe for romance. That's fine with Andy and Hanna, but their attempts at making love are forever interrupted by Hanna's bedridden mother (Grania O'Malley), a devout religious fanatic. Egged on by her nosy neighbor (Beulah Garrick), mother rings a cowbell whenever she hears silence coming from the downstairs, where Andy and Hanna are frolicking on the couch. Andy and Hanna try solving this problem with a steady stream of banter between kisses; Andy, at one point, recites all thirty-two verses of Gray's *Elegy in a Country Churchyard* and has to start again when he continually gets distracted by Hanna.

"I was a little worried having to play with a big American star, but I couldn't have asked for a more wonderful person to play with," Manahan said. "I found that Art hadn't been on the stage for a few years and was extremely nervous, but he felt very happy with me at this time because he felt he was with someone he could rely on. And he was very happy in the company of a number of the Irish players. If he was going to try something different, he would come to me and say, 'Is it all right with you, Anna, would it upset you if I introduced this?' You don't get that consideration from many people in our business."

Lovers didn't go through the usual out-of-town tryouts, and knowing that it would open immediately in New York was making Art extremely nervous once rehearsals got under way.

"I found myself thinking, 'I'd better get out of this now, it's too much for me,' " he said. "But my wife, Barbara, and Bill McCaffrey, my agent, made me realize that I just couldn't pack a bag and run away from it. The people involved in the play helped me too, and it worked out, though not without some pretty uncomfortable times. But each day I showed up at rehearsal it got better."

One of Art's biggest fears was that he would never remember all his dialogue, which encompassed both playlets and the thirty-two-verse *Elegy* recitation. Gottlieb recommended Art— for his role as the Narrator in "Winners"—keep the script in front of him as insurance. He told Art that should he forget his lines, his first three words of dialogue—"It says here"—would spark his memory. Art took Gottlieb's advice but never forgot his lines and never had to refer to the script.

With New York mayor John Lindsay in attendance, *Lovers* opened on July 25, 1968, and was immediately hailed as one of Art's greatest triumphs.

The *New York Times:* "Until you have heard Mr. Carney deliver Gray's 'Elegy' as he is frolicking on a couch with the ample Anna Manahan, there will be something missing from your life. . . . The actors, including the incomparable Art Carney, are a pleasure to watch."

The *Christian Science Monitor:* "Art Carney stars in both [playlets], and his performances are quite in keeping with the Irish players who complete the small cast. Yet he also adds a force of his own that is important in giving the unlabored pieces a punch just when they need it."

The *New York Post:* "Art Carney provides us with a half-evening that is both riotous and touching. . . . He and Anna Manahan, as the not-so-young or slim daughter, make these wonderful moments."

Lovers was doing brisk business, and within about three and a half weeks of its opening, Gottlieb had recouped the investment he made with his producing partner, Helen Bonfils. Gottlieb and Bonfils were overjoyed, and in mid-September they moved the show from the Beaumont to Broadway's Music Box Theater. Art starred at the Music Box until his contract expired in November and Peter Lind Hayes took over the roles.

"I remember Art had this extraordinary rapport with the audience, they just rose to him," Manahan said. "One night in the Music Box, the spotlight wasn't hitting him. Everywhere he walked and spoke in the beginning of the second play, the spotlight was in a different place. And he said, 'All right, fellas, we'll start from the beginning and let's get it together.' Well, the audience went up and he had them in the palm of his hand."

The critics were dutifully impressed, and Art received his first Tony Award nomination that winter, joining Manahan and the play itself. "I'm damned sure I'm not going to get it, but what I really care about is the honor in being nominated," he said in

April 1969. "I think James Earl Jones will win it for *Great White Hope*. I haven't seen it, but I've heard he acts up a storm. I'm just happy to be nominated, that's all."

Art's prediction came true when Jones won the Tony for Best Actor. Manahan and *Lovers* also lost their Tony bids.

"I remember at the Tony Awards ceremony I was sitting with Art and our stage director, and Rex Harrison came down the aisle and stood with his back to the stage," Manahan said. "By standing there he was facing up the whole theater, which was full of famous people. And Art turned to me and said, 'You know, Anna, what I like about this guy is he's so modest.' "

Art returned to *Lovers* in February for a four-month road tour that stopped in Los Angeles, Phoenix, San Francisco, Denver, Baltimore, New Haven, Boston, and Washington, D.C. Barbara joined the production as Manahan's understudy. The savvy Bill McCaffrey took out a full-page ad in the show business bible, *Variety*, that trumpeted Art's return to *Lovers*. But Art still couldn't escape the shadow of Ed Norton. At the same time he was touring in *Lovers*, he was invited by the mayor of Chandler, Arizona, to dedicate the city's new sewage treatment plant. McCaffrey politely declined the offer: "For professional reasons, we are playing down the sewer image."

Said Manahan, "We had a lovely experience in Los Angeles. Art was a great personal friend of Jimmy Cagney's, who at that time didn't move around in society and lived a very secluded, quiet life. But when Cagney heard Art was coming, he insisted on inviting us all up to his home, and he gave us the most beautiful lunch. The most magical moment was when Art and Jimmy Cagney did a musical number and danced together. It was pure magic. And Art turned to Jimmy and said, 'You know, Anna sings "Won't You Come Home Bill Bailey," ' so Cagney insisted that I sing that. It was a very special memory of that tour."

19

MIAMI BLUES

If the social turbulence of 1969 perfectly symbolized the decade's schizophrenic upheaval, it also signaled the end of a television era. Hip shows like *Laugh-In, The Mod Squad, The Smothers Brothers Show,* and *Julia* were eclipsing Gleason's 1950s shtick. Suddenly, *The Jackie Gleason Show* seemed anachronistic and culturally insignificant. While the Classic Thirty-nine *Honeymooners* episodes from 1955–56 still performed well in reruns, audiences were tiring of the format. Gleason apparently shared the country's ambivalence, relegating Ralph, Ed, Alice, and Trixie to intermittent status for the 1969–70 TV season.

"Things were getting worse because Jackie wouldn't rehearse at all," said Sheila MacRae. "Art used to call him the Great White Whale, and Art would say, 'Well, there he is, that's the last we'll see of him.' I think Art resented that [Gleason never rehearsed] because they were equal in the series. And I believe, although he never acknowledged it, that Jackie was very depressed over his marriage and wanted to stop working altogether."

As 1969 turned into 1970, Gleason's negligent attitude toward *The Jackie Gleason Show* manifested itself in two areas of his life he particularly cherished: money and Art Carney.

Gleason's material appetites (he drove a Rolls-Royce to Art's Cadillac) were legendary. So too was his almost obsessive compulsion to spend money he didn't necessarily have. Gleason had insisted on being TV's highest-paid performer, and CBS had obliged his demands. But while Gleason's CBS contracts were huge, they always had this stipulation: Gleason was to use part of the money for projects created by his Peekskill Productions company. More often than not, the projects never materialized, and Gleason spent the excess cash on office expenses and/or staff retainer fees.

It was unusual, then, for Peekskill Productions, under Gleason's guidance, to actually produce something. And when it finally did, in early 1970, Gleason returned to familiar ground. More specifically, he returned to familiar *under*ground.

With Gleason spending more and more time away from the *Gleason Show,* CBS needed something to fill Gleason's Saturday-night time slot. Someone, perhaps even Gleason himself, had the brilliant idea to launch a *Honeymooners* spinoff, a sitcom that would showcase Ed Norton in his daily routine down in the sewer. This wasn't the first time the concept of a Norton spinoff had been explored. According to Jane Kean, Twentieth Century-Fox had previously approached her and Art about a possible Norton-Trixie series once the *Gleason Show* ended. That idea never materialized.

Art himself had, years earlier, voiced his resistance to the idea of transplanting Norton from *The Honeymooners* into his own series: "I have made up my mind about one thing. I'll never do a weekly series as the star of a show," he said. "And I wouldn't think of making Ed Norton a separate character, as happened when Gildersleeve broke off from *Fibber McGee and Molly.* It just wouldn't seem right to me. I'd be making a mistake. How many shows can you base around sewer jokes?"

But Peekskill Productions set its sights on a new Norton series, and Art reluctantly agreed to the idea. The pilot for the new series would be shot live in the 7,200-seat Miami Auditorium as the second half of a *Gleason Show* hour. George Burns would star in the first half hour.

Gleason writers Bob Hilliard, Walter Stone, and Rod Parker wrote the script for the Norton pilot, which would focus on Norton's workday life away from Trixie and the Kramdens. Character actors Al Lewis, Phil Leeds, and Ron Carey, a stand-up comic with whom Art had struck up a close friendship, were flown down to Miami to round out the cast.

It was, for all intents and purposes, a can't-miss proposition.

It did, for all intents and purposes, miss. Badly.

If Art objected to starring in his own series as Norton, he didn't verbalize his feelings. But it was apparent to those who watched the pilot's weeklong rehearsals and its subsequent live taping that, consciously or subconsciously, Art Carney quickly destroyed the notion he could or should star in a TV show.

"Art fucked it up," said Phil Leeds, recalling the scattershot, disorganized rehearsals held at Gleason's estate. "He was a brilliant talent, but he had a will to fail. He didn't remember his lines. I don't know if it was booze or pills that did him in, but I don't think Art had the confidence in his own talent. He fucked it up all the time in rehearsal and we kept looking at each other. We didn't know what to do with him."

Bob Hilliard remembered that time differently. "Art had no drinking problem whatsoever during that pilot," he said. "By the time it rolled around, he had cemented his lines and knew them very well. Art was just very sensitive and got a little nervous when he was in the limelight."

Rod Parker in hindsight admitted that the Norton pilot was "wrong" for Art and could never have worked because of its weak concept and structure.

"Art was so nervous; I never saw a man so nervous in my life," Parker said. "He was scared to death. But once he got out in front of that audience, he was wonderful. I'm not quite sure he thought the show was that good. But he was funny because everybody loved him."

One insider, however, described the pilot as a disastrous embarrassment, especially when it came time to shoot the show in front of a live audience.

No one connected with the project remembers much about plot details, and no scripts were filed. To the best of the principals' recollections, the two-scene pilot opens on Norton down in the sewer brushing his teeth and singing. Norton banters with coworkers Carey and Leeds, whose character always had a cold because he never wore the proper sewer gear. Then Lewis enters as Norton's irascible Irish boss. One of the writers remembered a scene taking place in a restaurant, although he wasn't sure why or how this related to the Norton plot.

According to one insider, the live taping was chaos. Art was dead drunk and obviously hadn't bothered to learn his lines. To remedy this situation, Ron Carey's character entered with a clipboard that was, in the context of the scene, ostensibly for Norton to peruse. The clipboard really contained a copy of the script, and when Art tried embellishing and doing shtick, he accidentally dropped the clipboard, scattering the pages—and his lines—all over the stage floor. So there was Art, center stage, reading lines from different pages in random order. His costars were confused, and the audience, dumbstruck, watched in amazement as Art fell apart onstage.

"People thought they were in an insane asylum," said one insider. "It was like a giant mural, with 7,200 people painted in their seats. They didn't know what was going on because there was no connection to anything. It was unbelievable. Why do you do that to a guy?"

The "you" was Gleason, who turned a blind eye toward his "pal's" plight. Gleason was present at a few rehearsals, and either knew Art was in no condition to tape the pilot or did his best to ignore the warning signs. Even though his production company was footing the bill for this impending disaster, Gleason failed to lift a finger to stop the madness.

"I don't think Gleason would have said anything because it would have been like he was shaming Art," Leeds said. "Art just couldn't remember his lines, and we thought he was kind of suicidal or he just didn't think he could cut it."

Neither did CBS, which never aired the edited pilot.

"I think deep in his heart he realized it was probably too heavy a load for him," said Ronald Wayne, who directed the pilot. "Remember, Art always had Jackie to depend on, and I think this was a little too much for Art. He wasn't comfortable."

To writer Hilliard, CBS's decision to kill the project was an obvious and easy one. "Let's face it, the network wasn't about to break up Gleason and Carney, because they weren't going to kill the goose that laid the golden egg," he said. "In that particular case, you don't break up the Yankees—you just don't do it. I don't have to tell you how strong the *Honeymooners* were."

Or weren't. Not any longer. In the winter of 1970, CBS officially canceled *The Jackie Gleason Show,* forever ending Gleason's weekly television career and TV's greatest comedic partnership.

Art soldiered on, continuing to thrive in television even after the Norton debacle and *Gleason Show* cancellation. He guest-starred on a Carol Channing special taped in London and appeared on the season debut of NBC's *Laugh-In,* where, among other characters, he portrayed Norton to Johnny Brown's (black) Ralph Kramden. He also filmed an episode of NBC's *Men from Shiloh.*

Art had stopped drinking, for now. But he faced yet another emotional crisis when he went to Las Vegas—a place he detested—to star in a stage show at the Hotel International's eight-hundred-seat Theatre Royal.

The show was called *An Evening of Three Broadway Comedy Hits* and featured Art in three one-act vignettes: as an aging, unsuccessful actor in Robert Anderson's "Shock of Recognition," from *You Know I Can't Hear You When the Water's Running;* as the father of a nervous bride-to-be in Neil Simon's "Visitor from Forest Hills," culled from *Plaza Suite;* and as an overaged draftee in "Next" from Terrance McNally's *Adaptation—Next.*

The show's producer, Stan Irwin, had assembled an impressive supporting cast, including Salem Ludwig, Barra Grant, Joan Shea, and Elsa Raven. Directing the show would be Joshua Shelley, a strict adherent to the Stanislavsky "method-acting" school.

Art should have thrown in the towel then and there. He was no method actor, and once rehearsals began—and he silently clashed with Shelley—Art's manic-depressive emotional state kicked in. He was at turns "enthused, way up" about returning to the stage, other times deeply depressed, confused, and angry at Shelley's prodding.

"Shortly after I got into rehearsal I took a nosedive," Art said. "What caused it, I don't know. I had no trouble, either at home or with the plays, but it happened. I couldn't learn my lines. I couldn't get with it. I was going through what the doctor calls the dip after being way up."

Art's problems were aggravated by Shelley, a well-meaning, earnest stage veteran whose insistence on the "method" style sharply contrasted to Art's homegrown acting approach. While Art disagreed with Shelley's rigidity, he refused to voice his displeasure and anxiety.

"The thing that really impressed me about Art was that he used a technical approach that must have come from the Moscow Art Theater," said "Shock of Recognition" costar Salem Ludwig. "During rehearsals, he would verbalize out loud images which would color the lines that he used. In other words, he would give his own image of something he had experienced and then say the author's line, and that gave it a color he couldn't have gotten any other way. But then Shelley stopped him, treating Art as though he were an errant child and insisting Art be disciplined and use the author's words and not fool around. And of course poor Art froze; he thought, 'Gee, there's something wrong with me, I don't know how to work with these high-class, legit people.' And he spent a couple of days in the hospital, which I'm sure was a psychological result of that terrible frustration."

There were no screaming matches, no fights, no outward hostility between Art and Shelley. Had Art been so inclined, he could have had Shelley fired. At the very least, he could have insisted on utilizing his own style of acting.

But it wasn't to be, and it was obvious Art was rattled when the show opened on November 5, 1970, before a packed house. Art forgot some of his lines and completely disintegrated in the third act, "Next," when he announced to the astonished audience, "I drew a blank," when he was supposed to recite an important, dramatic soliloquy. Art quickly vanished from the stage, returning only for a brief curtain call.

"He lost some lines opening night and toward the end he completely blanked and went out altogether," Ludwig said. "The technique he used was disturbed, and he couldn't make the adjustment. It all became by rote, instead of being organic."

Although *Variety*'s reviewer was enthusiastic enough— "Carney displays a mastery of vocal and physical comedy"—the show lasted only four weeks.

"Once the work goes sour, everything is hateful," Ludwig

said. "After we opened, [Shelley] disappeared, so we had some fun after that. But the damage was done. Art really lost a lot of the spontaneity he normally had."

"I'd prefer to forget about it," Art said. "I was very unhappy there. Vegas is not theater-oriented. I mean that they're not ready for theater and they don't want to come in and sit down for a couple of hours and watch a play. I think the gambling and the drink is what they go there for. I wasn't happy doing what I was doing there. I couldn't wait to get out of there. I don't care if I ever see it again."

$$===\ 20\ ===$$

THE PRISONER OF
SEVENTY-THIRD
STREET

If Art's drinking had been under control prior to the Las Vegas
debacle, the temptation to hit the bottle might have easily
arisen once the show closed and Art returned to Manhattan.

While Gleason had forsaken television to try repeating his
early-sixties success in Hollywood, Art had thought about pursuing a sitcom—until the disastrous, unaired Norton pilot. After
that, the TV industry wasn't exactly beating a path to Art's door
with offers, and as 1971 approached, Art entered a phase of
depression and professional inactivity. The TV and movie jobs
had dried up, and Barbara tried keeping Art busy by renting a
house in Nyack, New York, a picturesque town about twenty
miles north of Manhattan overlooking the Hudson River. Here,
Art and Barbara would visit with friends or walk the quaint
downtown streets shopping for antiques. There were times, Art
would recall, "that were just murder, a time of doubting myself,
my talent, my ability. . . . When I wasn't working—well, I have
no hobbies. My vocation is acting. It's also my avocation. And
when I wasn't acting, I was nothing. I'd retreat into sleep. I'd

dread the day coming. I'd pad around the apartment trying to shake my depression."

Art's weight had ballooned to nearly 220 pounds, nearly 30 pounds heavier than normal. He was emotionally frazzled and physically winded. Throughout 1971 his TV appearances were few and far between: a *David Frost Revue* guest shot and visits with Dean Martin and Perry Como. Barbara tried her best to ease Art's spiraling depression, but it was mother hen Bill McCaffrey who was instrumental in saving Art from going off the deep end.

Neil Simon's dark Broadway comedy *The Prisoner of Second Avenue* had opened in late 1971 in Broadway's Eugene O'Neill Theater. Peter Falk starred as Mel Edison, a recently unemployed New York ad executive. With his long-suffering wife, Edna (Lee Grant), Mel undergoes a series of hellish, dead-of-summer Manhattan experiences that leave both characters teetering on the brink of madness.

The show was played for laughs, but its core retained more than a touch of pathos—perfect, McCaffrey thought, for Art, who could certainly identify with Mel Edison's creeping paranoia, his feeling that life was suffocating him in a blanket of aggravation and futility.

With Falk, Grant, and costar Vincent Gardenia scheduled to leave *Prisoner* in June 1972, McCaffrey had an idea. He approached producer Saint Subber and director Mike Nichols—the same team who guided Art through *The Odd Couple*—and asked them to consider Art as Falk's replacement.

"[McCaffrey] knew that Saint Subber liked me and Neil Simon liked me and that Nichols had worked with me before," Art said. "He knew that Peter Falk was leaving the play. After I saw the play, I said, 'Gee, I'd love to do it.' Subber and Simon were very happy about it, which made me happy. I said to Subber, 'Maybe I can make up for that time I pulled out of *The Odd Couple,* and he said, 'Don't say that. You don't have to make up for anything. We're happy to have you in this play. We're glad you're doing it.' "

Along with Art, Barbara Barrie was brought in to replace Lee Grant, while Jack Somack would now play the role of Mel's brother Harry (replacing Vincent Gardenia).

Art's return to Broadway meant a return to the spotlight, and that meant facing the same worries he had fretted about four years earlier with *Lovers*. "I'm no go-getter, but my second wife, Barbara, helped me," Art said. "I'm basically a very shy, sensitive, maybe even insecure guy. I never considered myself a comic or comedian. I'm an actor. It hurts to think that people will read about me. Sometimes I have people phobia, like in a department store I'll get uptight. But on a stage I don't care how many people there are out in front as long as there is that dividing line."

Although *Prisoner* had been running for quite a while by the time Art, Barrie, and Somack assumed their roles, it was by no means on autopilot. Art's style differed from Falk's, and he asked that Nichols, rather than the stage manager, direct the show for a few weeks. Nichols agreed.

"Art was perfect for the part because he was older than Peter and worked totally differently from the way Peter worked," Barrie said. "Art was a big star and had his own style, and Mike wanted it to be very realistic. He kept saying, 'We've got to play this like Chekhov,' and Art was resistant to that. It was a struggle for him, but after a while he realized Mike was right. Neil [Simon] came in, too, and he and Mike really refashioned the play."

The New York critics were generous in their praise for the new *Prisoner* cast. *New York Times* critic Clive Barnes, reassessing the play in July, wrote that Art was "splendid. He stresses the pain of the play as well as its ebullience. Mr. Carney—no newcomer to the neurotic schizophrenia of Mr. Simon's wit—is in particularly happy form."

Said *Variety*: "There is perhaps a greater sense of desperation in Carney's performance, enhanced by his slightly older appearance. So while Carney gets every laugh in the role, he brings added dimension."

The Prisoner of Second Avenue continued its Broadway run through September. In October Art and the cast embarked on a road tour, stopping for a month in Los Angeles's Ahmanson Theatre and for three months in Chicago's Blackstone Theatre.

Jean had remarried in October. Art, now planning his post-

Prisoner project, was reunited with *Honeymooners* writer Leonard Stern. Stern was developing a pilot for NBC called *The Snoop Sisters* and wanted Art to take a supporting role as the harried chauffeur to amateur sleuths Helen Hayes and Mildred Natwick. Art filmed the pilot but declined a regular role when NBC picked the series up in December.

"I wasn't interested in playing a glorified chauffeur," he said. "For me, it was a one-shot deal. But if the right script comes along, I'd like to do my own series. I never have before, but now it interests me."

While *The Prisoner of Second Avenue* was in Chicago, Art signed another pilot deal, this time to costar with Anne Jackson in a sitcom called *Up the World!* Produced by Twentieth Century-Fox, the show was targeted for ABC and had a plot with which Art could identify: A man spends most of his time in bed, fed up with the world around him.

The pilot for *Up the World!* was shot in March 1973, but ABC passed on the show. "It was lousy," Art said. "It was about a guy who gets in his car, fights the morning traffic and the noise and bad weather. He tosses it all up and returns home, goes back to bed, and lets the world fight around him. It would have been nice to do a whole series in bed."

Barbara, meanwhile, had accompanied Art to Los Angeles and Chicago as Barbara Barrie's *Prisoner* understudy. Art and Barbara had always wanted to work together on the stage. After *Prisoner* ended its road run, they decided they would open the show in Ogunquit for a short summer run. Barbara would take over the Barbara Barrie role, costarring with Art.

Back on the West Coast, filmmaker Paul Mazursky was having problems. Mazursky, who had directed *Bob & Carol & Ted & Alice,* had cowritten a script with Josh Greenfeld called *Harry and Tonto.* The story revolved around a philosophical seventy-two-year-old teacher named Harry Combes. Evicted from his New York apartment, Harry embarks on a liberating cross-country odyssey with his marmalade cat, Tonto.

But Mazursky was having trouble raising the necessary capital to turn *Harry and Tonto* into a movie. "I had reached the point where everyone was afraid to make this movie about an old man," he said. He was getting desperate. His first choice to play Harry was James Cagney, who was in a self-imposed retirement and turned the role down. Mazursky had also approached Cary Grant, Laurence Olivier, Jimmy Stewart, and Frank Sinatra, all of whom declined the role for various reasons.

"I heard Jimmy Stewart wanted to do it, but there was something about him I didn't think was right," Mazursky said. "I sent it to Laurence Olivier and he read it, but he said he felt I would be better off using a real American. Finally I found somebody at Fox who said if worst comes to worst they could make [the movie] for a million dollars and get a TV name. Or they could make it into a TV movie."

Mazursky, however, was going to direct *Harry and Tonto* and was adamant it be made for the big screen, even if he had to use a "TV name" to sell the project. Notwithstanding his pursuit of Cagney, Grant, and the others, Mazursky and Greenfeld hadn't written *Harry and Tonto* with any one particular actor in mind. Mazursky had always been a big fan of Art's *Honeymooners* work. "He was brilliant, and I knew he could act," Mazursky said. So he now thought of Art, who was up at the Ogunquit Playhouse with Barbara doing *The Prisoner of Second Avenue*.

Mazursky sent Art the script, but Art was reluctant. How could he, only fifty-four, possibly play seventy-two-year-old Harry Combes? But Mazursky didn't give up, and he flew to Ogunquit to try and persuade Art he was right for the part.

As Mazursky recalls: "Art said, 'Don't you think I'm too young?' And he was already quite balding and already hard of hearing with the hearing aid and the gimpy leg. I said, 'Art, I don't think there will be much trouble playing you as seventy-two.' So I had this real strong talk with him, and by the time I finished the day with him in Ogunquit, I desperately wanted him to do it. But he was on the fence—he wasn't sure, and he was afraid. But Barbara assured me she'd get him [to do it] somehow."

The problem for Art wasn't the *Harry and Tonto* script, which he enjoyed. He just couldn't picture himself playing an older man. Despite the big hearing aid he wore publicly—he had inherited his father's nerve deafness—and his noticeable war-wound limp, Art felt insecure about tackling the role. With only two real movie experiences under his belt (*The Yellow Rolls-Royce* and *A Guide for the Married Man*), Art felt he had to be extremely careful in choosing his first starring role. He hadn't spent all those years declining numerous movie offers to throw it all away now.

"I was worried. For my first starring role I didn't really want to play an old man traveling across the country," he said. "It sounded depressing, like a dull travelogue, so I turned it down. But Paul asked me again and again, and Barbara helped me to see the light. If Paul wanted me so badly for the part, she said, he must have his reasons."

Bill McCaffrey was more terse in advising Art to take the role: "Do it," he said. "You *are* old."

21

HARRY & TONTO & ART & OSCAR

Mazursky was delighted when, despite overwhelming doubts, Art finally agreed to star in *Harry and Tonto*. With Art's commitment firmly in hand, Mazursky immediately began the laborious production process. He planned to shoot the movie—in sequence and on location—from October through December 1973.

Mazursky's timetable gave Art a small window for one last project, and in mid-September he reunited with Gleason for a comedy/musical revue shot in Miami that aired in early October. Gleason revived many of his stock characters—Reggie Van Gleason, The Poor Soul—and Art was on hand as Ed Norton to Gleason's Ralph Kramden. It was the first time Art and Gleason had worked together in more than three years.

By mid-October Mazursky was ready to begin shooting in New York, where Harry begins his cross-country journey. Rounding out the cast were Ellen Burstyn—a former Glea Girl who toiled on *The Jackie Gleason Show* back in the fifties—who would play Harry's only daughter; *Gleason Show* veteran Phil Bruns; *I Dream of Jeannie* star Larry Hagman; and newcomers

Melanie Mayron and Josh Mostel (Zero Mostel's son), who would be making their movie debuts. In a magnificent casting coup, Mazursky had landed the legendary Geraldine Fitzgerald for a heartbreaking cameo that anchored the film's emotional core.

But tantamount to casting, locations, etc. was Art's relationship with his whiskered costar—the cat who would play Tonto. Art and Tonto were in virtually every scene together, and it was important that Art at least *pretend* to like the cat.

Eileen, Brian, and Paul Carney had had cats and dogs while growing up in Yonkers. And Uncle Rich owned a beloved dog, who lived with the Carneys in the Bedford Avenue house back in Mount Vernon. But Art was never much of an animal lover. Making matters worse, he was allergic to cats. Art's idea of the perfect domesticated companion was the "pet rock" given to him by pal Jonathan Winters.

"After we did the casting we were going to have a week's rehearsal in New York, and I wanted him to spend a week with the cat," Mazursky said. "Art told me that he hated cats, which I thought was absolutely hilarious. He opened his drawer and took out his pet rock. 'It doesn't piss and doesn't shit,' he said."

Throughout the movie, Mazursky used three cats to play Tonto, although only one cat was used extensively. "Art pretended to hate the cat, but actually he liked it and the cat loved him," Mazursky said. "They would walk down the street in New York rehearsing, and Art would sit there while the cat jumped up on his lap. They established a brilliant relationship that was basically unsentimental."

Costar Phil Bruns, however, remembers it differently. "Quite frankly, Art didn't like cats, and if you watch real closely—you really have to look hard when he's petting the cat—you'll see his nose just turned up a bit," Bruns said. "Although there's such love coming across on film, you really had to know Art to catch that [distaste]."

Having tried to establish a tenuous relationship between his two main stars, Mazursky left it up to makeup man Bob O'Bradovich to transform Art into seventy-two-year-old Harry Combes. For starters, O'Bradovich had Art grow a mustache, which came in completely snow white. Next, he added bushy eyebrows and some subtle makeup shading around Art's eyes, temples, and chin to highlight his naturally gray hair. "I wore my own tortoiseshell bifocals, dressed in clothes just a bit too big and baggy, and used my World War II shrapnel limp," Art said. "I wanted [Harry] to be a lively, youngish old man, not a doddering, cranky old throwaway."

To further enhance the illusion, Art instructed the wardrobe department not to pad Harry's shoulders, and to make his collars a little loose with some padding around the back. He also parted his hair in a style that suited a man of Harry's age.

"I knew when I finally accepted the role and Paul and I talked about it, there wasn't much I could do in terms of preparation," Art said. "That is, I didn't have to visit a whorehouse, or live in a tent, or what have you." For inspiration, Art drew on his recollections of Uncle Rich, who used to talk to his dog while patiently deboning the dog's fish dinner. Like Harry, Uncle Rich was a freethinker, liberated in his attitude toward the younger generation.

When we first meet Harry Combes, he's a widowed, retired professor who walks his cat, Tonto, on a leash and passes his time sitting on a park bench chatting with his socialist friend (Herbert Berghof). When Harry's Upper West Side apartment building is condemned, he's crushed. An independent soul, he can't imagine living anywhere else and refuses to leave the apartment until he's forcibly removed by the police. With nowhere else to go, Harry moves in with his oldest son (Bruns), a Riverdale (Bronx) businessman whose own son Norman (Mostel) has taken a vow of silence.

Harry moves into Norman's room and tries his best to communicate with his mute grandson but soon discovers he's not cut out for the quasi-suburban lifestyle. So he does what any normal seventy-two-year-old widower would do: He boards a bus with Tonto and sets out on a cross-country journey. Harry eventually buys a used car and visits his daughter Shirley (Burstyn) in Chicago. Father and daughter have never seen eye to eye— they're both stubborn—but they reach a loving truce before Harry leaves Chicago. Norman, meanwhile, has joined Harry in Chicago, though he still isn't talking.

Harry decides to head to Los Angeles to visit his other son, Eddie (Hagman). Along the way he and Norman get sidetracked when they pick up a runaway teenaged hitchhiker (Mayron). She, in turn, convinces Harry to visit an old flame, Jessie (Fitzgerald), who's now senile and living in an Indiana nursing home. Jessie barely remembers Harry but, locked in her own far-away fantasy world, asks him to dance, thinking Harry to be a romantic suitor. The old lovers touchingly waltz in the nursing-home cafeteria.

Back on the road, the runaway and Norman—who's now speaking!—decide they want to join a hippie commune. Not one to pass judgment, Harry drops the young couple off in the middle of nowhere. In his next adventure Harry has a liberating sexual encounter with a friendly prostitute and gets arrested for public drunkenness in Las Vegas. He's thrown into a jail cell with an old Indian (Chief Dan George), who promises to fix Harry's aching back for a price: Harry's electric blender.

"Chief Dan George didn't know his lines, and Art used that," Mazursky said. "Every time the Chief would say something and have a long pause because he didn't know the next line, Art would just stare at him. That made it even funnier."

By the movie's finale, Harry finally reaches Los Angeles and his son, swinging bachelor Eddie. Blustery and self-confident, Eddie lives in a plush condominium, drives a Cadillac, and brags about his financial security. But it's all a false front, and Eddie finally breaks down and admits to Harry that he's flat broke and a total failure.

"I had trouble controlling myself in the scene with Larry Hagman, the other son," Art said. "He was crying, and he's broke, and he says, 'Pop'—it'd break your heart—'Pop, I'm on my ass.' And here I'm supposed to be a pillar of strength and I had to put my arm around him to keep from crying myself."

Harry knows that Los Angeles is the end of the line. He's found peace and tranquillity finally, spending time on the beach with Tonto and chatting with new friends. But the cross-country trip proves too much for Tonto, who dies quite suddenly. Harry is heartbroken, until he sees a look-alike cat roaming the beach. He's found his new Tonto.

The reservations Art had going into *Harry and Tonto*—Could he carry the movie? Was he projecting as Harry?—were quickly forgotten once filming began.

"I knew within two or three days after we had started work . . . that I made the right decision," he said. "I looked forward to getting up early every day and getting to work. I told Paul after, 'I don't want to do anything else but work for you from now on!' "

Mazursky realized, as time went on, that he was making a special movie. His faith in Art was rewarded. Art's drinking was under control, and he stopped drinking entirely toward the end of shooting because of his herniated diaphragm. He knew his lines, was enthusiastic, and most of all, he kept Mazursky and his crew loose with his offscreen antics.

"Art was funny as hell," Mazursky said. "His biggest problem was taking a good crap in the morning, and if he did he'd have a great day. He was a very wonderful person to be around. I think he liked me very much, and I never laughed so hard as when he used to regale us with imitations of Arthur Godfrey—and of all the famous people in the world—farting. He imitated animals just before they would pee or shit—he did a lot of jokes about farting and shitting, no question about it."

Mazursky completed *Harry and Tonto* under budget and on schedule in December 1973. The film earned an R rating—"We had a mad love affair," Art joked about his relationship with Tonto—but didn't open until August 1974. Already, though, the buzz in Hollywood was good, and there were whispers about possible Oscar nominations for Art and Mazursky.

Art had been in show business for thirty-seven years. He'd won five Emmys, two Sylvania Awards [for TV work], and a Tony nomination. Hollywood loved comeback stories, especially among its own, and Art certainly qualified. His drinking was Hollywood's worst-kept secret, and his peers knew he'd been to hell and back through the years of alcoholism, depression, and pill popping. The majority of Academy members—the people who would vote for the Academy Awards—were of Art's generation or older. Suddenly it wasn't beyond the realm of possibility that Art could be nominated for an Oscar, although *Harry and Tonto* was his first major film role.

But success, as we've seen, was anathema to Art Carney. Would it be any different now that *Harry and Tonto* had completed filming and the Oscar talk had begun? Art struggled to stay away from the bottle, knowing how his manic highs often spiraled into crashing depressions. To try and counteract what seemed to be inevitable, he was undergoing psychotherapy and attending Alcoholics Anonymous meetings. He was also taking daily doses of Antabuse, a prescription drug that produced violent illness or even convulsions if mixed with alcohol. "It's just a reminder," Art said, of the days when he would mark "L.D."— last drink—on his calendar.

"I am so elated over *Harry and Tonto,* and I have to watch it because I have difficulty coping with exhilaration," he said. "But now when I recognize the danger signals, I don't open up a bottle and get blind drunk the way I used to. I go talk to a doctor. As for booze, I hope I never take another drink in my life because I know I'm better off without it. I function better as a human being and as an actor."

Art transferred his craving for alcohol to doses of heavily sugared iced tea and/or orange juice and water. Through thick and thin, the chocolate-and-marshmallow Mallomars, Art's trusted standby, remained a staple of his diet and satisfied his sweet tooth.

Harry and Tonto was generating a lot of talk, yet Art still wasn't being swamped with movie offers. His next role was a supporting turn as a detective-turned-parson in *W.W. and the Dixie Dancekings,* shot in Nashville and starring Burt Reynolds.

Without much movie work coming his way, Art returned to the stage in early 1974 for a second go-round in *The Odd Couple.* This time, however, he was far removed from Broadway, playing the slovenly Oscar Madison to Don Knotts's prissy Felix Unger in a production staged in Arlington Park, Illinois. Knotts was ill and almost forced the show to be canceled, but he recovered and made it to Arlington Park about two days before the show was set to open.

Harvey Medlinsky, who had served as stage manager during Art's ill-fated *Odd Couple* run on Broadway, was directing the Arlington Park show. He remembered the "joy" Art felt at finally playing Oscar. Also in the Arlington Park production was Sidney Armus, another holdover from the Carney-Matthau *Odd Couple.* He jokingly referred to Art as "Olivier" because he so easily slipped into the role of Oscar.

Harry and Tonto wouldn't open nationwide until September. It was set to premiere in New York in mid-August, which was crucial: If it passed the litmus test of New York's exacting—and influential—movie critics, that would bode well for *Harry's* (and Art's) future.

Just four days after President Richard Nixon's resignation, the *New York Times* applauded Art's performance for its "gentle dignity and resilience throughout, though [Carney] has to address too many of his lines to a cat named Tonto."

With the lull preceding *Harry and Tonto's* nationwide opening, Art returned to television. Since the *Gleason Show* and failed Norton pilot in 1970, Art's TV appearances had been few and far between, consisting mostly of one-shot guest appearances. In the interviews he gave throughout 1974, Art spoke time and again of his desire to star in a sitcom. That was quite a change from his previous "I never want to carry a show" attitude. Whatever offers did come his way, however, he declined for unspecified reasons.

In early September Art teamed with his old CBS stablemate Lucille Ball, with whom he'd shot his memorable cameo in *A Guide for the Married Man.* Lucy was headlining an hour-long comedy special called *Happy Anniversary and Goodbye* and wanted Art to play her husband. So Ball and Carney became the Michaelses, a married couple (she's a housewife, he's a dentist) celebrating their twenty-fifth wedding anniversary. Once svelte, she's now overweight; once sporting a thick head of hair, he's now balding and paunchy. They call it quits but fall back in love after she slims down and he discovers the magic of a good toupee. Ultimately forgettable, *Happy Anniversary and Goodbye* includes one historical footnote: a cameo appearance by a muscle-bound, thick-tongued actor named Arnold Schwarzenegger.

Like so many of his stage roles, *Happy Anniversary and Goodbye* eerily mirrored Art's offscreen life. Not only did Malcolm Michaels drink to excess—yet another of Art's drunken characters—but his marital problems probably struck closer to home than Art would have liked (shades of *The Odd Couple*).

And here's why: Art and Barbara's eight-year marriage was showing signs of wear and tear. Up to this point they had been, by all accounts, as happy as could be expected under the trying circumstances of Art's emotional crises. It was Barbara who urged Art to continue working, who guided him through the tough times after his divorce from Jean and his reemergence into the spotlight. Next to Bill McCaffrey, Barbara was the driving force behind Art's life and career, and he turned to her for guidance. It was often noted in various newspaper and magazine articles how Barbara prodded Art, supporting him through the dreaded interviews by interjecting a comment here or there, cajoling, praising, and needling (good-naturedly). Art, in turn, often credited Barbara with helping him keep his sanity, although he always sounded as if he was trying to convince himself that he enjoyed life in their Manhattan duplex.

By late 1974 Art and Barbara were talking about starring together in a production of Eugene O'Neill's *Ah, Wilderness!* that would be directed by Jose Quintero in Washington's Kennedy Center. In early January 1975, *Variety* reported that rehearsals for *Ah, Wilderness!* would get under way in March, with Zoe Caldwell costarring, if she were available. The show would, according to *Variety,* open in April before making its Broadway debut in the fall.

But however united Art and Barbara appeared in print, privately the cracks were beginning to show. Art's close friend and *Honeymooners* costar Sheila MacRae noticed a lot of tension the previous summer when Art and Barbara had rented a house in Los Angeles and thrown several pool parties, inviting friends like Steve Lawrence and Edye Gorme. Jane Kean remained convinced that no matter how happy he seemed to be with Barbara, Art had never recovered from his divorce.

By 1975 Art and Jean had three grandchildren, and Art still kept in close contact with his children. Sons Brian and Paul, now twenty-eight and twenty-two, were pursuing musical careers. Paul had dropped out of high school when he was eighteen to form a band and cut an unsuccessful jazz album. Brian, married and a new father, played his guitar in nightclubs like New York's Scotland Yard.

"When I get in trouble I very often call Brian. . . . There's something about his makeup," Art said at the time. "I call and say, 'Can I drive out and see you? Have a cup of coffee or something?' Because who the hell else can I bullshit with? And he's made it all on his own. He's never traded on my name."

The problems brewing between Art and Barbara were swept under the rug, for the time being, when *Harry and Tonto* opened to rave reviews. Several critics immediately put Art on the inside track for an Oscar nomination, while a shocked Hollywood was astounded at the low-budget film's brisk performance at the box office. It was obvious that *Harry and Tonto* crossed generational barriers and meant something to people of all ages. For the first time since 1966 and his reemergence with Gleason in Miami, Art's face graced many a major newspaper and magazine. *Newsweek, People,* the *Los Angeles Times,* and the *New York Times* all focused on his "comeback" and the remarkable poise and talent Art displayed in his first starring movie role.

For once, Art basked in the attention. Instead of dreading face-to-face interviews, he now told reporters how he enjoyed talking to them, because he was proud of his work and was ecstatic over how *Harry and Tonto* had turned out.

"*Harry and Tonto* is the biggie for me," he told one newspaper reporter. "Imagine, the first movie I've starred in, even though I've been in the business for thirty-seven years. I'm feeling so high that I'm beginning to wake up in the morning with a sober hangover."

As the accolades poured in, Art's stock in Hollywood began to rise. Just a year before, Art was considered a high-strung, undependable drinker who could jeopardize a project. Now, the scripts began piling up in Bill McCaffrey's office. CBS even offered to turn *Harry and Tonto* into a weekly series starring Art.

"My first reaction to this was, I don't want to dissipate the character in a weekly half-hour series," Art said. "It was too special to me and I didn't think the people involved with making such a sensitive film would want it either. What I would like to do—and maybe I'm wrong—is in a year or two make another movie based on the same character, to find out what happens to this guy after the picture ended. But I wouldn't want to water him down."

One of Mazursky's stated goals in cowriting and directing *Harry and Tonto* was to change the perception of senior citizens as humorless, "silly eccentrics." Art's Harry Combes not only accomplished Mazursky's goal but continued a cinematic trend that had begun with Ruth Gordon's performance in *Where's Poppa?* (1970) and with *Kotch* (1971), Melvyn Douglas in *I Never Sang for My Father* (1971), and Ruth Gordon (again) in *Harold and Maude* (1972).

The euphoria Art felt over *Harry and Tonto*'s success was elevated on February 24, 1975, when he was nominated for an Academy Award in the Best Actor category along with Jack Nicholson (*Chinatown*), Al Pacino (The Godfather, Part II), Albert Finney (*Murder on the Orient Express*), and Dustin Hoffman (*Lenny*). Mazursky and Josh Greenfeld received a nomination for Best Original Screenplay. Ellen Burstyn, Art's costar, was nominated as Best Actress for her role in *Alice Doesn't Live Here Anymore,* another movie she filmed the same year. A one-time Mount Vernon neighbor of Art's, United Artists chairman Arthur Krim, was cited for his humanitarian work.

Art was thrilled by the nomination but convinced he would never win an Oscar. The odds were overwhelmingly against Art's overcoming his television background; his fierce competition (Nicholson, Pacino, et al.); and *Harry*'s status as a "small" movie lacking a proven, bankable star. "You always figure you're going to lose with a small picture," Mazursky said.

"How can you compare, or put in the same category, Pacino's performance, Dustin Hoffman, Albert Finney, Nicholson, myself," Art said. "The characters, the characterizations are all different. I'm not a better actor than these other guys . . . maybe they can come up with a different phrase, instead of Best Actor perhaps Outstanding Performance."

Hollywood oddsmakers picked Art as a long shot. Several critics sniped in print that Art wasn't worthy of a nomination. The experts were split: Would it be Pacino or Nicholson?

They were all wrong.

April 8, 1975, was a rainy night in Los Angeles, and when Glenda Jackson ripped open the envelope, she sent a gasp through the Dorothy Chandler Pavilion.

"And the winner is . . . Art Carney for *Harry and Tonto!*

Art, sitting with Barbara, was stunned. As he limped to the podium, the TV cameras clearly showing his hearing aid, he pumped his fist in triumph. The roaring crowd greeted Art with a standing ovation, showing him—and the world—how much they cared. They weren't only cheering for Art's acting prowess, but for the joy he had given to so many people over the years.

Art Carney was the Comeback Kid.

"Ladies and gentlemen and members of the Academy . . . and what other words besides 'Thank you,' " Art said, cradling his Oscar like a newborn baby. "Paul Mazursky and Josh Greenfeld for a gem of a script, and particularly for my wife, Barbara, and my agent/manager/father confessor William Francis Xavier McCaffrey for twenty-five years, who said two words: 'Do it! You *are* old!' Thank you very much."

Art was the first winner to ever thank his agent while accepting his Oscar. "It made me bawl," an astonished McCaffrey said afterward. "We figured it would be hard for him to win, being alien to that Hollywood crowd. But he's an actor's actor."

After the ceremonies, Art partied the night away, telling reporters he was "numb" and "very happy." His win made front-page news in New York—"Carney & Burstyn Win Oscars" blared the *Daily News*—and his face was splashed across newspapers and TV screens nationwide. The next morning, Art answered a congratulatory phone call from Gleason, who good-naturedly asked Art where he had been the night before. "I went to see *Chinatown,*" Art replied.

It was a time to celebrate, to bask in the accolades and telegrams that came flooding into Art's Beverly Hills Hotel suite, and to read the inevitable "No More Second Banana" headlines. Art had thought of saying "You're looking at an actor whose price has just doubled" when he accepted his Oscar, but the offers now came flooding in, his hotel phone already ringing off the hook.

Before heading back home to New York, Art found time, in all the media crush and hoopla, to renew some old acquaintances. Horace Heidt called and offered to take Art out to dinner to celebrate. The two men quietly broke bread at Chasen's, thirty-seven years after the gangly eighteen-year-old kid from Mount Vernon had impressed the stern bandleader with his FDR impersonation.

Art was high on life, living in the moment, reveling in his extraordinary success . . . and it soon all came crashing down. Shortly after returning to New York, he began to feel the sense of despair that seemed to dog his every triumph, the suffocating blues that sucked him into an abyss of depression and anxiety.

The worries began. Would he forever be typecast as a senior citizen? Now that he finally wedged his fifty-six-year-old foot in Hollywood's door, would it remain open only for stereotyped roles? Earlier in the year, Art had taped a syndicated TV special called *The Middle Age Blues*—an apt description of his post-Oscar mood.

"All of a sudden, the miseries would hit him, even without drinking," Sheila MacRae said. "He would go into this real depressed state. I remember after *Harry and Tonto* he was thrilled he won the Oscar. But then Barbara called and said, 'Sheila, I wish you would come over, because Art likes the fact that you talk to him about God and the light and everything else without mentioning religion.' So I went over there, and I'd never seen him like that: He was sitting in a chair with scripts all around him. He was like Rodin's *Thinker*, except he had both hands on the side of the chair and he was wearing a blue robe. And I said, 'Well, gee, it's a letdown, I guess; maybe the four of us will take a trip.' And he said, 'I don't know what to do with my life.' And I said, 'What's all this?' and he said, 'I don't want to do any of it.' For some time he was really depressed. Barbara would say, 'I don't know what to do, I don't know what I'm doing wrong. He won't talk to me.' "

22

THE LATE SHOW

Back in 1966, Jackie Gleason had thrown Art an emotional life preserver when he resurrected *The Honeymooners* down in Miami. Gleason now talked of staging a live *Honeymooners* show in Las Vegas with Art, Sheila MacRae, and Jane Kean. The show, as envisioned by Gleason, would be similar to the 1952 summer *Honeymooners* tour: a *Honeymooners* sketch sandwiched between musical-comedy numbers. Gleason thought that if the show worked, it could continue onward to Lake Tahoe.

Art, in the wake of his Oscar and battling his depression, was making the rounds of TV talk shows. He hadn't yet committed to his next project and was interested in Gleason's idea. But the project never got off the ground.

The same couldn't be said for Art's movie career, which now shifted into high gear. Art's fears of being typecast never came to pass; realistically, he couldn't be considered for any character younger than fifty, but neither was he pigeonholed into playing elderly, Harry Combes–like men who talked to their cats. He followed his costarring role in *W.W. and the Dixie Dancekings* with a broad comic turn as flamboyant studio president J. J. Fromberg in *Won Ton Ton, The Dog Who Saved Hollywood,* which featured Bruce Dern, Madeline Kahn, Phil Silvers, and Teri Garr, among others.

But Art hadn't turned his back on television. With his newfound clout, he now shuttled freely between movies and TV, pursuing whatever projects appealed to him.

The rush of working with Gleason still appealed to Art, who had listened with interest to Gleason's plans for the Las Vegas *Honeymooners* show. In 1973 Gleason's hundred-thousand-dollar annual contract with CBS had expired. He had left the network for ABC, which asked him to reconsider doing some *Honeymooners* specials. Gleason said he'd think about it. Three years later, in 1976, he corralled Art, Audrey Meadows, and Jane Kean for *The Honeymooners: The Second Honeymoon,* a twenty-fifth-anniversary special that, Gleason hinted, would be the first in a series of nonmusical, hour-long *Honeymooners* specials.

The Second Honeymoon was taped in Miami Beach and aired on February 2, 1976. (Ralph Kramden was the only Brooklyn bus driver with a "playboy suntan," noted *Washington Post* TV critic Tom Shales.) The plot was typical *Honeymooners* fare, with Ralph suspecting Alice of being pregnant (!), Norton performing his slapstick ballet—this time while teaching Ralph how to change a diaper—and the boys getting "drunk" on nonalcoholic punch. To lend some authenticity and nostalgia to the occasion, Gleason had the original *Honeymooners* set trucked down from New York.

"Gleason and Carney are not only funny, one realizes, they are terrific actors—and this is terrific television," Shales wrote. "Carney's Norton has always been incalculably important to the comedy; he may be the most crucial second banana in TV history." ABC, encouraged by the show's ratings, urged Gleason to formulate plans for future *Honeymooners* specials, possibly for the following year.

Art followed the *Honeymooners* reunion by reteaming with Lucille Ball for her CBS special *What Now, Catherine Curtis?* With the retro hit sitcom *Happy Days* topping the Nielsen charts, fifties kitsch was in heavy demand. TV viewers could mistakenly think it was 1956 and not 1976, what with Jackie Gleason, Art Carney, and Lucille Ball popping up all over the place. (Ball had also teamed with Gleason the previous year, with mediocre results. The chemistry between the two TV icons was nonexistent.)

In California, meanwhile, filmmaker Robert Benton, who had cowritten *Bonnie and Clyde* and *What's Up, Doc?,* was huddled with his mentor, director Robert Altman. In 1974 Benton had written a screenplay called *The Late Show,* which was a homage to forties film noir updated to present-day Los Angeles. The story revolved around aging, paunchy, ulcer-ridden detective Ira Wells, who's hired by spacey Margo Sperling to find her stolen cat. Wells eventually finds himself avenging his ex-partner's death and investigating another murder while striking up a just-short-of-romantic friendship with frenetic, freewheeling Margo.

Benton rewrote the *Late Show* script in 1975 and submitted it to agent Sam Cohn, who in turn handed it to Altman. Altman agreed to produce the movie for Warner Bros., with Benton directing. Benton, who had based Ira Wells partly on his father, didn't have any one actor in mind for the role. That soon changed when he and Altman sat down to cast *The Late Show.*

Bill McCaffrey had entered semiretirement by the mid-seventies, entrusting his stable of clients, including Art, to International Creative Management. ICM's most powerful agent, Sam Cohn—legendary for his nervous habit of eating paper—handled Art while the seventy-six-year-old McCaffrey kept an office at ICM's New York headquarters. McCaffrey had never steered Art wrong, and by handing Art over to Cohn, McCaffrey now helped him land one of the biggest roles of his career. As luck would have it, Cohn also represented Benton and Altman.

Said Benton, "We started the [*Late Show* casting] list with Art Carney and ended it with Art Carney, and once we said Art Carney it seemed like such an absolutely natural idea. I guess because of *Harry and Tonto* he was foremost in people's minds as far as casting. I spoke to Paul Mazursky about *Harry and Tonto* and about how Carney looked older than he really was because of his hearing aid and bum leg."

Benton met with Art in New York, explaining how he based Ira Wells on his father, who had survived on Alka-Seltzer in his declining days because he feared an operation. Art was famous for regaling interviewers with a laundry list of his health problems. He felt an immediate kinship with Ira Wells.

"I told [Benton] I could relate to that," Art said. "I've got the hearing problem . . . I've got the bum leg. I've got the paunch, the middle-age spread. I mean, I really brought the paunch to the part. I've got cataracts. And for the perforated ulcer, I've got a hiatus hernia. I get mad at my infirmities. I can't play tennis anymore. I can't go bowling. I can't ride a bike. I mean, the character was well defined before we got started. I told Benton, 'You've got the right guy.' "

Benton said, "Everything [Art] would tell me about we would just incorporate into the character. What I wanted early on was for him to play as much of himself as he could, because I didn't want him to fight anything he had. And anything that was wrong with him was a plus for me: The worse off Ira Wells was, the better off I was."

The Late Show was mostly a two-character study centering around the relationship between Ira and Margo. Central Casting couldn't have provided Benton a better lead in the broken-down, limping Art Carney. But it was just as important that Benton find the quintessential actress to play the laid-back, EST-influenced, psychobabbling Margo.

That actress turned out to be Lily Tomlin, a bright, multitalented stand-up comedian and actress who earned an Oscar nomination for her role in Altman's 1975 epic, *Nashville,* her first movie. Before starring in *Nashville,* Tomlin had won acclaim, and several Emmy nominations, for her funny vignettes on NBC's *Laugh-In* as the lisping Edith-Ann and sarcastic switchboard operator Ernestine. (Tomlin subsequently won an Emmy for her 1974 special, *Lily Tomlin.*) While Tomlin was masterful at slipping into a number of characters, she was also a noted feminist—the perfect foil for Ira, an anachronistic, chauvinistic throwback who still called women "dolls" and could not comprehend the idea of women's liberation.

"Originally I didn't want to do the movie, but it wasn't because of Art," Tomlin said. "When I got the script, my character said 'shit,' 'turd,' and 'crap' about 153 times. In retrospect, the overkill of it probably would have been funny, but I felt it was going to be so heavy-handed for my character. But then I talked to Altman and Benton about it and we made a few changes."

Tomlin was also represented by Sam Cohn, who sent her the script and brokered a deal with his four clients. Shooting was scheduled to begin in the summer of 1976, and Tomlin met with

Art and Benton for a get-acquainted session at the Polo Lounge in Beverly Hills.

"It was easy to have a naturalness with Art because he was someone who invited a certain affection, the memory and knowledge of him over the years," Tomlin said. "When people do comedy and you respond to it, I think you kind of always hold a simple affection for them."

Whether that affection sustained itself over the course of *The Late Show*'s shooting schedule is debatable. While Art and Tomlin certainly connected onscreen—they were believable, touching, and delightfully quirky—Tomlin's improvisations repeatedly clashed with Art's by-the-book acting method. "I was inclined to do improvisation a little bit, and Art didn't like me to do that too much," Tomlin said. "He wanted to stick to the script, which is not unusual. So I stopped doing [improv] in scenes with him. I'm pretty flexible that way, so the fact he didn't want me to [improvise] didn't bother me."

Said Benton, "Art would go back to his dressing room because he hated being on the set. He has a kind of claustrophobia, especially in those tiny areas, but Lily would stay on the set all the time, never leaving. And she would be on the telephone all the time, until I would say, 'OK, start to roll.' It was her way of keeping herself fresh. Art and Lily worked out of utterly different systems, but they really did respect each other. They never became good friends, but they got along.

"Lily is a wonderful actor but she's also a performer in a different kind of way than Art. And when things get tough for an actor, they go back to the things they know the best. I think what both of them understood about one another was that they could depend on the other's wit and energy to be there when they reached out. They both really did love each other as a performer. At least I felt that."

The years of working with Gleason, who never rehearsed and often ad-libbed, should have prepared Art for Tomlin's high-wire, "in the moment" work habits. Apparently, though, Art was having a tough time dealing with his costar's quirks.

Phil Bruns, who costarred with Art in *Harry and Tonto*, visited Art one day on the *Late Show* set. Bruns said Art told him, "Phil, I cannot stand that woman! She's telling me how to act and how to be funny! I'm going nuts! I've never hit anybody onstage, but if I did, it would be her."

Costar John Considine, who played a well-dressed, curly-haired thug, also noticed some tension between Art and Tomlin. "Art had a lot of trouble with Lily, because of her improvising," Considine said. "It made him a little crazy, especially in the beginning. He always used to say something like, 'I don't care what you do, but let me know, wave to me or something. Let me know when I come in.' "

But Benton managed to keep his troops under control, despite a grueling schedule, shooting in cramped sets, and mid-morning Los Angeles temperatures that often reached nearly one hundred degrees. Art chipped in by noodling on the piano between breaks and, in one instance, feigning a massive heart attack and collapsing into a motel swimming pool (having warned Benton beforehand of his "joke").

"It's a defense in a way. You find it hard to concentrate on your lines so you fool around to relieve the tension," Art said. "I thank God I'm still able to do that . . . and still be as depressed as I am. But it's also wanting to be liked. That's a paralyzing thing, too."

While Art sang ditties, played the piano, and planned practical jokes, costar Bill Macy broke the ice infamously: The former *Oh, Calcutta!* cast member completely disrobed during the first day of rehearsal.

"The crew we had on that movie was pretty macho. This goes back to the mid-seventies, and things were even more overt," Tomlin said. "I remember there was an instance where one of the stand-ins was a woman, and one of the guys poured beer on her T-shirt; then they kind of tossed her between each other. You'd hear racist, sexist, and homophobic jokes, and I'd say, 'Don't tell those jokes in front of me.' Art was much more loved by the crew—he was outgoing, easygoing, played the piano, and was always telling jokes and communicating with the crew. I was always challenging them in some way, but it didn't affect the relationship between Art and me."

Tomlin energized Art's *Late Show* performance, ignited an

electric chemistry between Oscar winner and Oscar nominee, old guard Art Carney meshing seamlessly with upstart Lily Tomlin.

"No actress could have played that role better than Lily," Art said. "A lot of it came out of her ability to improvise and chatter. You can't write that kind of stuff into a script. Lily and I had a lot of fun working together, but she's a loner, not at all the gregarious person most people assume she is."

In *The Late Show,* as Ira gets more deeply dragged into the case of Margo's missing cat, he begins to rely on Margo's good sense—however convoluted—and her companionship. Margo, in turn, grows to understand, and even respect, Ira's old-world values and sense of despair at growing older and losing his purpose. ("He was so goddamn mad about being over the hill," Art explained.) Best of all, this mismatched pair feeds off each other's anxieties, while Margo, always up for new experiences, gets high off the action and intrigue into which she's plunged by Ira.

In one of *The Late Show*'s best scenes, Margo and Ira embark on a high-speed chase, careening madly through a suburban neighborhood and cementing their unspoken spiritual bond. Benton shot the scene in an actual neighborhood near the Los Angeles airport. Luckily, the area was slated for demolition and no one was living there at the time.

"Lily insisted on driving and I thought Art was going to die, but he said, 'OK, all right, we'll do it,' " Benton said. "And at the end, when they slap hands [in the scene], believe me, that's not acting, that's Art saying, 'My God, we lived through it.' They were both so high from that. I think Art loved the sense of danger. God knows he was a great sport about it."

The Late Show ends with Margo asking Ira to move into the vacant next-door apartment so they can start their own detective agency. Not only was it poignant, but it left the door open for a sequel, or maybe even a television series. Either option seemed to be a foregone conclusion when filming was completed and Warner Bros. executives raved about their new comedy team.

"There maybe was that kind of speculation," Tomlin said. "Before [the movie] was released in theaters, everybody was real high on it and they were saying we worked well or had chemistry. They thought the movie had charm."

Art was still talking about a sequel in May 1977, three months after *The Late Show* opened in theaters to critical praise but tepid box office business.

"The reason Robert Benton called it *The Late Show* was that if it turned out to be a hit, he could follow it with *The Late Late Show*," Art joked. "He's being very closemouthed about the plot, but my suspicion is that I'll be moving into the spare room in Lily's house and that we'll set up a private investigating agency. I don't think we'll ever get married, because there is no sexual attraction between us. What we have is a respect for one another's ability and brainwork."

Art had chosen his post–*Harry and Tonto* roles wisely, and the accolades he garnered for *The Late Show* almost equaled those he had received for his Oscar-winning performance. This helped cement Art's reputation as a first-class screen actor. Although Art wasn't nominated for an Oscar (Benton felt both Art and Tomlin should have been nominated), he was cited as Best Actor by the National Society of Film Critics.

Art's marriage to Barbara, meanwhile, had deteriorated while he was shooting *The Late Show* (costar Joanna Cassidy remembered engaging in "a lot of flirting" with Art). After ten years together, Art and Barbara separated at the end of 1976; one gossip columnist linked Art to a "new love," actress Bebe Kelly. "I just got a note one day saying, 'Here at the Beverly Hills Hotel. Barbara and I are not together anymore.'" said Art's friend, Mitzi Gaynor. "I don't know what happened there."

Art's breakup with Barbara was painful and was made even worse in December, when Art's brother Phil died in New York's Lenox Hill Hospital after a brief illness. Remembered by many of Art's boyhood friends as one of the funniest Carney brothers, Phil had entertained wounded servicemen during World War II and spent his later years organizing the entertainment on cruises to the West Indies and South America. He had lived only a block away from Art and Barbara, on East Seventy-third Street.

In June 1977 Barbara filed suit for divorce in Manhattan Supreme Court, asking for temporary alimony and possession of the couple's Seventy-second Street apartment. Art was ordered to pay five hundred dollars a week temporary support pending divorce proceedings; he filed a countersuit in July.

But a funny thing happened on the way to divorce court. Jean had separated from her second husband, and in 1976 she and Art were spotted together several times. By the spring of 1977, Art and Jean were seeing each other on a fairly regular basis, sometimes going together to see son Paul perform his musical nightclub routine. Their appearances sparked talk of a possible reconciliation.

"Art's been coming here to Connecticut to see his family— particularly Paul and his new grandchild," Jean said. "Art and I have been out a few times, but that doesn't mean we're going to get married again. Some people who've seen us out together are jumping to that conclusion. But we don't have any plans in that direction."

Bill McCaffrey told the press that "Art and Jean are seeing each other a lot, but Art doesn't want to talk about it. It's a very delicate thing right now because Art's involved in divorce proceedings. But it's right that he and Jean have become pretty close again. After all, Jean is the mother of his three children, and there are grandchildren. It's a very happy situation."

Rounding out this familial atmosphere was Art's reunion with Leonord Stern, the former *Honeymooners* writer who had cast Art for the *Snoop Sisters* pilot. Stern was in the process of adapting Harry Kemelman's popular series of Rabbi novels—*Friday the Rabbi Slept Late,* etc.—which would be part of NBC's rotating *Sunday Mystery Movie* shows (*McMillan and Wife, McCloud, Columbo*). Ray Wagner, Stern's co–executive producer, owned the rights to Kemelman's books and had come close to making a movie with Dustin Hoffman in the role of sleuthing rabbi David Small. When that failed, Wagner and Stern pitched the idea as a TV series. George C. Scott had shown some interest.

"The only thing the network felt was that the emphasis had to change to accommodate the times," said Stern, alluding to NBC's concern that it wouldn't be a good idea to make the series' lead an overtly Jewish character. "So it went from the rabbi to the police captain as the principal character."

Art would play the captain, Paul Lanigan, the police chief of a small California town who often collaborated with his close friend, amateur sleuth Rabbi Small, to crack tough cases. Art teamed with Stuart Margolin for the *Lanigan's Rabbi* pilot, which was shot in the spring of 1976, before Art began work on *The Late Show*. According to Stern, however, Margolin was dropped from the project because he was "too Jewish." He was replaced by Bruce Solomon, while Janis Paige was hired to play Art's onscreen wife, Kay Lanigan. Just as Gleason had done for him in 1966, after his flight to the Institute for Living, Art now helped Paige get back on her feet after the death of her husband.

"Art called me one day and said, 'Are you ready to go to work? I just think you ought to go to work, and I've got something I want you do to with me,' " Paige said. "He really saved my life. He got me back and focused and concentrated and helped me get through a terribly difficult time."

Rounding out the *Lanigan's Rabbi* cast was Janet Margolin as Miriam Small, the rabbi's wife. Barbara (this was before the separation) had a small role as Bobbie Whittaker, the local newspaper reporter.

At the time, Art was dealing with a painful knee and would often come to work with brochures of the latest knee operations, telling anyone within earshot he thought he needed a prosthesis. Whatever physical pain Art was feeling seemed to be matched by his marital problems.

"I knew that he was having marital problems, but not from anything he said to me," Solomon said. "You could talk about anything with Art, but I never felt I could discuss his personal life. I think there was an undercurrent that he had a lot on his mind."

Art admitted as much in February 1977, when he interrupted a lengthy explanation of his physical ailments to tell an interviewer, "There are days I would like to escape, to just stay in bed and not show up for work. Right now my mental house is not in order. I hate New York, but when I finish my television commitment here, I must go back. I've tried to grow accustomed to New York, but I haven't been so successful."

What Art failed to mention was that he and Barbara were already separated. "It's really not enough to be working and have a show," he said. "If you have personal or emotional problems then it's difficult to concentrate on lines and give a good performance. I realize many people resent this kind of talk when it seems, from the outside, that I'm successful and earning a good salary. But if there's a way to shut off the things that hurt you, then show me. Please show me."

In January 1977 *Lanigan's Rabbi* had the dubious distinction of debuting opposite the premiere episode of *Roots,* ABC's epic miniseries that shattered all ratings records. *Rabbi* never gained momentum and aired only sporadically through July—the same month Art countersued Barbara, his *Lanigan's Rabbi* costar and soon-to-be ex-wife.

By that time, however, Art was busy shooting another movie, *House Calls,* a comedy in which Art played the eccentric chief surgeon overseeing a staff of hospital doctors, including Walter Matthau, who spent the movie chasing after divorcée Glenda Jackson. Although Art had contributed a cameo to Matthau's *A Guide for the Married Man* back in 1967, this was the first time the *Odd Couple* combatants had performed face-to-face since 1965. Both men, by this time, had mellowed considerably, and they shot their scenes without incident.

While ABC's *Roots* had killed *Lanigan's Rabbi* (probably to Art's relief), the network had been successful in its efforts to talk Gleason into reviving *The Honeymooners.* Gleason had, in fact, declined a similar offer from CBS and Atlantic City's Palace Hotel. The Palace had offered Gleason $350,000 a week for a live *Honeymooners* stage show (twice a night) with segments featuring Gleason's characters like Joe the Bartender and the Poor Soul.

In September 1977 Art, Audrey Meadows, and Jane Kean flew down to Miami's Gusman Hall for a three-week taping of two *Honeymooners* specials for ABC, one airing in December 1977 and the other in February 1978. In late September Art was stricken with "gastrointestinal distress" and was hospitalized for several days, forcing Gleason and crew to rework their production schedule. The incident was minor and certainly not serious, but it was an omen of the medical problems that would plague Art for the rest of his career.

$$\equiv\!\!\!= 23 \equiv\!\!\!=$$

A NEW CAREER

The physical maladies suffered by Art through the years
were many: the gimpy leg (which required further
surgery in the mid-seventies), hiatal hernia, nerve deafness, cataracts, and ulcers, to name just a few. They had taken
their physical toll by the time Art turned sixty in November 1978.

Art's paunch, his bushy sideburns, and his glasses combined
with his limp and his large hearing aid to age him well before his
time. Art poked fun at his appearance, but it was a professional
blessing. It kept him a marketable and much sought-after actor.

While Art was a semiregular TV presence in the late seventies, appearing in miniseries, guest-shots, and several *Honeymooners*
reunions shot in Atlantic City, he maintained a moviemaking pace
that would have winded an actor half his age. Art shot two
movies in 1978, *House Calls* and *Movie Movie* (opposite *Yellow Rolls-
Royce* costar George C. Scott). In 1979 he increased that pace,
ignoring his constant physical pain to shoot *The Ravagers, Sunburn,*
and *Going in Style.*

After a lengthy court battle, Art's divorce from Barbara was
in the final stages, and he was now dating first wife Jean on a regular basis. ("We're living in sin," he told *Sunburn* director Richard
Sarafian while he and Jean shared a trailer on the Acapulco set.)

Bill McCaffrey was still Art's trusted advisor, though he was enjoying his semiretirement. Sam Cohn, meanwhile, had relinquished his role as Art's agent, handing the baton to fellow ICM agent Joe Funicello (Annette Funicello's brother, who was based in Los Angeles).

This was a happy time for Art. Working steadily, he was dating his ex-wife—with remarriage a strong possibility—and proudly watching his sons Brian and Paul establish their own show business careers without riding on their old man's coattails. Brian had appeared with Art in *The Ravagers* and was acting and doing voice-overs for TV and radio commercials. Paul was living in Old Lyme, Connecticut, performing his rock 'n' roll piano act in local nightclubs. Art's daughter Eileen also lived nearby and was raising a family.

While Art had spoken freely in the sixties and early seventies about his alcoholism and emotional problems, he now seemed tired of rehashing these episodes. He now limited his press interviews to a strictly enforced forty-five minutes, preferring to talk about his TV and movie work rather than about personal problems. In January 1978 *People* magazine profiled Paul Carney and alluded to Art's drinking and the Carney family's alcoholism ("granddad and several uncles too"). Art was peeved at the complimentary profile, and dashed off an uncharacteristically nasty letter to the magazine, which was published the following month.

"It pains me to write this because I was so looking forward to an intelligent, constructive article on my talented son, Paul, who, incidentally, has made it on his own," Art wrote. "I must tell you that I quit reading this piece of garbage after the first sentence or two because of the old drivel about me being a 'recovered alcoholic' etc. etc. and then the reference to my brothers (Paul's uncles) and then his grandfather! Thank you for absolutely NOTHING!"

Art was working steadily in Hollywood, although his post–*Harry and Tonto/Late Show* movie appearances were mostly in supporting roles. It kept him in the spotlight but didn't give him much of a chance to flex his dramatic muscles.

That all changed in 1979, when first-time director Martin Brest hired Art to star opposite legends George Burns and Lee Strasberg in *Going in Style*. The movie was an understated affair about three elderly men who, bored with their dreary everyday existence, decide to rob a bank. Once again Art would play a character older than sixty, but the chance to work with Burns and Strasberg (an Oscar winner and nominee, respectively) doused any qualms he might have had about the role.

In March 1979 Art and Jean remarried in a quiet ceremony conducted at the Grace Episcopal Church in Old Saybrook, Connecticut. The press was barred, with only Eileen, Brian, Paul, and their spouses and children in attendance. "I've never been happier," Jean said afterward. Said family friend William Huston: "It didn't surprise me that they got back together. Jean was his high school sweetheart and the woman he's always loved."

Three months later Art began filming *Going in Style* on location at the refurbished Astoria Studios in Queens, New York. Director Brest was a twenty-seven-year-old Bronx native who had grown up watching *The Honeymooners.* He had been given the plot of *Going in Style* by a carpenter in Queens, who read his fictional story into a tape recorder. Brest heard the tape and convinced Warner Bros. to let him write the screenplay and make his professional directorial debut.

"Out of all the three [main actors], Art was the one who sort of crept into the writing the earliest," Brest said. "I wouldn't say the role was written for him, but he was the first one I felt was right."

Art played Al, a retired bartender who lived with pals Joe (Burns) and Willie (Strasberg) in a modest three-bedroom Queens apartment. The men pass their time idly arguing about nothing and everything, shuffling over to the neighborhood park or sitting at the kitchen table staring at each other. Of the three men only Al has any family, and he frequently visits his nephew, Pete (Charles Hallahan), to have some dinner and entertain Pete's young children.

Fed up with doing nothing, Joe suggests the men put a little spice into their lives and rob a bank. The way Joe figures it, the worst that could happen would be the men would be arrested and sent to jail for a few years. Meanwhile, they would still collect their Social Security checks and get three square meals a day. Could it be any worse than the dreary existence they're now leading?

Willie—timid, withdrawn, and frightened—isn't so sure he wants to rob a bank, but he's overruled by Joe and Al. The men take a train into Manhattan and choose their target, casing the joint to check its security setup. A few days later, after methodically and quietly loading their guns in their Queens apartment (a great scene), Joe, Al, and Willie are ready for the big heist. Donning Groucho Marx nose/mustache/glasses disguises, they storm the bank, rob the stunned tellers, and walk off with nearly one hundred thousand in cash. Al, without telling his nephew, gives Pete a chunk of the loot so he can open up his own business.

Willie, still not convinced he did the right thing, suffers a heart attack and dies. But Al and Joe are thrilled with their new-found wealth. Like two giddy schoolkids, they fly to Las Vegas and embark on a wild gambling spree. With Lady Luck still on their side, Al and Joe win a lot more money in Vegas, adding to their bank loot (and giving Art a chance to do some Ed Norton–type shtick in the casino). But shortly after they return to New York, Al dies in his sleep. Joe, left all alone, is arrested and sent to prison. When Pete comes to visit, Joe tells him where the money is hidden.

If Brest was ever worried about a clashing of three egos—Carney, Burns, and Strasberg—his fears were allayed once filming on *Going in Style* got under way. Art and Strasberg both deferred to the eighty-three-year-old Burns, who called Strasberg, seventy-seven, "kid."

Art talked excitedly about working with one of his idols. "He's the remarkable one," he said of Burns. "I admire this man tremendously. I've known him for years. Someday I'd like to sit down with him and talk to him deeply about his philosophy of life. But for now I just watch him and admire him and scrutinize him. His moderate life appeals to me."

Brest noticed the unique interplay of these three show business giants working together on an ensemble movie comedy.

"I had nothing to compare it to at the time, but looking back on it, I realize it was a really unique dynamic having three guys who, on their own, were all used to being the senior talent on any given project," Brest said. "It was like a bunch of brothers, with George being the oldest. And because he was the oldest in terms of professional experience, the others were very respectful of that, particularly Lee, who was amazed by George's theatrical accomplishments."

Strasberg spoke warmly of his costars. "[Art's] capable of so many things," he said. "Unfortunately, he got typed on television and didn't get the opportunity to show what he could really do. Beneath the natural comic quality, beneath the seeming ebullience and joviality is something else, something more: an inner man. He touches me and moves me very much."

Brest recalled a scene that didn't make the movie, in which Al, Joe, and Willie are sitting silently around the kitchen table the night before the robbery, contemplating their fate while eating dinner.

"Art was brilliant in [the scene] because he did what he does best, which is a sort of silent comedy," Brest said. "The way he ate his meal, using his tongue to clean a piece of food out of his teeth. The way he ripped a piece of bread off the loaf and the finger he chose to shove in his mouth—it broke your heart. Somehow it was riveting and funny and sweet. It's amazing how much of a ballet he was able to make out of eating."

For Hallahan this was only his second movie. He was thrilled to be working with Art, especially with *The Honeymooners* having been required viewing in his house during the fifties. Although Hallahan thought Art was having trouble with his hearing throughout the movie shoot, Art's offhanded compliments made the novice actor Hallahan feel comfortable and welcomed.

"He never made a big issue of [any scene]," Hallahan said. "He'd say, 'Oh, yeah, that's great!' or, 'Oh, sure, try that, that's fine.' It took me a while to realize that that was his way of being positive, and it was disarming. When I look back on it, it set standards for me, in terms of working relationships with people, that I still strive to maintain."

Going in Style got off to a smooth start, but trouble hit two weeks into production when Art, walking alone at night near his Sixth Avenue hotel, was mugged. He was approached by a panhandler who said he recognized Art, that he was a big fan, and who then demanded money. When Art refused, the man hauled off and punched Art squarely in the face, giving him a shiner and breaking a blood vessel in his eye. Shooting was halted for two weeks while Art, who was embarrassed by the incident, recuperated back in Connecticut. When he returned to the set, he refused to discuss what had happened.

By August 1979 Art and Burns were in Las Vegas shooting their casino scenes at the Aladdin Hotel. *Going in Style* was now behind schedule, and the set was becoming tense as Brest fretted about completing his movie with studio executives breathing down his neck. Art remained implacable, joking with the crew, following Brest's directions, and laughing at Burns's corny jokes. But Las Vegas brought back bad memories—the 1971 stage appearance—and Art hated the city. Making matters worse, he had developed a hacking cough, a byproduct of the dry desert air and hotel air conditioning. "When the jobs come too close together, I get overtired and the blood pressure rises," he said.

Art's words were prophetic. On August 23, shortly after filming his last scene and flying back to the East Coast, Art had to be hospitalized in the intensive-care unit of Middlesex Memorial Hospital, near his home in Westbrook, Connecticut. Complaining of chest pains and suffering from an irregular heartbeat, Art was diagnosed as suffering from elevated blood pressure and severe exhaustion. Art's doctor cited his patient's "burning the candle at both ends" as the culprit.

"I worked him so hard on the movie, and I was sort of a fanatic about doing a lot of takes," Brest said. "When we did the last shot, Art said, 'Excuse me,' and he went upstairs. I saw him down in the lobby about five minutes later and his mustache was shaved off. And I said, 'Why did you shave your mustache off?' and he said, 'Because I know you. And I'm done.' "

Art remained hospitalized for two weeks. Just before being discharged he made a quick visit to Jerry Lewis—hosting his annual Muscular Dystrophy telethon in nearby West Hartford— and gave him a plastic bag filled with donations from hospital staff members. While in the hospital, Art's weight had dropped from 210 to 197 pounds. "I think I'll watch my diet and stay away from any form of the grape," he told reporters waiting for him outside the hospital after he was discharged. "You know what the grape is—the sauce." A month later, dressed as Ed Norton, Art served as grand marshal of a fund-raising parade for leukemia held in Westbrook.

Going in Style was charming and featured excellent performances by Art, Burns, and Strasberg. But like *Lanigan's Rabbi,* which had premiered opposite *Roots,* the movie was a victim of bad timing. It opened in late December 1979 opposite two highly hyped, much anticipated movies: Francis Ford Coppola's *Apocalypse Now* and Robert Benton's *Kramer vs. Kramer.* Up against this stiff competition, *Going in Style* was largely ignored, its box office appeal not helped by a tepid review in the *New York Times.*

But Art's career didn't miss a beat, and as 1980 approached he resumed a hectic moviemaking schedule that was peppered with TV appearances. While his physical health was obviously a priority, just as important was Art's push to keep working. This way he could avoid the periods of inactivity that inevitably triggered his depression and anxiety.

"I still go through stages," he said at the time. "When I'm up, I say, 'Please keep me here because I love it.' Then something happens and I find myself losing confidence, being afraid I can't be a good actor anymore, feeling guilty, guilty, guilty, taking all kinds of responsibilities on my shoulders. I've tried a lot of treatments, but I think the most help I get is from my loved ones—my wife and children and grandchildren."

So with a lot of help from his friends and family, Art forged ahead. He costarred with Gleason—Redmond Gleason, not Jackie—as a construction foreman in the forgettable movie *Steel* (a stuntman plunged to his death during filming, putting an understandable damper on the shoot). And Art costarred in two other "small" movies that year, *Defiance* and the quirky, offbeat *Roadie.* On television he had a leading role as Robert Stroud, the legendary Birdman of Alcatraz, in NBC's four-hour miniseries *Alcatraz: The Whole Shocking Story.*

All the late-seventies talk of a *Honeymooners* road show had led nowhere. ABC's last *Honeymooners* reunion was already two years past, and the prospects of Art and Gleason working together again seemed a near impossibility. Gleason was drinking heavily during this time and making only sporadic forays into movies, scoring big in Burt Reynolds's *Smokey and the Bandit* series with a recurring role as a redneck sheriff. But Gleason's days as a bankable television personality had long since vanished.

In March 1981 Art was one of the first ten alumni to be inducted into Mount Vernon High School's Hall of Fame, along with Dick Clark, E. B. White, and Susan Harris, who had created ABC's hit soap-opera parody series, *Soap*. Although Art no longer lived in Westchester County, he had maintained close ties with the area throughout the years, always willing to grant interviews to local journalists and help in various local fundraising drives. He no longer had his hair cut by Mount Vernon's Johnny "Johnny Cake" Coschigano or Bronxville's Phil Marano, but he still enjoyed reliving old times with Bedford Boys like Al Tepe and Whitey Fryer.

In early May 1981 Art flew to Dallas, where he was supposed to begin filming his role as Candy in a television version of John Steinbeck's *Of Mice and Men*. Sometime around May 10 he abruptly left the production and was transported to St. Paul's Hospital, where he was admitted "for a recurring illness he's had over the years," according to his production manager, Bob Hargrove. Newspaper accounts speculated that Art had suffered a heart attack.

When Art was discharged from St. Paul's and had returned to Westbrook, Bill McCaffrey would only say that Art was resting "very comfortably." The New York *Daily News,* however, reported that "sources in New York" said Art was having heart problems similar to the ones he suffered in 1979 after completing *Going in Style*. Art decided not to return to Dallas and *Of Mice and Men*. Lew Ayres took over his role when shooting resumed on May 27.

Another of Art's movies, *Take This Job and Shove It,* was released in 1981. *Take This Job* was a blue-collar comedy that borrowed its title from Johnny Paycheck's popular country music hit. In the movie, Art played the manager of a midwestern brewery that was in chaos because of workers versus management labor squabbles. *Take This Job* was shot on location at Pickett's Brewery in Dubuque, Iowa. James Karen, a veteran actor and well-known Pathmark Supermarket pitchman, costarred in the movie. Karen had jumped at the chance to work with Art; he was a close friend and confidante of Buster Keaton, who also suffered from alcoholism and the same sense of isolation that seemed to plague Art.

After shooting began, Karen noticed that Art took his lunch breaks in his trailer, away from the rest of the cast and crew. Gossip soon began about Art's apparent "star" attitude.

"I went up to his trailer, knocked on the door, and said, 'Art, it's beautiful out here, would you like to come out and join us for lunch? We'd love to have you,' " Karen said. "He looked at me and said, 'Would it be all right? I didn't want to impose on you guys.' And from then on he came out every day and joined us, and he was the life of the party, telling stories and singing and dancing. He was the spark plug, but Jesus, he was too self-effacing."

Despite the fact that *Take This Job and Shove It* was filmed in an actual brewery—which provided free beer to any takers—Art didn't drink while he was working on the movie. That all changed, however, once the production ended.

"He never touched a drop, but then he came out [to California] the day after we finished shooting and went on a terrible drunk," Karen said. "His wife called me and asked for a little help, and he ended up hospitalized here. Art would say, 'We moved a little closer to the sanitarium—less driving to do.' "

Art was back on the wagon by the time he was hired to costar with fellow Oscar winners David Niven and Maggie Smith in *Better Late Than Never.* The movie was scheduled to be filmed on location in Nice, France. In a twist of irony, Art won the role after the film's "junior" producers—David Niven Jr. and Jack Haley Jr.—had already approached Bob Hope and then Jackie Gleason, both of whom had passed because of other commitments. (Gleason was filming *Smokey and the Bandit III* in Las Vegas.) To get Art to accept the role, it took a series of long-distance phone calls from the "juniors" and some extraordinary persuasion from Art's agent, Joe Funicello. Money wasn't the issue.

"Art was so fearful because he had only been in recovery a short time," Haley said. "He'd say, 'Jack, I don't think I can do this, I don't think I can go to Europe and do a picture.' He was so fearful of himself and of exposing himself to temptations. He was drying out and didn't know if he could ever perform again."

Both Haley and Funicello assured Art he would be surrounded by people, including Jean, who would make sure he stayed on the straight and narrow. This would be Art's first return to France since the war, and despite his overwhelming concern, *Better Late Than Never* turned out to be a rewarding (and nonalcoholic) experience.

David Niven didn't know at the time that he was in the early stages of Lou Gehrig's disease, a debilitating nerve paralysis that would kill him a few years later. For now, the disease manifested itself in Niven's slightly slurred speech but didn't impede his performance in any noticeable way (though some of his dialogue had to be looped, or rerecorded, after the film was shot). Niven and Art struck up an immediate friendship. The suave, debonair British lady's man was completely at ease with Art, whose famous trick of sucking air into his gut and emitting a loud, distressed-seal grunt was included in the movie.

"They loved each other," Niven Jr. said. "There was a great friendship and great admiration, and the two of them just gobbled up the scenery, with the possible exception of Maggie Smith."

Better Late Than Never revolved around the two men. Niven was a past-his-prime singer, while Art was a broken-down photographer. The men had once slept with the same woman during World War II, one of them fathering a daughter. The daughter, in turn, had her own daughter and then died tragically young—leaving her mother with custody of her granddaughter. When the grandmother died, she stipulated in her will that both men were to be summoned to the south of France, where one of them would inherit a quarter of a million dollars per year and custody of their "granddaughter" once the little girl decided which man she'd like to live with. Child actress Kimberley Partridge played the little girl, while Smith played her legal guardian.

Better Late Than Never was financed by Golden Harvest, which at the time was also financing Tom Selleck's movie *The High Road to China*. When *High Road* bombed, the entire deal fell apart and *Better Late Than Never* was never distributed in America but was seen in Europe (it was finally released in 1983). Warner Bros. eventually purchased the American rights and frequently shows the movie on late-night television.

═══ 24 ═══

UNFINISHED
BUSINESS

A rt had, by the mid-1980s, settled into a comfortable pattern in his professional life. He was nearing his sixty-fifth birthday, yet he still pushed himself extremely hard, working on two or three movies a year and appearing intermittently on television. The rigors of Broadway no longer appealed to him; nor was Broadway even a viable alternative given his physical condition.

Had he chosen to retire now, Art could have looked back at a long, fruitful career. He had been immortalized in pop culture with *The Honeymooners,* and in the minds of the American public it wouldn't matter if Art never worked another day: Ed Norton would live forever in TV-rerun heaven. But Art and television had matured together and he wasn't about to forsake the medium on whose airwaves he had ridden to stardom—especially if it meant working with his idol, James Cagney.

Midway through 1983, producer Joseph Sargent approached Art about costarring with Cagney in *Terrible Joe Moran,* a made-for-TV movie. *Terrible Joe* dealt with curmudgeonly, wheelchair-bound ex-boxer Joe Moran (Cagney) and his relationships with those around him, including his niece (to be played by Ellen Barkin). Art would play Troy, Terrible Joe's aide-de-camp, trusted personal valet, and whipping boy.

Art had perfected his razor-sharp impression of Cagney when he was a kid back in Mount Vernon. Later in life, Art was lucky enough to meet Cagney and strike up a friendship with the legendary actor. Art often visited Cagney when he was out in California (for example, the memorable visit during the *Lovers* road tour back in 1969) and recalled how Cagney told Art he didn't want to work anymore when he turned down Paul Mazursky's offer to star in *Harry and Tonto.*

In his later years Cagney was weakened by various health problems; still, he returned to show business in 1981 when he made a triumphant appearance as the racist police chief in Milos Forman's movie *Ragtime.* Shortly thereafter, however, a massive stroke had left Cagney, eighty-four, immobilized and unable to speak clearly. Though his mind was sharp he was trapped in a lifeless body, a virtual cripple forced into a wheelchair.

A *Life* magazine story published around that time portrayed Cagney as the unwitting dupe of his caretaker/agent, Marge Zimmermann, who was accused by some of pushing Cagney to continue his acting career against his doctors' advice. For better or worse, the article helped publicize *Terrible Joe Moran,* which Art and Cagney were now shooting on location in New York for director Sargent.

"Art was on our wish list, but we never thought we'd get him," Sargent said. "Frankly, when he was available and interested, I jumped for joy. Cagney at that point was almost a vegetable, but he was such a dear man. He was very touching, very moving. It was just instant love between the two guys, but it was at a distance, because Jimmy wasn't able to relate that fully [to anyone]. He had all of his marbles, but it was painful for him because he couldn't speak and communicate the way he used to."

To protect Cagney's fragile health, Sargent decided not to include him in rehearsals. A stand-in was used, and Cagney would be wheeled in just before the cameras rolled, reading his lines off a TelePrompTer (an electronic device from which he could read his dialogue). "In several instances he was beyond fully comprehending the scene he was in," Sargent said. "I had to lay it out for him, and once I did that and he was reminded what was going on, he fell right into it. It was incredible. He summoned all those years of professionalism and experience and just cut through that curtain that had suddenly fallen over him."

Art was in almost every scene with Cagney, tenderly pushing his wheelchair and helping Terrible Joe cope with his relationship problems. In one particular scene, Terrible Joe sits in his wheelchair watching old films of himself boxing. Cagney really *was* watching his old boxing movies. "Art had a lot of moisture in his eyes," Sargent said.

Terrible Joe Moran would be Cagney's final screen performance, and he died shortly after the CBS movie premiered in March 1984. While *Terrible Joe Moran* received only mediocre reviews, Art's performance was widely applauded. He was nominated for an Emmy Award, and in September he won his sixth, as Best Supporting Actor in a Limited Series. This time the award was extra special: It was Art's first Emmy for a dramatic role. His five previous Emmys had all been for his work on *The Honeymooners.*

Ironically, Ralph Kramden and Ed Norton made national headlines again in early 1985. Gleason, strapped for cash, had "uncovered" a mother lode of "lost" *Honeymooners* episodes, which in reality were sitting in an air-conditioned vault in Florida. These episodes were fuzzy kinescopes of varying lengths (four minutes to one hour) and quality that hadn't been seen since they first aired as part of *The Jackie Gleason Show* in the early fifties. These "lost episodes" were predecessors to the so-called Classic Thirty-nine. "Nobody asked about them," Gleason explained. "They were nicely stacked, waiting for the phone to ring."

Gleason's "discovery" was front-page news, since all America had seen for the last thirty years were the same *Honeymooners* episodes shown time and again. Television historians and fans couldn't wait to see these alternate looks at Ralph, Alice, Norton, and Trixie. Gleason knew he would start a media feeding frenzy, and shortly after announcing he'd found the episodes he signed a lucrative deal with Viacom, which agreed to package and air them on the Showtime cable network. At a press conference in February 1985 at New York's 21 Club, Gleason announced that Showtime would begin airing the episodes later that year. (Art had the flu and didn't attend the press conference.) Gleason also said that the episodes would be made available to noncable (broadcast) stations in 1986. That August, MPI, a distribution company, paid Gleason nearly one million dollars for the rights to release the "lost episodes" on home video. (Viacom had reportedly paid Gleason six million, the money to be spread out over seven years.)

Audrey Meadows was the only *Honeymooners* star to have earned residuals from the original programs. Meadows's brothers were lawyers, and when they had written up her *Honeymooners* contract they had been savvy enough to include a residuals clause. This time around, Art received a lump sum from Viacom. It was belated justice for Art, who had won three back-to-back Emmys in the fifties and two more in the sixties for his work on the show.

The year the lost *Honeymooners* episodes surfaced also found Art and Gleason working together on a new project: *Izzy and Moe,* a made-for-TV CBS movie produced by Robert Halmi and directed by Jackie Cooper. *Izzy and Moe* marked the first time Art and Gleason would star together outside the sketch-comedy sphere, notwithstanding *The Laughmaker* (in 1953) and several dramatic episodes of the *Gleason Show* in the sixties.

Art and Gleason had already rejected three scripts before agreeing on *Izzy and Moe.* In one scenario, they were retired men who find a carful of money in Las Vegas. In another script, they were two men impersonating a husband and wife so they could win a free luxury cruise. A third movie cast them as owners of a golf course.

According to Gleason biographer William A. Henry III, neither Art nor Gleason was exactly thrilled at the idea of working together. Art, far removed from his second-banana days, refused to work for anything less than equal pay and equal star billing. Gleason, as usual, wanted a higher salary, which no doubt rankled Art.

"In the beginning, neither of them wanted to do it. They

didn't want to work with each other," Halmi said. "Finally Carney, whom I already knew well, said, 'You get Gleason and then you come talk to me. I won't let you down. Just get him first.' To get Jackie I had to go to Florida four or five or six times to talk conceptually. Later on, Jackie insisted on involving himself in every line of the script. It was rewritten for three solid months under his supervision. But the problem was still that Gleason wanted to be paid more than anyone else."

Halmi discovered a way to appease Gleason yet still assure Art he would earn the same starring salary: He paid Gleason a composing fee after Gleason insisted he could write the movie's jazzy score. (Gleason's composition turned out to be nothing more than old sheet music. Several of Gleason's cronies later told William Henry that Gleason—who'd made a fortune "conducting" and "composing" albums such as *Music for Lovers*—couldn't read a note of music. It was an elaborate sham.)

The Gleason who showed up to film *Izzy and Moe* was surly, drunk, and belligerent. He often mocked Cooper behind the director's back and usually couldn't work in the late afternoon, after consuming a liquid lunch. One day actress Nandrea Lin Courts knocked on Gleason's trailer door to introduce herself as his onscreen daughter. Gleason looked her up and down, then sneered, "Who the fuck cares?" before slamming the door shut in her face.

"We were all prepared for Jackie Gleason to bowl us over with great old stories and be wonderful and kind of pass the baton from his generation to ours, but he was such a fool," Courts said. "He was just angry and awful. And Art Carney dealt with [Gleason] in the most amazing way I've ever seen. He wasn't near Gleason much, but Art had this peace about it. Gleason was really being awful to people and Art just kind of stayed out of that. He told funny stories and stuff but never when Jackie was around. I think he was afraid to incur [Gleason's] wrath. Art looked apologetically at everyone but without any words, and it didn't look in any way like he agreed with Gleason. There was that look of, Please understand he's a sick man, which is what Art did. It's amazing what eyes can tell you."

One insider remembered that "Carney would arrive in the morning on the set and say, 'Is King Farouk here yet?' He was letting the crew know that he knew about Jackie's behavior. There was no malice in his remarks, but it was like, I know what you're going through. There was humor in Art's remarks, but it wasn't spiteful."

During the five weeks of shooting *Izzy and Moe,* Art and Gleason spent very little time with each other. They ventured into each other's on-set trailers only for publicity purposes, to give joint interviews or pose for photos. "In all that time Jackie never once invited Art to lunch or dinner," Halmi said. "Twice he had Carney into his trailer while he was being interviewed, and both times Art came back after about fifteen minutes and told me he couldn't get a word in edgewise so he left."

CBS was looking for ways to capitalize on this Gleason-Carney "reunion" and assigned someone to hover around the two stars as the shoot progressed, ostensibly to glean the "fun" comments they made to each other. CBS planned to publicize the comments to show how chummy the men still were with each other after all these years—that the old *Honeymooners* magic was still there.

"But they didn't talk to each other," a person on the set said. "There was no communication. Gleason would sit there and wait to be told what to do. He didn't talk to Art, Jackie Cooper, or the other cast members. Carney, who was not a gregarious man, would just sit a few feet away and mind his own business."

Art recalled one conversation he had with Gleason away from the lights, cast, and crew. "It was the first time I had seen Gleason look really old," he said. "He seemed genuinely miserable. He took no pleasure in what he had achieved or what he had amassed. My heart just went out to him. I knew he was a diabetic, but he wouldn't stop drinking, which was crazy. His spirit was just not there. The joy had gone out of him."

Said Cooper: "Art was just constantly apologizing to me for Gleason, who made Art so uncomfortable. But with all that discomfort, Art was still professional and wonderful. In front of the camera, Gleason was more comfortable around Art; he would even take a suggestion from Art, not for the good of the scene, necessarily, but for the good of Jackie [Gleason]. If Jackie had trouble getting into a chair a certain way, Art would say, 'If I pretend to bump into it, it would move it away from the table and then it would be easier for you.' Art made him more comfortable, to whatever extent you could make Gleason comfortable at that point."

Gleason's sour, nasty mood contrasted with Art's good-natured personality, but Gleason managed to pull it together for Cooper once the cameras began rolling. *Izzy and Moe* encompassed the true story of washed-up vaudevillians Izzy Einstein (Gleason) and Moe Smith (Art), who became 1920s Prohibition agents and used disguises in their undercover work. The story was light and fluffy and gave Art and Gleason the chance to demonstrate—one final time—the remarkable chemistry they always seemed to generate before the cameras. In large part, they succeeded. *Izzy and Moe* wouldn't win any awards, but it was a benign, lighthearted movie that wasn't embarrassing to either man, and it ended their historic comedic partnership on a sweet note.

"There must have been a way, week after week on the *Gleason Show,* where Art was used to this and that and they got along," Cooper said. "The only thing I gathered here was that Art was the only one around who could sometimes put Jackie at ease. I think poor Art was embarrassed for Jackie a lot, because it was very obvious Jackie never bothered to read this script. Art agreed with me that Jackie had never read the script and probably had someone tell him the story."

Art's experience with *Izzy and Moe,* however, ended on a sour note. He was invited to a wrap party celebrating the movie's completion and agreed to attend only if the press was kept away from the event.

"Gleason came to the party and absolutely took his corner of space with everyone hovering around him," one partygoer said. "There were a lot of press people there, and when Art came in he felt that he had been immediately betrayed. He was in and out of the party in fifteen minutes." It was the last time Art would ever see Gleason.

Another of Art's longtime partnerships ended on August 28,

1985, when mentor/agent/friend Bill McCaffrey died after a lengthy battle with cancer. He was eighty-six. McCaffrey's impact on Art's personal and professional life was inestimable, his devotion to Art as his mother hen and father confessor second only to Art's immediate family.

It was McCaffrey to whom Art's beloved oldest brother, Jack, had entrusted Art's career; McCaffrey who proudly labeled Art's acting "primitive"; McCaffrey who carefully massaged Art's career, guiding his star pupil from *Gleason Show* regular to Broadway to Hollywood; McCaffrey who understood his client's alcoholic despair and tried to protect Art from the spotlight's harsh glare; and McCaffrey whom Art respected, admired, and loved.

Although years before he had turned over the day-to-day management of Art's career to Joe Funicello, Bill McCaffrey was, up until his death, a guiding force in Art Carney's life and work. He was one of the family.

= 25 =

FINALES

A rt had spent years trying to shake the image of sewer worker Ed Norton. He lamented, time and again, how he was always identified as Ralph Kramden's goofy sidekick.

But Gleason's announcement of the "lost" *Honeymooners* episodes had spurred new interest in the show. There was talk of a *Honeymooners* movie, and Gleason was fielding more offers from network bidders to stage *Honeymooners* reunion shows. In the beginning of 1987, longtime Gleason writer Walter Stone was writing the final *Honeymooners* show. In the episode, Ralph and Alice retire to Florida, leaving Norton and Trixie behind in Brooklyn. Norton, it turned out, couldn't leave the sewer until he had handed his shovel and boots to a family member. It was a Norton family tradition passed down from generation to generation.

In the late fifties journalists and industry pundits had wondered if television's greatest comedic partnership would be irretrievably lost when the Gleason-Carney team broke up. Time, of course, had solved that riddle. But the enigmatic relationship between Jackie Gleason and Art Carney was another matter.

Gleason had been feeling ill in the spring of 1987. In April he was told he had colon cancer. When Gleason underwent an operation in May to remove a tumor from his colon, doctors discovered that the cancer had spread to his lymph nodes. Gleason was given six months to live, and he quietly went home to die in his Florida mansion.

Art had one final conversation with Gleason, phoning him shortly after his release from the hospital. Five days later, on June 24, 1987, Gleason died at the age of seventy-one.

"I told him how much I thought of him, and that he was in my thoughts and prayers," Art said. "He said, 'I know that, pal. I know that.' I didn't think I was going to be able to talk to him because he was a pretty sick man. We hung up, [glad] that we had made contact with each other. I'll miss our friendship. Our respect and love for each other, that's what I'm going to miss most of all."

Gleason's funeral mass was held at St. Mary's Cathedral in Miami. More than two thousand people mobbed the cathedral, yet Audrey Meadows was the only *Honeymooners* costar to show up. Art sent a bouquet of flowers.

"Art had this very strange reaction [to Gleason's death], to tell you the truth," said Joan Reichman Canale, who had worked with Art and Gleason back in the fifties. "I don't know what his reactions are today, and I don't know what's happened, but something is wrong. I know Art had great respect for Jackie and Jackie certainly did for Art. He adored Art. But after Jackie passed away I wanted to have a big celebration. I called Art and all he kept saying was, 'Let him rest in peace. Forget it. Let him rest in peace.' That's all he says now."

After Gleason's death, Art concentrated on keeping busy. He disdained Los Angeles, preferring instead to remain in his house on the Connecticut shoreline. But Connecticut wasn't exactly a moviemaking hub, which drastically reduced Art's career opportunities.

Art didn't seem to mind. When he did travel out to California now, it was mainly for television appearances or made-for-TV movies. In 1987 he appeared sporadically on *The Cavanaughs,* a CBS sitcom about an Irish family headed by patriarch Francis "Pop" Cavanaugh (played by Barnard Hughes). Art bore a distinct physical resemblance to Hughes, and he was cast in a recurring role as Pop Cavanaugh's younger brother, Jimmy

"The Weasel" Cavanaugh. (Hughes, incidentally, had almost costarred with Art in *Going in Style*. He was offered a part but couldn't accept it because he was committed to an NBC pilot that never materialized.)

"When you're the oldest living guy on any show you're on these days and you get anybody that's even close to your age, it's a real treat," Hughes said. "At least you have some frame of reference. I remember Art and I used to sit around and try to top each other with vaudeville acts. He didn't want to do too many shows, as I remember, because he wanted to keep the part alive, and I thought it was just great. Art was a big plus we never expected."

Art had watched *The Cavanaughs* and had admired Hughes's work. After hearing Pop Cavanaugh refer time and again to the Weasel, Art told agent Joe Funicello that he'd like the part if it was ever offered.

"This is the first job I [personally] ever went after," Art said. "My daughter, Eileen, told me that I should look at the show because there's a man who reminded her of me. I did, and I realized the resemblance. I also loved the show and the Irish flavor."

In September 1990 Art and Audrey Meadows reunited for the last time on an episode of the short-lived CBS sitcom *Uncle Buck,* which was adapted from a movie starring John Candy as an irascible, slobbish uncle forced to babysit his niece and nephew. (Stand-up comedian Kevin Meaney played Candy's role in the TV series.) Meadows had a regular role in *Uncle Buck* as the kids' grandmother. In his one appearance, Art played Uncle Buck's old friend and mentor, who has eyes for grandma. That same year Art costarred as Michael Landon's father in the TV movie *Where Pigeons Go to Die,* Landon's final project (he died from cancer shortly thereafter). Art's work in *Pigeons* earned him his seventh, and final, Emmy nomination. But Art wouldn't take home his seventh Emmy—the award went to Hume Cronyn.

Remaining close to his Connecticut home might have reduced Art's visibility in Hollywood, but it opened up a new door: television commercials. In the late eighties Coca-Cola launched an advertising campaign for Coca-Cola Classic. Art was hired for a few commercials, playing a wise old grandfather who dispenses wisdom to his young grandson, played by child actor Brian Bonsall.

In the ad, Art and his grandson are walking together after the child's soccer game. The boy is dejected because his team lost. "So you lost," Art says. "The ball didn't work." Grandfather and grandson stop for a Coke, without realizing they don't have any money. Art reaches behind the boy's ear and, with some grandfatherly magic, pulls out a few coins to pay for the soda.

The last time moviegoers saw Art on the big screen was in 1993, when he made a cameo appearance in *Last Action Hero,* a big-budget flop. The movie starred Arnold Schwarzenegger, who was now an international star—a far cry from the muscle-bound no-name actor who had given Lucille Ball a quick massage in *Happy Anniversary and Goodbye* almost twenty years before.

In *Last Action Hero* Schwarzenegger played fictional onscreen movie hero Jack Slater, who literally comes off the screen to help his number-one fan, a kid played by Austin O'Brien. Art played O'Brien's wise old uncle. *Last Action Hero* was universally ripped to shreds by the critics and closed almost immediately. Because of its huge budget (said to be close to a hundred million dollars), *Hero* had the infamous distinction of becoming one of the costliest flops in Hollywood history.

Art has kept an extremely low profile since *Last Action Hero.* His last television appearance came in 1995, when Audrey Meadows was honored with a Lifetime Achievement Award by the American Comedy Awards. The special aired on ABC, and at the end of the show Art congratulated Meadows by appearing (via videotape) in character as Ed Norton, dressed in a robe and Norton's famous felt hat. Art resurfaced briefly when Meadows died of lung cancer in February 1996 after keeping her illness hidden for more than a year. He granted a few newspaper interviews and told reporters how much he'd miss Meadows. He also reminisced about the *Honeymooners* days, when Meadows would learn everyone else's dialogue and help Gleason when he drew a blank.

While Art remains an extremely private, nearly unapproachable figure, his show business legacy lives on. *The Honeymooners* still airs in syndication around the country, and in New York it is often the highest-rated show in its late-night time slot (usually 12:30 or 1:00 A.M. on WPIX, Channel 11). *Honeymooners* conventions and societies have sprung up around the country, and Hollywood is again talking about making a *Honeymooners* movie that would put Ralph, Alice, Ed, and Trixie on movie screens around the world.

Art's failure to be inducted into the American Academy of Television Arts and Sciences Hall of Fame has been a glaring omission in need of remedy. Along with Milton Berle, Sid Caesar, Jackie Gleason, Lucille Ball, and Desi Arnaz, Art was a seminal figure in popularizing the new medium of television. His six Emmy Awards make him one of the top all-time winners, while Ed Norton is, without a doubt, one of TV's most popular and enduring characters.

Back in the early fifties, when Art and Gleason were just beginning their remarkable television relationship, Gleason was stopped in a New York nightclub by suave actor Adolphe Menjou. "Your television show comes on in California in the middle of our dinner hour, but we never miss it," Menjou said to Gleason. "We carry our plates from the table to watch it. This fellow Art Carney is great, isn't he? Since he's been with you, Jackie, he's made himself."

"You got it wrong, pal," Gleason shot back. "Art Carney's made *me*."

ART CARNEY IN
TELEVISION, FILMS,
AND THEATER

TV SERIES

1948–49, *The Morey Amsterdam Show,* CBS
1949–50, *The Morey Amsterdam Show,* DuMont
1950–52, *Cavalcade of Stars,* DuMont
1951, *Henry Morgan's Talent Hunt,* NBC
1952–57, *The Jackie Gleason Show,** CBS
1959–61, Art Carney Specials,** NBC
1966–70, *The Jackie Gleason Show,** CBS
1977, *Lanigan's Rabbi,* NBC

TV MOVIES AND MINISERIES

1972
December 18, *The Snoop Sisters,* NBC

1975
September 26, *Death Scream,* ABC
October 5, *Katherine,* ABC

1976
June 17, *Lanigan's Rabbi,* NBC

1979
November 22, *Letters from Frank,* CBS

1980
November 5–6, *Alcatraz: The Whole Shocking Story,* NBC
December 7, *Fighting Back,* CBS

*EMMY AWARDS: 1953, 1954, 1955, 1966, 1967
**EMMY AWARD: 1959, OUTSTANDING PROGRAM ACHIEVEMENT IN THE FIELD OF HUMOR

1981
May 18, *Bitter Harvest,* NBC

1984
March 27, *Terrible Joe Moran,**** CBS
April 23, *A Doctor's Story,* NBC
December 13, *The Night They Saved Christmas,* ABC

1985
May 5, *The Undergrads,* Disney Channel
September 23, *Izzy and Moe,* CBS
November 17, *The Blue Yonder,* Disney Channel

1986
April 3, *Miracle of the Heart: A Boys' Town Story*

Episodic TV Shows

1953
January 12, *Lux Video Theatre:* "Thanks for a Lovely Evening," CBS
May 18, *Studio One:* "The Laughmaker," CBS
August 4, *Danger:* "I'll Be Waiting," CBS
September 4, *Campbell Sound Stage:* "The Square Hole," NBC
November 30, *Studio One:* "Confessions of a Nervous Man," CBS
December 29, *Suspense:* "Mr. Nobody," NBC

1954
January 14, *Kraft Television Theatre:* "Burlesque," NBC
April 20, *Suspense:* "The Return Journey," CBS
May 5, *Kraft Television Theatre:* "Alice in Wonderland," NBC
May 14, *Studio One:* "A Letter to Mr. Gubbins," CBS
August 26, *Kraft Television Theatre:* "Uncle Harry," NBC
November 10, *Best of Broadway:* "Panama Hattie," CBS

1955
January 6, *Climax:* "The Bigger They Come," CBS
June 13, *Studio One:* "The Incredible World of Horace Ford," CBS

1956
Air Power: "Fools, Daredevils and Geniuses," CBS
March 16, *Star Stage:* "The Man Who Was Irresistible to Women," NBC

1957
March 28, *Playhouse 90:* "Charley's Aunt," CBS
June 27, *Playhouse 90:* "The Fabulous Irishman," CBS

***Emmy Award nomination

1958

September 22, *DuPont Show of the Month*: "Harvey," CBS
Some Facts About Benedict Arnold, syndicated
November 23, *Alfred Hitchcock Presents*: "Safety for the Witness," CBS

1959

January 22, *Playhouse 90*: "The Velvet Alley," CBS
April 5, *Art Carney Meets the Sorcerer's Apprentice,* NBC
May 3, *Art Carney Meets Peter and the Wolf,* NBC
November 4, *At the Movies,* NBC
America Pauses for the Merry Month of May, CBS
November 13, *Our Town,* NBC
A Tribute to Eleanor Roosevelt on Her Diamond Jubilee, CBS

1960

January 16, *Call Me Back,* NBC
February 5, *Three in One,* NBC
February 5, *Hooray for Love,* CBS
April 8, *Victory,* NBC
May 6, *Full Moon Over Brooklyn,* NBC
October 24, *The Right Man,* CBS
December 23, *The Twilight Zone*: "Night of the Meek," CBS

1961

The Chevy Show: "O'Halloran's Luck," NBC
Westinghouse Presents: "The Sound of the Sixties," NBC
The Chevrolet Golden Anniversary Show, CBS

1963

June 9, *DuPont Show of the Week*: "The Triumph of Gerald Q. Wert,"
NBC

1964

April 19, *DuPont Show of the Month*: "A Day Like Today," NBC
October 30, *Bob Hope Presents Chrysler Theatre*: "The Timothy Heist,"
NBC
November 28, *Mr. Broadway*: "Smelling Like a Rose," CBS

1966

September 7, *Batman*: "Shoot a Crooked Arrow," ABC
September 8, *Batman*: "Walk the Straight and Narrow," ABC

1970

October 7, *Men from Shiloh*: "With Love, Bullets and Valentines," NBC

1974

November 19, *Happy Anniversary and Goodbye,* CBS

1975

April 10, *Happy Endings*: "Kidnapped," ABC

1976

February 2, *The Honeymooners: The Second Honeymoon*, ABC
March 30, *What Now, Catherine Curtis?*, CBS

1977

November 28, *The Honeymooners Christmas Special*, ABC

1978

February 13, *The Honeymooners Valentine Special*, ABC
December 12, *The Honeymooners Christmas Special*, ABC

1979

May 15, *You Can't Take It With You*, CBS
December 9, *Alice*: "My Cousin, Art Carney," CBS

1981

December 23, *The Leprechaun's Christmas Gold*, ABC

1982

April 15, *Fame*: "A Big Finish," NBC

1987

February 23, *The Cavanaughs*: "He Ain't Heavy, Father . . . ," CBS
March 12, *Faerie Tale Theater*: "The Emperor's New Clothes," Showtime

1988

August 8, *The Cavanaughs*: "Weasel Waltz," CBS

TV GUEST APPEARANCES

1957

The Dinah Shore Chevy Show, NBC
The Tonight Show, NBC

1958

The Arlene Francis Show, NBC
The Dinah Shore Chevy Show, NBC
The Perry Como Show, NBC
The Jack Paar Show, NBC
The Sid Caesar Show, NBC

1961

The Jackie Gleason Show, CBS
The Jane Powell Special: Young at Heart, NBC
The Connie Francis Special: Kicking Sound Around, ABC
The Ed Sullivan Show, CBS

1962
Jackie Gleason and His American Scene Magazine, CBS

1963
Andy Williams Special, NBC
The Danny Kaye Show, CBS

1964
Jackie Gleason and His American Scene Magazine, CBS
The Danny Kaye Show, CBS
Jonathan Winters: A Wild Winters Night, NBC

1968
The Dick Cavett Show, ABC

1970
The David Frost Show, syndicated

1971
The David Frost Revue, syndicated
The Dean Martin Show, NBC
Perry Como's Winter Show, NBC

1973
ABC Comedy Hour, ABC
The Jackie Gleason Special, CBS

FILMS

1941, *Pot o' Gold*
1964, *The Yellow Rolls-Royce*
1967, *A Guide for the Married Man*
1974, *Harry and Tonto**
1975, *W.W. and the Dixie Dancekings*
1976, *Won Ton Ton, The Dog Who Saved Hollywood*
1977, *The Late Show*
1977, *Scott Joplin*
1978, *House Calls*
1978, *Movie Movie*
1979, *The Ravagers*
1979, *Sunburn*
1979, *Going in Style*
1980, *Steel*
1980, *Defiance*
1980, *Roadie*

*ACADEMY AWARD, BEST ACTOR

1981, *St. Helen's*
1981, *Take This Job and Shove It*
1983, *Better Late Than Never*
1984, *Firestarter*
1984, *The Naked Face*
1984, *The Muppets Take Manhattan*
1993, *Last Action Hero*

THEATER

1957, *The Rope Dancers*
1961, *Take Her, She's Mine*
1965, *The Odd Couple*
1968, *Lovers**
1972, *The Prisoner of Second Avenue*

*TONY AWARD NOMINATION

INDEX